Professional Risk Manager Exam Handbook Exam 1

Jaffar Mohammed Ahmed, FRM

HARRIMAN HOUSE LTD
18 College Street
Petersfield
Hampshire
GU31 4AD
GREAT BRITAIN
Tel: +44 (0)1730 233870
Email: contact@harriman-house.com
Website: www.harriman-house.com

First published in Great Britain in 2015

Print ISBN: 9780857193445
eBook ISBN: 9780857194794

British Library Cataloguing in Publication Data

A CIP catalogue record for this book can be obtained from the British Library.

To the soul of my father.
To my wife, Warda, for her love,
encouragement and all her support.

Acknowledgements

This book would not have come into existence without the inspiration, support and encouragement of my wife. She inspired me to write and persistently supported me during the whole process, tolerating my hours of absence while writing and researching.

I should also like to thank Craig Pearce at Harriman House Inc. for his meticulous editing of the manuscripts of this book.

Preface

The Professional Risk Managers' International Association (PRMIA) sponsors the Professional Risk Manager (PRM) designation, which is awarded to candidates who pass the exam and the work experience requirements. To satisfy the examination requirements, a candidate must go through the following exams (which do not need to be taken in order):

- PRM Exam I: Finance theory, financial instruments and markets.
- PRM Exam II: Mathematical foundations of risk measurement.
- PRM Exam III: Risk management practices.
- PRM Exam IV: Case studies, PRMIA standards of best practice, conduct and ethics, by-laws.

There are limited resources and options available to help candidates prepare for these exams and there is no compulsory set of materials that candidates must use for their preparation.

From my extensive experience in teaching PRM preparatory courses to PRM candidates, I have seen that they find preparation for the exams using the official material from PRMIA extremely difficult. Due to the limited number of study manuals that are available in the market for these exams, PRM candidates rely on various books on finance and financial instruments to learn the information they need. This approach is time-consuming and does not make the candidate, especially the new entrant to the field of risk management, confident about their readiness for the exams. The *Professional Risk Manager (PRM®) Exam Handbook – Exam 1* has been put together to address this problem and help PRM candidates sitting the PRM exams. My intention is to remove the need to refer to many different reference works and to make the obscure concepts comprehensible.

The *Professional Risk Manager (PRM®) Exam Handbook – Exam 1* covers the Learning Outcome Statements (LOSs) issued by PRMIA for **Exam 1 only**. I cover the different requirements of the four exams in four different volumes because PRMIA gives candidates the option to sit the exams in any order. Also, I have noticed that PRM candidates tend to sit one exam at a time. So, it is convenient for the candidates to have one book for each exam and also to avoid having a bulky book combining materials for all four exams. This book should be read with the PRMIA official material, the *PRM Handbook*, which is available from the PRMIA online store.

The *Professional Risk Manager (PRM®) Exam Handbook* is LOS-structured. PRMIA issues these LOSs on its website. The LOSs for Exam 1, as in *PRM Self Study Guide – Exam 1*, have remained pretty much the same over time.

In Exam 1 LOSs, PRMIA divides the material for each topic into different chapters. For example, PRMIA discuss bonds in three separate chapters (analysis of bonds, bond markets, general characters of bonds). In my opinion, and from my experience in teaching PRM exam preparatory courses, this could create confusion for candidates and cause them not to properly see the sequences of concepts and their application.

So, I designed this *Handbook* to include all the materials related to each topic under one chapter. For instance, **Chapter 4: Bond Markets and Contracts** encompasses all the PRMIA LOSs related to the basic characteristics of bonds, bond pricing, types of bonds, the bond market, convertible bonds, etc. I have also combined the sub-topics discussed in different chapters by PRMIA into single chapters under one dedicated section.

Structure of this book

Chapter 1 – Corporate Finance encompasses the LOSs related to risk and risk aversion, capital allocation, CAPM and capital structure. I have combined these topics because they are all concerned with corporate finance and they are interrelated.

Chapter 2 – Portfolio Mathematics discusses the math of portfolio theory.

Chapter 3 – Term Structure of Interest Rates outlines the theory of the interest rate term structure.

Chapter 4 – Bond Markets and Contracts addresses bonds. This chapter includes all the LOSs in *general characteristics of bonds*, *analysis of bonds* and *bond markets*, which are discussed in separate chapters by PRMIA official material.

Chapter 4 starts with bond basics, including terminology and reasons for issuing or investing in bonds. It then moves on to discuss how bonds are priced and the cash flows involved in the calculation of the price. After learning the concepts of bond pricing and working on some examples of this, the candidate will be ready to look at the relationship between the bond price and the interest rate, and the tools available to measure this relationship. This is the toughest part of the chapter. The remainder of the chapter discusses the different types of bonds available in the market and peculiarities of bond markets.

Chapter 5 – Options Markets and Contracts addresses options markets and contracts. Again, PRMIA official material scatters the topics on options across different chapters in the following sequence: *basic principles of options pricing*, then *vanilla options* and *caps and floors*. I have combined the LOSs of these three topics into one chapter. I believe concepts of options and their types should be established and demystified, then the discussion should flow, in the same chapter, to the methods of pricing options and the factors affecting this.

Chapter 6 – Forward Markets and Contracts addresses the forward market and contracts. In this chapter I have covered the LOSs related to forward contracts only from *futures and forwards* and *valuing forward contracts* as indicated in the PRMIA official material.

Chapter 7 – Futures Markets and Contracts addresses the futures market and contracts. In this chapter I have covered the LOSs related to futures contracts only from *futures and forwards* and the *futures markets* as indicated in the PRMIA official material.

Chapter 8 – Swap Market and Contracts.

Chapter 9 – Credit Derivatives.

Chapter 10 – Stock Market discusses the fundamental concepts, structures and terminologies in financial markets, in general, then moves on to discuss the stock market in particular. I have combined the LOSs from *structure of financial market* and *stock market* as indicated in the PRMIA official material, because they are interrelated.

Chapters 11-14 discuss the money, foreign exchange (FX), commodity and energy markets, respectively.

With the necessary combinations of interrelated topics, you can read the *Handbook* in any order – there is no need to go through the chapters in sequence. It is worth mentioning that the chapters are designed based on very minimal prerequisite knowledge in risk and finance. Hence, PRM candidates coming from a non-financial background should face no difficulty using this book as a reference to the intricacies of financial markets and risk management.

Every owner of a physical copy of

Professional Risk Manager Exam Handbook: Exam 1

can download the eBook for free direct from us at Harriman House, in a format that can be read on any eReader, tablet or smartphone.

Simply go to:

ebooks.harriman-house.com/riskexamhandbook1

to get your copy now.

Contents

Introduction

Risk management is no longer merely a passive cost center in financial and non-financial organizations. Regulators, shareholders, executive management and investors look to risk managers for advice on risk budgeting. Since the financial crisis erupted in 2007, risk managers are expected more than before to make a thorough internal assessment of their organization's risk management frameworks and advise the board of directors and investors on their findings.

To undertake these responsibilities, risk managers must be equipped with an in-depth understanding of:

- Their firm's risk profile, tolerance and their methodologies.
- Expected returns from accepting risks.
- Capital available and the trade-off between capital regulation, risks and return.
- Tools available to identify, quantify, monitor, report and hedge risks.

Through its Professional Risk Manager (PRM) examination, the Professional Risk Managers' International Association (PRMIA) offers an outstanding tool of education for risk managers in financial institutions. PRMIA is a non-profit professional association with 90,000 members worldwide and 65 chapters in major cities around the world.

To be awarded the PRM designation, PRM candidates must successfully pass four exams. The PRM exams are multiple-choice and computer-based, and administrated by PRMIA at four intervals throughout the year. There are around 5,000 testing centers in 160 countries worldwide. According to PRMIA, over 2,400 companies worldwide employ PRM holders.

Chapter 1. Corporate Finance

This chapter includes the following sections:

1. Risk, utility and interest rate.
2. Capital allocation.
3. Capital structure.

1.1 Risk, Utility and Interest Rate

In this section we will address the LOSs related to the following topics:

- Continuous and discrete compounding.
- Nominal and effective interest rate.
- Utility maximization and function.
- Risk aversion.
- Mean-variance criterion.
- Risk adjusted performance measurements (RAPM):
  1. Sharpe ratio.
  2. Jensen alpha.
  3. Treynor ratio.
  4. Information ratio.
  5. Risk adjusted return on capital (RAROC).
  6. Return over value at risk (RoVaR).
  7. Sortino ratio.
  8. Omega index.

LOS. Differentiate between continuous and discrete compounding

As the name implies, in **discrete compounding** interest is compounded in a discrete number of periods during the year. With quarterly compounding, for instance, interest is compounded four times per year, and with monthly compounding, interest is compounded 12 times a year.

On the other hand, in **continuous compounding** money generates income every second. So the period is infinitesimally small in continuous compounding. In mathematical terms, when a variable value (the time per year in this context) reduces to a smaller amount, it goes to infinity. This is called continuous compounding.

Therefore, for an investment with a given present value, the future value of the investment is *larger* with continuous compounding than with discrete compounding. Similarly, for an investment with a given future value, the present value of the investment is *smaller* with continuous compounding than with discrete compounding.

For example, the future value (FV) of $100 invested today for six months at an interest rate of 7%, if compounded on a continuous basis, is:

$$FV = \$100 \times e(0.07 \times 0.5) = \$103.562$$

But if discretely compounded annually:

$$FV = \$100 \times (10.07)0.5 = \$103.441$$

LOS. Differentiate between the nominal interest rate and effective yield

The nominal interest rate is the rate at which money will grow in a specified period prior to any adjustment for inflation. For example, if you invested $100 in a bank account on 1 January 2009 at an interest rate of 10% for one year, on 31 December 2009 your bank account will have the following balance:

$$100 \times (1.1)1 = \$110$$

The 10% is the nominal interest rate. This is the rate at which your money has grown from 1 January 2009 to 31 December 2009. Assume that the $100 invested had the power to buy a couple of shirts, for instance, but on 31 December 2009 it could only buy one shirt. This means that the $100 has lost some of its purchasing power over the course of the year. So you, as an investor, invested $100 to generate interest of 10%, but lost the purchasing power of one shirt. The net effect is that your real residual benefit is 10% less the loss of purchasing power. The residual return is called the real interest rate.

real interest rate = nominal interest rate – inflation

Assume that an investment opportunity (A) earns a 10% nominal interest rate for two months and another investment (B) generates a 12% nominal interest rate for three months. *Which investment opportunity would you choose?*

Since the two investment opportunities have two different maturities, it would need some consideration to decide which one is more profitable. To make a prudent choice between the two investment opportunities that have different interest rates and maturities we need a standardizing measure to enable us to evaluate these opportunities. This measure is the **effective interest rate of return.** The effective interest rate of return is typically stated on an annual basis. The formula for the calculation of the effective interest rate is as follows:

$$r = \left(1 + \frac{i}{m}\right)^m - 1$$

Where:

r = effective interest rate

i = nominal interest rate

m = number of compounding periods

Let us take another example that differentiates between the nominal interest rate and the effective interest rate of return. Assume that today you have $100 to invest either in a bank account that pays 12% compounded yearly (Bank A) and an account that pays 12% compounded quarterly (Bank B). *In which bank will you choose to deposit your $100?*

Bank A

Time	Value	Calculation
Today	$100.00	
end of year	$112.00	(100 × 12%)+100

Bank B

Time	Value	Calculation
Today	$100	
End of Q1	$103.00	(100 × (1+12%/4))
End of Q2	$106.09	(103 × (1+12%/4))
End of Q3	$109.27	(106.09 × (1+12%/4))
End of Q4	$112.55	(109.272 × (1+12%/4))
holding period return is equal to :	12.55%	(112.5509-100)/100

The table shows that investing in Bank B you would end up with $112.55, while in Bank A you end up with only $112. This indicates that you *earn* more in Bank B than in Bank A, despite their nominal interest rates being the same. From that we can conclude that the more you compound the interest rate per year, the higher the difference between the effective interest and the nominal interest rate.

LOS. Explain the concepts of utility and utility maximization
LOS. Explain the ways to determine the utility function

With limited income, consumers buy as much as they get satisfaction from and as long as their income allows them to buy. With each extra unit they purchase this satisfaction decreases. If you are hungry, the first sandwich you buy gives you huge satisfaction; the second one will give you satisfaction, but not as much as the first. You continue buying more sandwiches until you reach a point where you cannot eat any more and it does not make economic sense to buy more.

The satisfaction you got from eating sandwiches is the **utility** from eating them. Your utility was maximized at the point you were totally full and could not eat another sandwich. **Marginal utility (MU)** is the *extra* utility you receive from buying one more unit of the product. The marginal utility will increase until your utility, i.e. satisfaction, gets lower. In this case the marginal utility will decline and could be negative (if you continue eating sandwiches once you are full, you would cause harm to your stomach and the satisfaction will turn to illness).

Utility maximizing rule:

1. Rational consumers should compare the extra utility they receive from each product with the extra price they pay for this product. MU per dollar is found by taking the marginal utility per product over the price of each product. This can be used to determine a buying pattern, and to help figure out which product will be bought and when.
2. If marginal utility increases, that means the extra utility or satisfaction one gets from buying a certain product exceeds the additional price paid for it.
3. If marginal utility decreases, that means the extra utility or satisfaction one gets from buying a certain product is less than the additional price paid.

Algebraically this can be written as:

$$\frac{MUa}{Pa} = \frac{MUb}{Pb}$$

For example, if MU of product A is 6 units, and the price of A is $1, while MU of product B is 18 units and the price of B is $2, MU/$ for product A is 6 and MU/$ for product B is 9.

This concludes that the consumer can increase total utility by purchasing more of product B than product A. So, we may conclude that utility is the value a person attributes to an asset, while the price of the asset is what the market considers as the value of the asset. Thus, utility from a single asset varies amongst participants in the market.

Swiss mathematician Daniel Bernoulli found that utility from an asset depends on the financial status of the participant.

St. Petersburg Paradox

Bernoulli studied the utility issue in light of what is known as the St. Petersburg game. In this game, a gambler is given a coin to toss. If the gambler gets a tail he should toss the coin again until he gets a head. If he gets a head from this first toss, he gets $1 and the game is over. But if gets a tail in the first toss, he should toss the coin again. If he gets a head in the second toss he gets $2, if he gets a head in the third toss he gets $4, etc. The payoff keeps doubling with every toss of the coin that results in a tail, until a head comes up and the game ends.

The formula of payoff in the Bernoulli game is as:

$$\text{payoff} = 2^{\text{number of coin tosses - 1}}$$

We denote the number of tosses as *K*

$$\text{payoff} = 2^{K-1}$$

Since the gambler can continue tossing the coin indefinitely, the payoff is also infinite.

The paradox is that although the payoff is theoretically infinite and one should enter the game at any price if offered to do so, most people would be unwilling to pay much to enter the game as they do not trust the result. It has been suggested that many people would not even pay $25 to take part.

Bernoulli suggested a solution to this paradox by proposing that the payoff (i.e. the money) has marginal utility. This means even if the payoff is infinite that does not mean that a game would be played infinitely. Even though it is theoretically possible, in practice it is not, because there is an inverse relationship between money and utility. The richer the person, the lower the expected utility from the game and the poorer the person, the higher the utility of the game.

Based on that, Bernoulli formulated the **utility function** to be:

$$\text{utility of } (x) = \text{logarithm } (x)$$

Utility function

The utility of a decision or process (p) if it could lead to multiple outcomes is the result of multiplying the utility of each outcome (a,b,c) by the probability of its occurrence.

$$U(p) = U_a.P_a + U_b.P_b + U_c.P_c\ldots\ldots$$

Where:

Ua = Utility of outcome (a)

Pa = probability that outcome (a) will occur

LOS. Explain the concept of risk aversion

The risk-averse investor seeks to avoid two things: uncertainty and volatility. So, for the same level of risk, the risk-averse investor will choose an investment alternative that gives the highest return and for the same level of return would choose an alternative that results in lower risk.

According to Bernoulli's utility function, the utility of the three types of investors (risk averse, risk taker and risk neutral) would be as follows:

Type of investor	Bernoulli utility function	Description
Risk averse	u(x) = log(x)	Utility of expected return > expected utility of investment (x)
Risk taker	u(x) = x^2	Utility of expected return < expected utility of investment (x)
Risk neutral	u(x) = 2x	Utility of expected return = expected utility of investment (x)

LOS. Discuss the mean-variance criterion

The mean-variance criterion means an investor, when presented with two or multiple investment opportunities each with different rates of return and risks (measured by variance and standard deviation), looks at the return and risk of each and selects her investment by choosing the level of return and risk according to her profile. If she is risk averse, she would choose the highest return for a given level of risk, or the lowest risk for a given rate of return.

LOS. Define the Sharpe, Treynor and Information ratios
LOS. Define the Sortino, Omega Index and Kappa ratios
LOS. Define Jensen's alpha, RAROC and RoVaR

Sharpe ratio

The Sharpe ratio is defined as a reward-to-variability ratio. It is used in investment performance measurement to measure the risk adjusted return (i.e. it measures how much excess return per unit of risk the investment achieved). Since the Sharpe ratio indicates the return per unit of risk for each investment, it is used to rank alternative investments. Generally, the higher the Sharpe ratio the better, because it indicates a higher return for a lower level of risk.

Excess return is measured by the difference between the expected return on an investment and the risk-free rate. Risk is measured by the standard deviation. It is written algebraically as follows:

$$\text{Sharpe ratio} = \frac{\mu - r}{\sigma}$$

Where:

r = risk-free rate

μ = expected return from investment

σ = standard deviation of investment return

Treynor ratio

The Treynor ratio measures the differences between the average excess return on an investment portfolio and the average risk-free rate per unit of systematic risk. Systematic risk is measured by beta. So it is similar to the Sharpe ratio, except that the Treynor ratio divides the excess return by beta instead of by standard deviation. It is written algebraically as follows:

$$\text{Treynor ratio} = \frac{Rp - r}{\beta}$$

Rp = average return on the portfolio

r = risk-free rate

β = beta

Jensen's alpha

Jensen's alpha is a measure that compares the excess of the average actual return of a portfolio to the return predicted by the Capital Asset Pricing Model (CAPM). Similar to the Sharpe ratio, Jensen's alpha is also used for investment performance measurement. The higher the alpha, the higher the excess return.

$$\text{Jensen's alpha}(\alpha) = \text{actual return} - \text{expected return}$$

$$= R_a - [R_f + (R_m - R_f)\beta]$$

Risk adjusted return on capital (RAROC)

The risk adjusted return on capital is considered the most reliable performance measure in financial institutions as it measures the return each business line achieves per unit of risk assumed in relation to the economic capital. Economic capital is the size of the firm's equity that would absorb all the risks assumed.

$$\text{RAROC} = \frac{\text{expected return net of expected loss and all costs}}{\text{economic capital}}$$

Return over Value at Risk (RoVaR)

Return over VaR is similar to RAROC, but in relation to VaR instead of the economic capital.

$$\text{ROVAR} = \frac{\text{expected return net of expected loss and all costs}}{\text{VaR}}$$

Sortino ratio

The Sortino ratio is a modification of the Sharpe ratio. In the Sharpe ratio the excess return is divided by the standard deviation of the return. Standard deviation of all the returns, in the normal distribution as assumed by Sharpe, includes positive deviation from the mean as well as negative deviations. What is of concern to the investment manager or investor is the downside, i.e. the negative deviations from the average return. So, Sortino proposed that the excess return is divided only by the standard negative deviation of the returns.

$$\text{Sortino ratio} = \frac{\mu - r}{\sigma d}$$

Where σd is the standard deviation of the left side of the mean on the normal distribution.

Omega ratio

The Omega ratio is also a modification to the Sharpe ratio. The Sharpe ratio is a useful performance measure in a limited context because it assumes a normal distribution of investment returns. There are other investments in which the return does not show a normal distribution and the use of the Sharpe ratio in these cases would be misleading. For non-normal distributions, a performance measure should take into consideration the skew and the kurtosis of the return distribution, as does the Omega ratio.

$$\text{Omega ratio} = \frac{\int_r^b 1 - F(x)dx}{\int_a^r 1 - F(x)dx}$$

It can be simplified as follows:

$$\text{Omega ratio} = \frac{E\left[Max(R - \tau), 0\right]}{E\left[Max(\tau - R), 0\right]}$$

Information ratio

The information ratio is designed with the same concept as the Sharpe ratio, but with the following differences:

- It measures the excess return in relation to a benchmark (typically an index), not in relation to the risk-free rate.
- It divides the excess return by the standard deviation of the observations in which the return varies from the benchmark, i.e. the tracking errors.

So, the information ratio not only measures whether the investment manager achieved a positive return in relation to the benchmark, but also measures, by dividing by the tracking errors, the consistency of doing so.

$$\text{information ratio} = \frac{Ri - Rb}{\sigma te}$$

Where:

Ri = Return of the investment

Rb = Return of the benchmark

σte = standard deviation of the errors, defined by the differences between the return on the investment and the return on the benchmark

1.2 Capital Allocation

In this section, I will discuss the LOSs related to the following topics:

1. Efficient frontier.
2. Capital market line (CML).
3. Market portfolio.
4. Capital asset pricing model (CAPM).
5. Arbitrage Pricing Theory (APT).

LOS. Describe efficient portfolios that satisfy the mean-variance criterion
LOS. Define the risk-free asset
LOS. Show the efficient frontier for two assets
LOS. Show the efficient frontier for a multi-asset portfolio
LOS. Describe the capital market line
LOS. Define the market portfolio
LOS. Derive and describe the capital market line
LOS. Derive the security market line

Investors are typically assumed to be risk averse. According to the mean-variance tradeoff, if an investor has the chance to choose from two portfolios, they would choose the one with the higher return or the one with the lower risk. Risk is measured by variance or standard deviation. Portfolios that meet this criterion are called *efficient portfolios.*

Two risky assets

Assume you have $100,000 and would like to allocate this within a portfolio comprising two assets. The expected return and risk of each asset is indicated below:

Asset	X	Y
Expected return	16%	14%
Standard deviation	20%	23%

The expected return of a portfolio that is totally invested in asset Y is 14% and the expected return of a portfolio that is totally invested in asset X is 16%.

We will discuss the underlying detailed calculations for this LOS in Chapter 2. The important thing to understand at this point is the concept, not carrying out the calculations.

The following table illustrates how the portfolio's expected return and risk change as we alter the weight of each asset in the portfolio.

	Weight of X	Weight of Y	Portfolio standard deviation	Portfolio expected return
Portfolio combination 1	0%	100%	23.00%	14.00%
Portfolio combination 2	20%	80%	17.99%	14.40%
Portfolio combination 3	40%	60%	14.42%	14.80%
Portfolio combination 4	60%	40%	13.50%	15.20%
Portfolio combination 5	80%	20%	15.69%	15.60%
Portfolio combination 6	100%	0%	20.00%	16.00%

The purpose of this table is to find the optimum combination. The optimum combination means constructing a portfolio using weights of assets X and Y that would yield the lowest risk for the same rate of return as other investment opportunities, or highest return for the same level of risk as other investment opportunities. To compare the combinations we use the table above and the chart below.

The chart shows that portfolio combination 4 has the lowest risk. This is called the optimal portfolio. It is the optimal portfolio because none of the other portfolio combinations gives you higher return for the same level of risk (13.5%). You can find a higher return if you move to the right, but that will also give you higher risk.

Standard deviation is the square root of the variance and since the optimal portfolio is the portfolio combination that gives the lowest risk as measured by standard deviation, we can say that the optimal portfolio is the minimum-variance portfolio.

Combination 4 is an optimum combination for the risk-averse investor only. Risk-taking investors would be happy to go for combination 6 – with a 16% return – even though that means taking more risk.

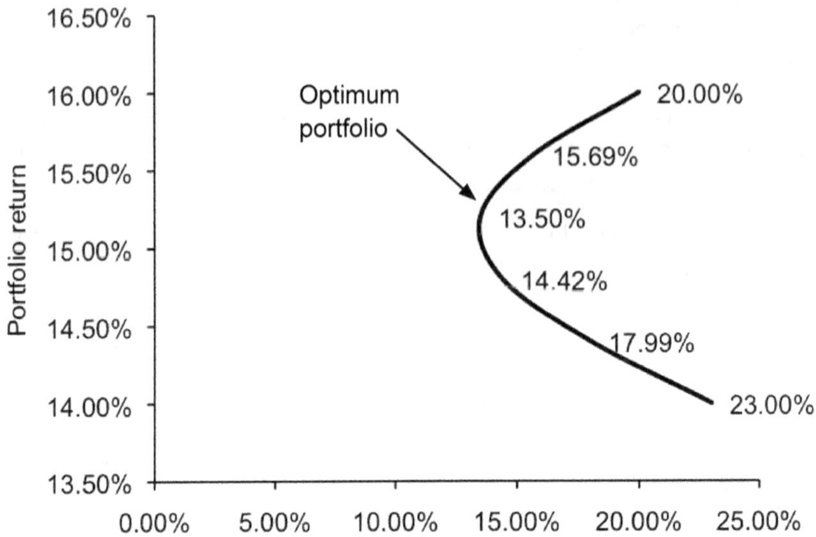

The optimum combinations on the curve that encompass all possible combinations between assets X and Y is the efficient frontier curve. It is called the efficient frontier because on this curve lies the optimum combination with the risk-return trade off. Combinations beyond it are unattainable, while combinations below it are not fully utilized.

Risk-free and risky asset

In the following example we assume that we have two assets. One of them (X) is risky (it has standard deviation higher than zero), while the other (Y) is risk-free, say a government security. It is called a risk-free asset because theoretically government securities bear no credit risk. So asset Y, as a risk-free asset, will have a standard deviation of zero.

We will say that risky asset (X) has an expected return of 16% and standard deviation of 20%. Risk-free asset (Y) has an expected return of 9% and standard deviation of 0%. Assume also that the correlation between the two assets is zero.

Why is the correlation between the assets assumed to be zero?

Since government securities are risk-free securities, they do not move *linearly* with any other asset. The risk of owning them depends solely on the government increasing or decreasing the interest rate, so the covariance between any government securities and any other risky asset is zero. If the covariance is zero then the correlation should also be zero.

Assume that we can have the portfolio combinations shown in the following table.

	Weight of X	Weight of Y	Portfolio standard deviation	Portfolio expected return
Portfolio combination 1	0%	100%	0.00%	9.00%
Portfolio combination 2	20%	80%	4.00%	10.40%
Portfolio combination 3	40%	60%	8.00%	11.80%
Portfolio combination 4	60%	40%	12.00%	13.20%
Portfolio combination 5	80%	20%	16.00%	14.60%
Portfolio combination 6	100%	0%	20.00%	16.00%

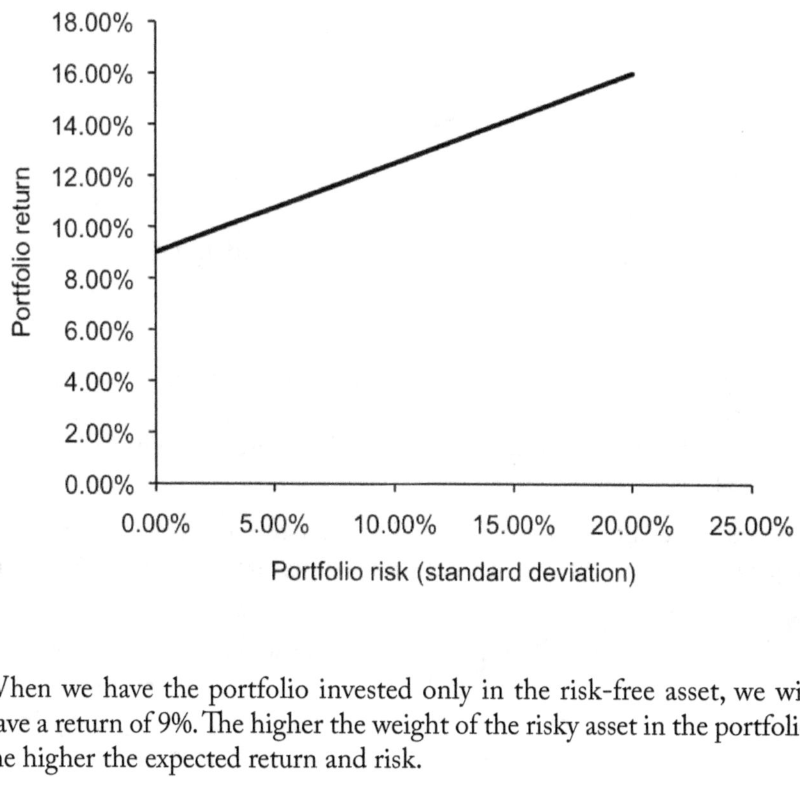

When we have the portfolio invested only in the risk-free asset, we will have a return of 9%. The higher the weight of the risky asset in the portfolio, the higher the expected return and risk.

Multiple-risky assets

So far we have discussed having two risky assets in the portfolio, and a portfolio with a risky and risk-free asset. In this section we will discuss having *N* number of risky assets in the portfolio.

Assume that we choose all the equities in an index and we are seeking the optimum combinations. We can vary the weight of each of these assets in a portfolio and assess the return and risk of each portfolio combination. The outcome of this simulation is illustrated in the chart below. P1 = portfolio 1, P2 = portfolio 2, etc.

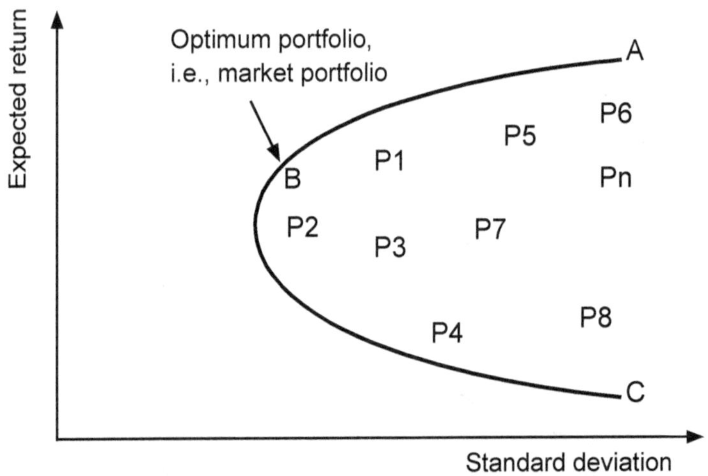

When we draw all the resultant combinations in our simulations we have a curved line – the efficient frontier curve. As mentioned before, this curve separates the inefficient portfolios from the unattainable ones, hence the name efficient frontier.

On the efficient frontier curve we can have many combinations. The objective is to find the optimum portfolio combinations of all the portfolios on the efficient frontier curve.

The optimum portfolio is at point B in the above chart. It is the optimum portfolio because it is the portfolio at a tangent to the straight line that crosses the curve. There is a mathematical reason why the optimum combination is the one at a tangent to the line, but that is beyond the scope of the PRM exam. For the exam you just need to understand this important concept.

The portfolio at point B is called the global or market portfolio. It gives the best combination of low variance and high return. It is called the market portfolio because it encompasses all the equities in the market.

By drawing the tangent line that crosses the optimum portfolio and the y-axis, the tangent line and the y-axis intersect at the risk-free rate point; the tangent line is called the capital market line (CML) and is illustrated in the following diagram.

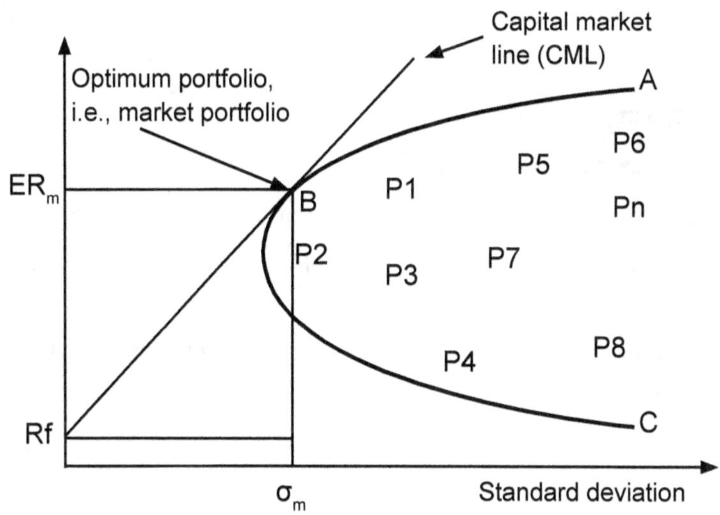

The investor's expected return would be the excess return over the risk-free rate of return (ERm-Rf) in relation to the risk of the portfolio.

$$\text{return} - \text{risk ratio} = \frac{ERm - Rf}{\sigma m}$$

Since the CML depicts a linear relationship between return and risk, we can algebraically express the CML in the following equation:

$$Y = a + bX$$

Where:

Y = the expected return from the investment. It is the dependent variable.

a = the y-axis intercept which equals to the risk-free rate

b = slope of the CML, which is equal to the return-risk ratio.

X = the standard deviation of the return. It is the independent variable.

Based on this we can rewrite the CML equation as follows:

$$ER = R_f + \left[\frac{ERm - Rf}{\sigma m}\right]\sigma m$$

CML characteristics:

- CML intersects the y-axis at the risk-free rate level.
- The slope of the CML is the reward-risk ratio (the Sharpe ratio).
- The slope of CML depends on the risk appetite of each investor. So there is a CML for each investor.
- CML intercepts the efficient frontier curve at the optimum, or market/global portfolio.

Beta

As a prudent investor, there is an issue that you should take into consideration in your investment decisions. To illustrate this point, assume that you have two stocks: one is a real estate company's stock and the other is an infant food company's stock (IFC). Assume also that the risk-free rate is 5%.

Will you expect the same premium from both assets? The answer should be no. At times of crisis, people do not behave in the same manner, including in their consumption of goods and services. At times of crisis, people and institutions might defer their investment decisions but they would still consume what they need of the infant's food. This reaction affects the demands and the prices of these two products and subsequently the risk and expected return of the companies' stock.

So we may conclude that the IFC stock is not strongly and positively correlated with the market, while the real estate company's stock is. IFC stock has lower sensitivity to market movements than real estate stock. This sensitivity to market moves is measured by **beta**. So, grocery stores have lower beta and real estate assets have higher beta.

Investors expect a premium that takes this beta effect into consideration. Thus, a more accurate expected return formula should be written like this:

expected return = risk free asset + (risk premium) × beta

Where:

risk premium = market return - risk free return

When we draw the relationship between the expected return and beta for each investment opportunity we would have a linear relationship, as shown in the following chart. The line shown in the chart is the security market line (SML).

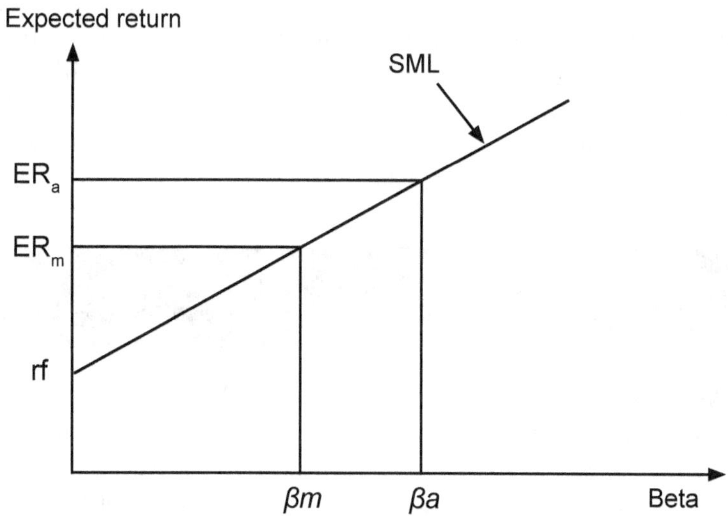

The equation to calculate the return according to the SML is called the capital asset pricing model (CAPM) and it is as follows:

expected return = Rf + (Rm–Rf)β

Where:

Rf = risk-free rate

Rm= return in the market

beta = sensitivity of the asset return to the market changes

LOS. Describe the separation principle

Separation is between the investment and the financing decision. The principle asserts that the optimum objective of the firm is to maximize its value through maximizing the present value of its assets/projects. So, the investment value depends on the firm's choices of the optimum opportunities that lead to that result. Decisions or choices of the best opportunities that maximize the firm's value have nothing to do with how these opportunities are financed, whether by debt or equity. In other words, the investment decisions are not related to the capital structure of the firm. This is also called the separation theorem.

LOS. Describe the capital asset pricing model (CAPM)
LOS. List the assumptions of the CAPM

The CAPM is used to explain the relationship between the investor's expected return and risk. The risk takes into consideration two parts: the idiosyncratic risk triggered by the firm business risk and the systematic risk, which is not diversifiable. In addition to that, the investor gains an opportunity as a result of the investment. The return the investor requires for assuming these risks and cost are the risk-free rate and the premium on top of the risk-free rate.

The security market line (SML) depicts this relationship in the CAPM. The slope of the SML is beta: the measure of the systematic risk of the firm.

The assumptions of the CAPM are:

1. Investors are risk averse and maximize the expected utility of their end-of-period wealth.
2. Investors have homogenous expectations (beliefs) about asset returns, i.e. everyone has the same information at the same time.
3. Asset returns are normally distributed.
4. There exists a risk-free asset and investors may borrow or lend unlimited amounts of this asset at a constant rate, i.e. the risk-free rate (Rf).
5. There are a definite number of assets and their quantities are fixed within the one-period world.
6. All assets are perfectly divisible and priced in a perfectly competitive market.
7. Asset markets are frictionless and information is costless and simultaneously available to all investors. (Implication: the borrowing rate equals the lending rate.)
8. Perfect market conditions exist with respect to taxes, regulations and restrictions on short selling.

LOS. Describe beta as a measure of relative risk

Beta is a measure that determines the tendency of an asset's price to increase or decrease relative to the market.

Beta measures the volatility of ABC stock price, for instance, in relation to the changes in the whole stock market. Theoretically, beta can assume any number. Beta of 2 means that if the stock market changes by 10%, the ABC stock price will change by 20%. Beta of 1 means that if the stock market decreases by 10%, ABC stock price will also decrease by 10%.

Beta is calculated as follows:

$$\text{beta} = \frac{\text{Cov}(Ri, Rm)}{\text{variance of the market return}}$$

Where Cov(Ri,Rm) is the covariance between the investment return and market return.

LOS. Define risk premium

I have highlighted the concept of risk premium, which is an additional return on the risk-free rate that an investor should expect as a result of accepting higher risk compared to a risk-free asset. The risk premium is justified because of the firm business risk, which relates to the risk surrounding a firm's operating cash flows.

Operating cash flows are the result of the firm's total revenue and expenditures from its core daily business. The more uncertain these cash flows, the higher the risk. Uncertainty of these cash flows affects the firm's earning, which would in turn affect its market share price. Therefore, an investor would ask for a premium to cover this uncertainty.

LOS. Describe the single index model

The CML and SML formulas depict the relationship between the return and the standard deviation and beta, respectively. What these two formulas tell us is that the return depends only on a single independent variable, measured by standard deviation or beta. Thus, CML and SML are called *single index models.*

These models assume there is only one variable that affects the return on the investment. On the other hand, there are multi-index models which assume that the return formula depends on various risk factors, such as the interest rate, inflation and GDP.

LOS. Describe systematic and specific risk

In diversifying your portfolio, you continue to add more securities to your portfolio to reduce the aggregate risk. With more securities added, the risk will be reduced until you can no longer reduce it further, even if you add all the uncorrelated securities in the market. The remaining risk that cannot be diversified is the systematic risk which is not triggered by factors related to the financial and economic system as a whole.

Specific risk, on the other hand, is a risk that can be diversified because as the name suggests, it is triggered by firm specific factors (qualitative and quantitative). This risk is also called idiosyncratic risk. An example of specific risk is plummeting sales as a result of unsatisfactory quality perceived by customers.

LOS. Describe the arbitrage pricing theory (APT)

Arbitrage means making a riskless profit with no investment. Arbitrage takes place by exploiting discrepancies in prices of the same asset in different markets. It entails purchasing a security or instrument in one market and the simultaneous sale (or purchase) of it, or its equivalent, in the same or another market. These discrepancies cannot be exploited easily due to transaction costs and other technological factors, but when an arbitrage opportunity is exploited at the right time it results in a positive return with zero risk. This kind of transaction is easier said than done because if such opportunities were readily available in the market, the whole world would be rich.

Assume GE stock trades on the New York Exchange and the Dubai Exchange. The price of the stock in New York is $50 and in Dubai it is $55. An arbitrageur (the person who engages in arbitrage) can buy the GE stock in New York and sell in Dubai, simultaneously, and generate a profit of $5. We called this transaction riskless because it involves a simultaneous buying and selling of the security.

We also describe it as 'no investment', because an arbitrageur does not have to put any money on the table. The amount to buy the GE stock in New York can be borrowed from a broker and the amount of the loan would be paid to the broker, plus interest, after the sale of the stock in Dubai.

Although it is typical for the arbitrageur to borrow instead of investing in the arbitrage opportunity, it is also possible that an arbitrageur invests directly in the transaction. There are two important points to be considered here before we move on to discuss the APT.

First, arbitrage opportunities are indicators of an inefficient market. Typically, the same asset should be priced equally in different markets. So, in finance theories, particularly in pricing assets, it is always assumed that arbitrage opportunity does not exist, i.e. there is a no-arbitrage assumption. Second, there are many barriers to engaging in arbitrage, such as transactions costs and taxes.

With zero risk, an arbitrage portfolio is said to be perfectly hedged. A perfectly hedged portfolio or investment is when the change in the value of the hedging instrument exactly offsets the change in the value of the hedged position.

Arbitrage Pricing Theory (APT) proposes an alternative to the Capital Asset Pricing Model (CAPM). APT indicates that the CAPM – which has only one sensitivity factor to the market, beta – is not enough to capture the true risk of the investment and subsequently is not enough to determine the required rate of return.

The assumptions of APT are:

- Investors choose portfolios on the basis of expected return and risk only.
- There is a single holding period that is the same for all investors.
- There is a riskless security in the world and all investors are able to borrow and lend at this risk-free rate.

$$R_{it} = a_i + \sum_{j=1}^{k} b_{ij} F_{jt} + e_{it}$$

Where:

a_i = alpha factor

b_{ij} = beta of the factor F

F_{ji} = the variable (such as inflation, interest rate, etc.)

e_{it} = error terms

1.3 Capital Structure

In this section we will discuss the LOSs related to the following topics:

- Firm value.
- Agency cost.
- Debt capital.
- Equity capital.
- Impact of leverage of return on equity (ROE).
- Optimum capital structure.

LOS. Explain and show the formula for the value of a firm
LOS. Characterize the impact of leverage on ROE volatility

The sources of a firm's capital are either debt or equity. These sources of capital are used to finance the assets on the balance sheet. So, the value of the firm is either the value of its assets or the value of its equity plus its debt.

From the investor's perspective, we can assign a value to the debt and equity from the cash flows available to the debtors and shareholders. These cash flows are called free cash flows, operating free cash flows or free cash flows to the firm. 'Free' means it is available after deducting all the working capital and capital expenditures planned to take place at the firm. So, the value of the firm is calculated as:

$$\text{value of the firm} = \sum_{t=1}^{\infty} \frac{\text{OFCF}}{(1+\text{WACC})}$$

Where:

OFCF = operating free cash flow

WACC = weighted average cost of capital

Then:

WACC = weighted cost of debt + weighted cost of equity

Since the weight of each component within the capital structure will determine the net impact on WACC, we can rewrite the WACC formula as follows:

WACC = (cost of debt × weight of debt) + (cost of equity × weight of equity)

cost of debt = interest rate on debt × (1-T)

cost of debt = rd × (1-T)

The cost of equity can be estimated from the CAPM as follows:

$$r_e = R_f + (R_m - R_f)\beta$$

or from the dividends discount model as follows:

$$r = g + \frac{D1}{P0}$$

Where

g = dividends expected growth rate

D1 = expected dividends

P0 = share current price

The question that should be asked is: *what is the optimum level of debt or equity in the capital structure?*

The answer is: we do not really know unless we do some calculations in relation to the value of the firm. The optimum combination is the one that maximizes the value of the firm.

From the above formula for calculating the value of the firm, we can also see that the value of the firm is maximized when the denominator (WACC) is minimized, or the numerator (OFCF) is maximized. Another question is this: *if interest on debt is tax-deductible, is it not prudent for the firm to structure its capital with 100% debt?* We will answer this question in the following comprehensive example.

Example 1.1: Capital structure

Assume the following information about a firm:

- Tax rate 35%.
- Can borrow at an interest rate of 8%.
- Would like to raise capital of $100,000.

The company explores the optimum combination of debt or equity, i.e. how much of the $100,000 it should borrow and how much it should issue in the form of shares (equity).

The beta of the firm is 1.5, the return in the market is 15% and the risk-free rate is 5%. Determine the firm's optimum capital structure through hypothesized scenarios.

Solution

At the beginning we would calculate the cost of debt and equity:

cost of debt = interest rate on debt × (1 - T)

8% × (1 - 35%) = 5.2%

cost of equity = $r_e = R_f + (R_m - R_f)$

5% + (15% - 5%) × 1.5 = 20%

Assume the initial scenario is that the firm's earnings before interest and taxes (EBIT) = $0. Also, assume that the firm will not borrow and designs its capital structure as 100% equity.

So:

EBIT - interest × (1- 35%) = net income

0 - 0 × (1 - 35%) = 0

ROE = 0/10,000 = 0%

Or ROE = ROI + (ROI - rd)(debt/equity)

Assume that the firm seeks 90% debt and 10% equity and its EBIT is zero:

net income = 0 - (90% × 100,000 × 8%)(1 - 35%) = -4,680

ROE = -4,680/10,000 = -46.8%

WACC = 5.2%(90,000/100,000) + 20% (10,000/100,000) = 6.68%

We will repeat the same steps for the scenarios as illustrated in the following table:

			When EBIT=0			
Debt	0%	10%	30%	50%	70%	90%
Equity	100%	90%	70%	50%	30%	10%
Debt	0	10000	30000	50000	70000	90000
Equity	100000	90000	70000	50000	30000	10000
EBIT	0	0	0	0	0	0
Interest	0	800	2400	4000	5600	7200
Net Income	0	-520	-1560	-2600	-3640	-4680
ROE	0.00%	-0.58%	-2.23%	-5.20%	-12.13%	-46.80%
cost of debt	5.20%	5.20%	5.20%	5.20%	5.20%	5.20%
weight of debt	0%	10%	30%	50%	70%	90%
cost of equity	20%	20%	20%	20%	20%	20%
weight of equity	100%	90%	70%	50%	30%	10%
WACC	20.00%	18.52%	15.56%	12.60%	9.64%	6.68%
Value of the Firm	0	0	0	0	0	0

When EBIT=10000						
Debt	0%	10%	30%	50%	70%	90%
Equity	100%	90%	70%	50%	30%	10%
Debt	0	10000	30000	50000	70000	90000
Equity	100000	90000	70000	50000	30000	10000

EBIT	10,000	10,000	10,000	10,000	10,000	10,000
Interest	0	800	2400	4000	5600	7200
Net Income	6500	5980	4940	3900	2860	1820
ROE	6.50%	6.64%	7.06%	7.80%	9.53%	18.20%

cost of debt	5.20%	5.20%	5.20%	5.20%	5.20%	5.20%
weight of debt	0%	10%	30%	50%	70%	90%
cost of equity	20%	20%	20%	20%	20%	20%
weight of equity	100%	90%	70%	50%	30%	10%
WACC	20.00%	18.52%	15.56%	12.60%	9.64%	6.68%
Value of the Firm	8333.333	8437.395	8653.513	8880.995	9120.759	9373.828

When EBIT=40000						
Debt	0%	10%	30%	50%	70%	90%
Equity	100%	90%	70%	50%	30%	10%
Debt	0	10000	30000	50000	70000	90000
Equity	100000	90000	70000	50000	30000	10000
EBIT	40,000	40,000	40,000	40,000	40,000	40,000
Interest	0	800	2400	4000	5600	7200
Net Income	26000	25480	24440	23400	22360	21320
ROE	26.00%	28.31%	34.91%	46.80%	74.53%	213.20%
cost of debt	5.20%	5.20%	5.20%	5.20%	5.20%	5.20%
weight of debt	0%	10%	30%	50%	70%	90%
cost of equity	20%	20%	20%	20%	20%	20%
weight of equity	100%	90%	70%	50%	30%	10%
WACC	20.00%	18.52%	15.56%	12.60%	9.64%	6.68%
Value of the Firm	33333.33	33749.58	34614.05	35523.98	36483.04	37495.31

From the three tables we can make the following important observations:

1. The value of the firm is maximized when WACC is minimized.
2. ROE improves as debt in the capital structure increases – the higher the leverage, the higher the ROE. This might seem fine at first glance when the firm is making a profit, as ROE increases disproportionately to the increase in the leverage, but the risk of leverage on ROE is that the reverse happens when EBIT decreases; in this case ROE will decrease dramatically.
3. Although the value of the firm increases as WACC decreases with the increase of leverage, we cannot conclude that the

combination at the lowest WACC level is the optimum capital structure. The criteria for the optimum capital structure combination is not the value of the firm but the firm's share price.

4. Although the three tables above show that the higher the leverage the lower the WACC and the higher the value of the firm, in practice, firms do not choose to use the 90% debt and 10% equity kind of capital structure. This is because there are two risks that make excessive debt an unattractive choice:
   - Bankruptcy cost: Legal and possible liquidation costs are considerably high and impact the residual interest of both creditors and shareholders.
   - Exposure to financial distress: Panic created by excessive leverage might give a signal to the stakeholders that the company might not be able to honor its obligations when they fall due. This might lead to lower sales, higher costs of funding, inability to raise funds from the market, lower cash flows, etc.

LOS. Describe the agency costs of equity
LOS. Describe the agency costs of debt

I will structure the discussion of *agency* by looking at agency relationship, agency problems and agency costs in turn.

Agency relationship

Generally, an agency relationship exists when an individual or an organization (referred to as the principal) hire(s) and/or delegates another individual or an organization (referred to as an agent) to act on behalf of the principal.

Agents are entrusted to act and take decisions to meet the objectives set forth by the principals in a manner that maximizes the value to the principals. Agents undertake these responsibilities in exchange for financial and non-financial compensations/benefits.

Specifically, shareholders' investments are used to create an organization. A board of directors is nominated and elected by the shareholders to manage the organization, which in turn delegates to a team of individuals to form a *management* of the organization. The management is the agent which should work to maximize the value of the shareholders' investments. There are reasons behind the separation between the ownership and management:

1. Expertise: shareholders might have the financial investments necessary to establish an organization but they might lack the know-how to run this organization.
2. The opportunity cost incurred to run the newly-established organization forgoing the management of other existing investments.

Agency problems

Agency problems arise when the management acts in a way detrimental to the interest of the shareholders, i.e. management acts in a way that maximizes its own value and interest at the expense of the shareholders.

The problem is when the interest of the management deviates from the interest of the shareholders. Management is motivated to increase the returns (to increase their bonus, prestige and remunerations), which is typically accompanied by assuming excessive risks. Excessive risks might not be in line with the shareholders' risk appetite and capacity, or might not even be well understood by the shareholders in order that they can approve the action. Management might also be inclined to increase the size of the organization in an unsustainable manner, contrary to the objective of shareholders, in order to increase their prestige in the market.

Agency costs

In order to align the interests of the shareholders with those of the management, mechanisms need to be set out to reduce information asymmetry[1] and ensure that management always aims to maximize shareholder value. The costs of these mechanisms are referred to as *agency costs*. Agency costs are all the costs of monitoring tools that are adopted by debt-holders and shareholders to align the interests of the management with the interests of debt-holders and shareholders.

One mechanism that the shareholders put in place is a *board of directors (BoD)*. A BoD oversees the conduct of the management and ensures the alignment of both parties' interests. Shareholders incur the costs of this mechanism by paying BoD remunerations. Another example of the

1 Information asymmetry refers to the gap of knowledge and/ or information about the organization between the management and the shareholders.

agency cost of equity is the remuneration and incentives of the executive management of the firm. The executive management should be well incentivized to reduce the inclination to compensate dissatisfaction through unacceptable conduct. The costs of appointing an external auditing firm to give an opinion on the financial statements, a compliance officer to ensure adherence to the laws and regulations, and internal auditors reporting to the audit committee of the board are all equity agency costs as they are tools adopted to give shareholders comfort that their interests are not disadvantaged by the management.

Debt-holders as capital providers would also aim to ensure that the management of the organization does not act or take decisions that might be detrimental to the interest of the debt-holders and result in the organization's inability to repay its debt. A bank, for example, which extends a loan to a corporation would strive to ensure that the company does not assume excessive risks that might jeopardize its ability to repay the loan. There are several ways debt-holders can protect themselves from the agency problems. Pursuing these is costly, and these costs are referred to as *debt agency costs*.

LOS. Describe the characteristics of debt and equity

Debt and equity are both sources of finance or capital for all firms. We can distinguish their features as follows:

Factor	Debt-holder	Equity-holder
Cash flows	Fixed or floating periodic contractual payments to the lenders. Upon maturity, the loaned amount is paid back.	Constant or variable non-contractual dividends.
Maturity	Contractual period through which the debt is repaid with interest.	Has no redemption date unless the shareholder decides to sell the share or the company closes down.
Risk for holder	Low, because they rank first ahead of shareholders as claimant on the firm's assets in liquidation.	High, because they rank last as claimant on the firm's assets in liquidation after debt-holders and creditors.
Legal requirement	Borrower must pay the obligations even when making losses.	A company is not obliged to pay dividends when it makes losses.

LOS. Compare the considerations of the chief financial officer (CFO) for issuing debt vs. equity

The CFO takes the following factors into consideration when deciding on the level of debt and equity:

- **Agency cost**: The greater the financial and tangible assets a firm has, the lower the agency cost, and vice versa. This is because these assets can be collateralized to satisfy the creditors and lower their risk in lending to the firm. This leads to a lower agency cost.
- **Distress cost**: The higher the firm's volatility in sales and earnings, the lower its capacity to have debt in its capital structure, because debt requires a constant reliable source of earnings to pay the periodic interest payments.
- **Tax**: Although interest is tax deductible, a firm will need to consider its expense structure as regards to its capacity to absorb the interest expenses. So, tax is not the only reason to choose debt over equity.
- **Flexibility**: Debt is more flexible than equity as it could be negotiated, optioned, etc. A firm leans on debt if it plans to embark on future expansionary projects.

Chapter 2. Portfolio Mathematics

On the completion of this chapter you will have learnt:

1. How to calculate the rate of return and standard deviation of single and multiple asset portfolios.
2. Correlation and its role in diversification.
3. Portfolio VaR and performance analysis.

2.1 Rate of return and standard deviation for single and multiple asset portfolios

LOS. Calculate the return, mean return, variance and standard deviation of a single asset

The return referred to in this LOS is the change in an asset's price between two dates of valuation. Let us take investing in stocks as an example. Assume that you buy an asset for, say, \$10 on t_0, and the price of the stock has jumped to \$14 on t_1. It is said that your return of investing in this stock is the difference between these prices, i.e. your return in dollars is equal to \$14-\$10 = \$4. In percentage terms, the return could be expressed as your dollars return/your initial investment, 4/10 = 40%.

We can express these relationships mathematically:

$$\text{dollar return}(\$) = S_0 - S_1$$

$$\text{dollar return}(\%) = \frac{S_1 - S_0}{S_0}$$

Example 2.1: Calculate rate of return

Assume that you observed the price of stock ABC for the past five trading days. The following table illustrates the price at the end of each trading day.

Day	Price	Return
Day 1	10	
Day 2	11.5	15%
Day 3	12	4%
Day 4	10.3	-14%

The return on day 2 is the difference between the asset price at the end of trading day 1 and trading day 2: (11.5-10)/10.

For investment analysis purposes, you might be interested to know how much your return was, in percentage terms, over the course of five trading days. You get this figure by averaging the daily rate of return over the five days as follows:

arithmetic mean investment return (average) = (15% + 4% -14% + 8%)/4 = 3.25%

The mean return, or average, is calculated based on the following formula:

(N1 + N2+ N3-----Nt)/t

Where:

N = observations

t = number of observations

We can see that the mean return of 3.25% in Example 2.1 is close to one observation (4%) and distant from some of the other daily returns (such as -14% or 15%). The difference between each observation and the mean indicates riskiness to the investor. The risk is simply due to the fact that the more each periodic observation deviates from the average, the more difficult it is to predict the new move. Thus, this deviation from the mean is measured through a statistical measure called *standard deviation*. Standard deviation is the square root of the variance.

Example 2.2: Calculate the standard deviation and variance

Assume an investor observed the price of ABC stock for five trading days as follows:

Day	Price
Day 1	10
Day 2	11.5
Day 3	12
Day 4	10.3
Day 5	11.1

Calculate the variance and standard deviation of the returns on the above stock data.

Solution

Before calculating the variance we need first to calculate the return on the stock over the five trading days. We calculate the return as a percentage change from one trading day to another. For instance, the return on Day 2 is = 11.5-10/100 = 0.15 = 15%

We can perform the same for the rest of the days, as illustrated in the following table:

Day	Price	Return	Variance
Day 1	10		
Day 2	11.5	15%	$(15-3.24)^2 = 0.013837$
Day 3	12	4%	$(14-3.24)^2 = 0.000123$
Day 4	10.3	-14%	0.030289
Day 5	11.1	8%	0.002052

Mean (M)		3.24%	
Variance			Σvariance/5 = 0.00926
Standard deviation			$\sqrt{}$variance = 0.09623

LOS. Calculate the return, mean return, variance and standard deviation of a portfolio

The mean return of a portfolio is not a simple average of the returns from the assets in the portfolio. The portfolio mean return is calculated in light of the weight of each asset in the portfolio. So, the portfolio return is a weighted average return. The weight is determined by dividing the value of each asset by the portfolio's total value.

$$\text{portfolio mean return} = (W_a \times R_a) + (W_b \times R_b) + \dots\dots\dots\dots$$

Where:

W_a = weight of asset a to the total portfolio

R_a = return on asset a

W_b = weight of asset b to the total portfolio

R_b = return on asset b

$$\text{weight of asset a} = \frac{\text{value of asset a}}{\text{total portfolio value}}$$

Variance, and subsequently the standard deviation of a portfolio, is calculated taking into consideration the weight of each asset in the portfolio in proportion to the total value of the portfolio *in addition* to the correlation between the assets within the portfolio. The following formula illustrates this:

$$\text{portfolio variance (two assets)} = W_a^2 \cdot \sigma_a^2 + W_b^2 \cdot \sigma_b^2 + 2 \cdot W_a \cdot W_b \sigma_a \cdot \sigma_a \cdot \rho_{a \cdot b}$$

$$\text{portfolio standard deviation} = \sqrt{\text{portfolio variance}}$$

Where:

W_a = weight of asset a to the total portfolio

σ_a = standard deviation of asset a

W_b = weight of asset b to the total portfolio

σ_b = standard deviation of asset b

$\rho_{a.b}$ = correlation between asset a and b

2.2 Correlation and its role in diversification

LOS. Calculate the correlation between two assets
LOS. Describe how diversification reduces risk

Correlation is the linear relationship between two assets. Correlation is measured by the correlation coefficient, which ranges between 1 and -1. It is important to note here that correlation measures the existence of a linear relationship between two variables. Zero correlation between two variables does not mean that there is no relationship between variables, but it only means that there is no linear relationship. There might be another strong relationship, but not a linear one. Correlation of +1 means there is a perfect positive linear relationship between two variables, while -1 is a perfect negative linear relationship.

correlation between assets A, B = covariance (A,B)/(standard deviation A × standard deviation B)

$$\text{correlation a,b} = \frac{\text{Cov a,b}}{\sigma a \cdot \sigma b}$$

Example 2.3: Illustration of correlation

Assume an investor is considering creating a portfolio of two assets A and B. The monthly rate of return on these assets is illustrated in the table below:

	A	B	$(A-X)^2$	$(B-Y)^2$
1	3.40%	11.00%	0.00052%	0.75589%
2	11.00%	-0.70%	0.61270%	0.09035%
3	10.00%	0.99%	0.46615%	0.01731%
4	2.00%	2.00%	0.01375%	0.00094%
5	0.87%	10.00%	0.05302%	0.59200%
6	-1.65%	6.70%	0.23257%	0.19309%
7	-3.56%	-1.07%	0.45327%	0.11396%

	A	B	(A-X)²	(B-Y)²
8	6.39%	-0.99%	0.10352%	0.10863%
9	-2.54%	1.23%	0.32633%	0.01157%
10	1.04%	1.01%	0.04548%	0.01679%
11	2.09%	-2.00%	0.01172%	0.18540%
12	9.03%	-0.50%	0.34310%	0.07873%
Mean (X)	3.17%			
Mean (Y)		2.31%		
Variance (X)			0.22184%	
Variance (Y)				0.18039%
Standard deviation (X)			0.047100091	
Standard deviation (Y)				0.042472117
Covariance				-0.000543853
Correlation				-0.27186636

If the investor created the portfolio with 40% of A and 60% of B, we would calculate the portfolio standard deviation as follows:

portfolio variance = $(40\%)^2 \times (0.0471)^2 + (60\%)^2 \times (0.0424\%)^2 + 2(40\%) \times (60\%)(0.0424)(0.0471)(-0.271) = 0.000743$

standard deviation = 0.027263

The chart below depicts the relationship between the return on both assets. As can been seen, there is weak linear relationship between the two assets. The correlation figure of -0.271 reflects this fact.

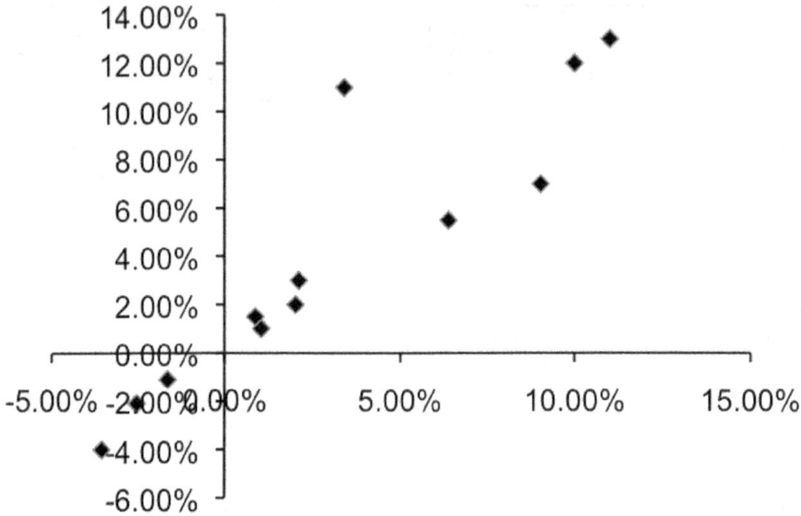

Next, we will examine how the change in the correlation affects the variance and standard deviation of the portfolio. If we change the correlation as a result of a change in the assumed portfolio returns, as illustrated in the table below, we will have a strong positive relationship between the two assets.

	A	B	$(A-X)^2$	$(B-Y)^2$
1	3.40%	11.00%	0.00052%	0.48060%
2	11.00%	13.00%	0.61270%	0.79790%
3	10.00%	12.00%	0.46615%	0.62925%
4	2.00%	2.00%	0.01375%	0.04275%
5	0.87%	1.50%	0.05302%	0.06592%
6	-1.65%	-1.10%	0.23257%	0.26703%
7	-3.56%	-4.00%	0.45327%	0.65085%
8	6.39%	5.50%	0.10352%	0.02052%
9	-2.54%	-2.10%	0.32633%	0.38038%
10	1.04%	1.01%	0.04548%	0.09348%
11	2.09%	3.00%	0.01172%	0.01140%
12	9.03%	7.00%	0.34310%	0.08600%

	A	B	$(A-X)^2$	$(B-Y)^2$
Mean (X)	3.17%			
Mean (Y)		4.07%		
Variance (X)			0.22184%	
Variance (Y)				0.29384%
Standard deviation (X)			0.047100091	
Standard deviation (Y)				0.054206813
Covariance				0.002526543
Correlation				0.98958019

We then calculate the portfolio variance as follows:

portfolio variance = $(40\%)^2.(0.0471)^2 + (60\%)^2.(0.054\%)^2 + 2.(40\%).(60\%)(0.054)(0.047)(0.989) = 0.002626$

standard deviation = 0.05124

We can see that the standard deviation of the portfolio has increased from 0.027 to 0.054 as a result of the increase in correlation. So, we conclude that the higher the correlation between the assets in the portfolio, the higher risk. To put it differently, the diversification of a portfolio, measured by the correlation of its assets, determines its riskiness. The more diversified a portfolio (i.e. weak or negative correlation) the lower the portfolio variance and risk, and vice versa.

LOS. Describe the impact of serial correlation on the standard deviation of returns

Serial correlation is the relationship of any variable values in different time periods (time-series data). For example, a stock price today might depend on the price yesterday and the day before that. Also, the up movement of the stock price today that might be followed by up movement the next trading day is a result of a positive serial correlation between the stock prices. Serial correlation is also called autocorrelation. If a down-move of the stock price today is believed to cause an up-move the next day, negative serial correlation would exist.

If the price movement of a stock on any day does not show any reliance on the movement in the previous trading day, the stock price observations are said to be independent, hence zero serial correlation.

So if financial data are correlated across observations within certain periods of time, we describe these data as *serially correlated.*

Observations that are positively serially correlated are showing mean aversion. This means that observations will follow subsequent changes which will eventually lead to moving away from the mean, hence higher standard deviation.

Conversely, if observations are negatively serially correlated they are said to be mean reverting. This means that the observations will eventually be close to the mean/average value, hence lower standard deviation.

2.3 Portfolio VaR and performance analysis

LOS. Calculate the minimum variance hedge ratio

The hedge ratio is the number of contracts needed to hedge (reduce the risk of) current exposure. This exposure could be in foreign exchange, equity, commodity or interest rate transactions.

For example, the hedge ratio tells us how many options, futures contracts or forward contracts we need to buy to reduce the risk of owning ABC Company stocks. This ratio is calculated by:

$$h = \rho \times \frac{\sigma S}{\sigma F}$$

Where:

ρ = correlation between the spot position and the hedging instrument (the future position, for instance)

σF = standard deviation of the spot position

σS = standard deviation of the future position

To determine whether this number of contracts constitutes an optimal hedge we use the following:

$$\text{optimal hedge} = \left(\frac{\text{size of the portfolio}}{\text{size of futures contract used in the hedge}} \right) \cdot \rho \times \frac{\sigma S}{\sigma F}$$

Example 2.4: Minimum variance hedge

Assume a farmer needs 10,000 tons of compost. The farmer is concerned there might be a surge in the compost price in the future. To hedge this risk of increasing prices he uses futures contracts. The size of a futures contract is 100 tons. To calculate the optimum number of contracts needed to hedge this risk, the farmer collected the following price changes in the spot and futures markets of the compost.

Month	Change in spot market	Change in future market
1	2.18%	2.13%
2	2.50%	2.11%
3	3.10%	2.99%
4	3.01%	2.88%
5	-1%	-1.09%
6	-2.90%	-1.77%
7	0.70%	0.54%
8	0.90%	0.31%
9	1.70%	1.32%
10	1.34%	1.00%
11	2.55%	2.23%
12	3.01%	2.44%

standard deviation of spot market = 0.017391

standard deviation of future market = 0.014613

correlation = 0.979167

So, the optimal number of futures contracts needed to hedge the farmer's risk is:

$$\left(\frac{10,000}{1000}\right) \times 0.979167 \times \frac{0.017391}{0.014613} = 11.65 \text{ contracts}$$

= 11.65 contracts

LOS. Calculate value at risk in a portfolio

The value at risk (VaR) of a portfolio is calculated according to the following formula:

$$v = -\mu + z\sigma$$

Where:

μ = the portfolio mean

z = standard normal distribution

σ = portfolio standard deviation

Example 2.5: Portfolio VaR

Assume a portfolio mean return of 2.36% and standard deviation of 5.31%. Calculate VaR for this portfolio at a confidence level of 99%.

Solution

At a confidence level of 99%, z = 2.33 as standard normal distribution.

$$v = -2.36\% + (2.33)(5.31\%) = 10.01\%$$

LOS. Calculate the probability that one portfolio will outperform another portfolio

---

Example 2.6: Calculate the probability of portfolio return

Assume an investor has two assets: Asset A and Asset B. Asset A has a mean return of 10% and standard deviation of 9%; Asset B has a mean return of 8% and standard deviation of 11%. Also assume the investor has $100,000 to invest and he considers the following portfolio composition alternatives:

1. $100,000 in Asset A only.
2. $100,000 in Asset B only.
3. $60,000 in Asset A and $40,000 in Asset B. The correlation between the two assets in this portfolio is 0.4.

Calculate the probability of earning $15,000 over a one-year horizon using these investment alternatives.

Solution

Earning $15,000 on the investment of $100,000 means we want to calculate the probability of earning 15% and above, i.e. [P>0.15].

In the context of the standard normal distribution, we are trying to find:

$$P\left[z > \frac{0.15 - \pi}{\sigma p}\right]$$

So, for the first portfolio composition:

$$P\left[z > \frac{0.15 - 0.1}{0.09}\right], P\left[z > 0.555\right]$$

From Excel: NORMDIST(0.15,0.1,09,TRUE) = 28.93%

For the second portfolio composition:

$$P\left[z > \frac{0.15 - 0.08}{0.11}\right], P\left[z > 0.636\right]$$

From Excel: NORMDIST(0.15,0.1,09,TRUE) = 35.81%

For the third portfolio composition, we will have to find first the mean and standard deviation of the portfolio:

portfolio mean return = 60% × 10% + 40% × 8% = 9.2%

portfolio variance = $(60\%)^2(9\%)^2 + (40\%)^2(11\%)^2 + 2(60\%)(40\%)(9\%)$

(11%)(0.4)= 0.3125

portfolio standard deviation = 0.3125 = 55.9%

$$P\left[z > \frac{0.15 - 0.092}{0.559}\right], P\left[z > 0.1037\right]$$

From Excel: NORMDIST(0.15,0.092,0.559,TRUE) = 45.87%

Conclusion: the portfolio comprised of 60% Asset A and 40% Asset B has the highest chance of meeting the target of 15%.

LOS. Calculate the probability of attaining a return goal

The performance of a portfolio could be assessed by comparing its parameters (return and standard deviation) to another portfolio comprised of identical assets but with different weights, or sharing some characteristics of these assets. This portfolio against which the portfolio parameters are compared is called a *benchmark portfolio.*

Example 2.7: Calculate the probability of attaining a return goal

We will continue from Example 2.6. Assume we want to create a portfolio of 60% Asset A and 40% Asset B. We call this Portfolio Q. We benchmark the performance of this portfolio with a portfolio comprised of identical assets but with different weights. The benchmark portfolio is comprised of 50% Asset A and 50% Asset B. The benchmark portfolio is Portfolio R.

We denote:

Π_Q = return of the portfolio in the question = Π_Q = 0.6 A + 0.40 B

Π_B = return of the benchmark portfolio = Π_B = 0.5 A + 0.5 B

The return of Portfolio Q will exceed the return of Portfolio R when:

$\Pi_Q - \Pi_B > 0$. The probability of the return from Portfolio Q exceeding the return of the benchmark Portfolio R = P($\Pi_Q - \Pi_B$ >0), P(0.6 A + 0.40 B - 0.5 A - 0.5 B >0). P(0.1 A - 0.1 b>0).

So, return of (0.10 A - 0.1 B) = 0.10 (10%) - 0.10 (8%) = 0.2%

And the standard deviation of (0.10 A - 0.1 B) =

$$((0.10)^2(9\%)^2 + (0.10)^2(11\%)^2 + 2(11\%)(9\%)(0.4)(0.10)(0.10))^{1/2} = 1.68\%$$

$$P[z > -002/0.0168] = P[z > -0.119] = 54.7\%$$

Conclusion: a portfolio of 60% Asset A and 40% Asset B stands a 54.7% chance of exceeding the return of the benchmark portfolio that is made of 50% Asset A and 50% Asset B.

Chapter 3. Term Structure Of Interest Rates

In this chapter we will discuss:

1. Spot and forward rates and yield curve analysis.
2. Theories of term structure.

3.1 Spot and forward rates and yield curve analysis

LOS. Define spot curve, spot rate and term structure
LOS. Define and describe the yield curve
LOS. Describe normal, flat and inverted yield curves

The spot rate is the current market interest rate on a zero-coupon bond. The term structure is a depiction of the relationship between interest rates and each maturity bucket. When graphed, this relationship results in a curve called the *yield curve*.

The yield curve can take various shapes. It is a depiction of the relationship between the interest rate and the time to maturity. The longer the time to maturity of a debt contract, the higher the interest rate. This relationship is called a normal curve. In a normal curve with a long maturity, the inflation risk, default risk and liquidity risk are all higher than with a short maturity. Hence, bonds with five years to maturity will cost a higher interest rate than bonds with two years to maturity.

A flat curve occurs when the interest rate is fixed across all maturities, i.e. five-year bonds will cost exactly the same interest rate as two-year bonds.

There could also be a negative relationship between the interest rate and time to maturity, which results in a downward sloping curve or inverted curve. In such a relationship, debt contracts such as five-year bonds would cost a lower interest rate than two-year bonds.

The illustrations below show respectively a normal, flat and downward sloping yield curve.

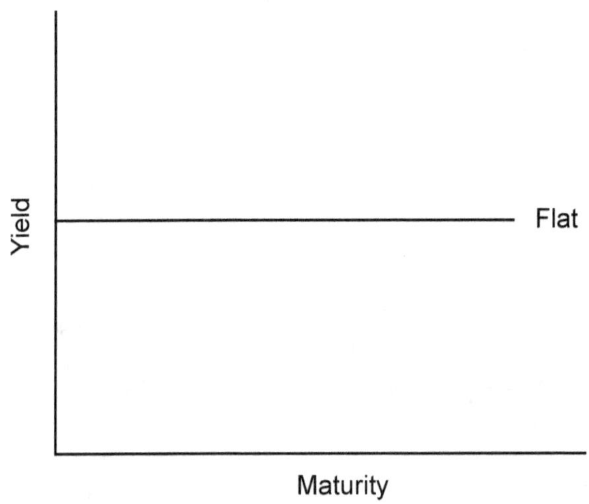

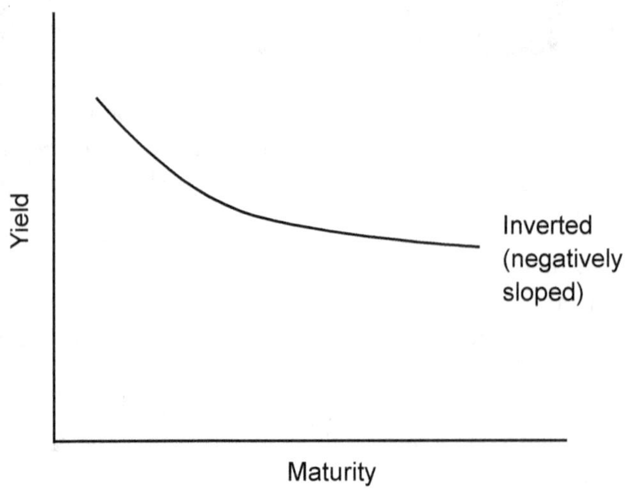

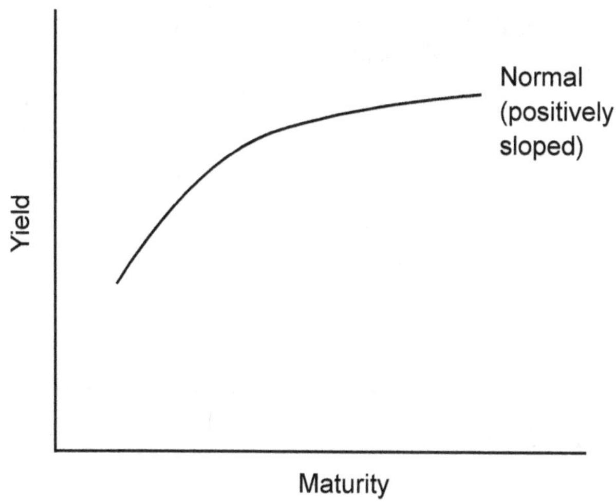

LOS. Demonstrate the process of bootstrapping
LOS. Calculate implied forward rates

We defined the spot rate as the current market interest rate on a zero-coupon bond. We denote the spot rate for a certain single period in the future as $r_{0,1}$. For example, the spot rate for a one-month, one-year or one-day security is denoted as $r_{0,1}$. The interest rate in the future is not known but it can be estimated from the spot rates. If we calculate the forward rate from the spot rates (r), we call this an *implied forward rate*, as seen in the time line below.

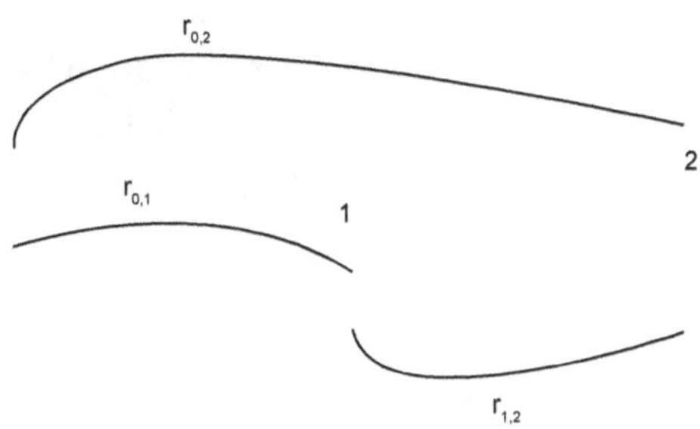

The time line tells us the following:

The spot rate for a one-year transaction is $r_{0,1}$; the spot rate for a two-year transaction is $r_{0,2}$; the forward rate for a one-year transaction that starts one year from now is $r_{1,2}$ and is paid in the second year.

So, $(1+r_{0,2})^2 = (1+r_{0,1})^1(1+r_{1,2})^1$

Or, $(1+r_{1,2})^1 = (1+r_{0,2})^2 / (1+r_{0,1})$

We can rewrite this as a general formula as follows:

$(1+r_{0,n})^n = (1+r_{0,n-1})^1(1+r_{n-1,n})^1$

Example 3.1: Calculating an implied forward interest rate

If you have a three-month note with an interest rate of 5.6% and a one-month note with an interest rate of 3.2%, calculate the interest rate of the two-month note in one month from now.

Solution

$(1+0.056)^3 = (1+0.032)^1(1+r_{1,2})^2$

$(1+r_{1,2})^2 = (1+0.056)^3 / (1+0.032)^1$

$r_{1,2} = 6.82\%$

I have introduced the concepts of forward and spot rate and did the above calculation to describe the process of **bootstrapping**. Bootstrapping in the context of interest rates refers to finding a spot rate for a certain period for a zero-coupon bond, using the prices of coupon-paying bonds to help us find this spot rate. The following example will clarify this concept.

Example: 3.2: Bootstrapping

Assume that an investor observed the following spot rates:

$R_{0,0.5} = 2.5\%$

$R_{0,1} = 3.4\%$

He wants to find $r_{0,1.5}$

Assume also that an 18-month coupon paying bond, with 2% semi-annual coupon is selling at par. Calculate the $r_{0,1.5}$

Solution

Assume the par value = 1000

We get the semi-annual coupon for the 18-month bond by dividing 2%/2 = 1% . So, 1% × 1000 = $10

Since interest rates are always quoted on an annual basis, the semi-annual spot rate would be 2.5/2 = 1.25% and 3.4%/2 = 1.7% respectively. We need these two rates to discount the future coupon payments.

The 18-month bond was issued at par; this means its price is equal to its par value = $1000

$$\text{price} = 1000 = (10/(1 + 1.0125)) + (10/(1 + 1.017)^2) + (10/(1 + r_{0,1.5})^3))$$

$$r_{0,1.5} = 1.325\%$$

LOS. Describe the pure expectations theory

The **pure expectations theory** attempts to explain the relationship between interest rate and maturity, i.e. it attempts to explain the shape of the yield curve. Theoretically, the shape of the yield curve is normally positively sloped and as the maturity increases, the interest rate increases. Pure expectation theory states that this might not always hold true. According to this theory, whether the yield curve is negatively sloped, positively sloped or flat depends on the investor's expectation of the short- and long-term interest rates.

If the yield curve is positively sloped, long-term loans would be at a higher interest rate compared to short-term loans because the longer the time to maturity, the riskier the investment or debt and the higher the interest rate charged. But under pure expectation, investors might view long-term bonds as riskier or less risky than short-term bonds; it all depends on their expectation. So, if the investor expects the future interest rate to be lower than the spot rate, the yield curve would be downwards sloping, and vice versa.

For example, if an investor expects the interest rate of a two-year bond (say an investment in a two-year bond that starts in 2007 and matures by the end of 2008) to be 9% and the interest rate of a one-year bond (interest rate for year 2007 only) to be 5%, then the interest rate expected to be earned in year 2008 only is:

$$(1 + \text{two year interest})^2 = (1 + \text{one year interest starts from today}) \times (1 + \text{one year interest rate starts one year from end of year 1})$$

$$(1 + 9\%)^2 = (1 + 5\%) \times (1 + i)$$

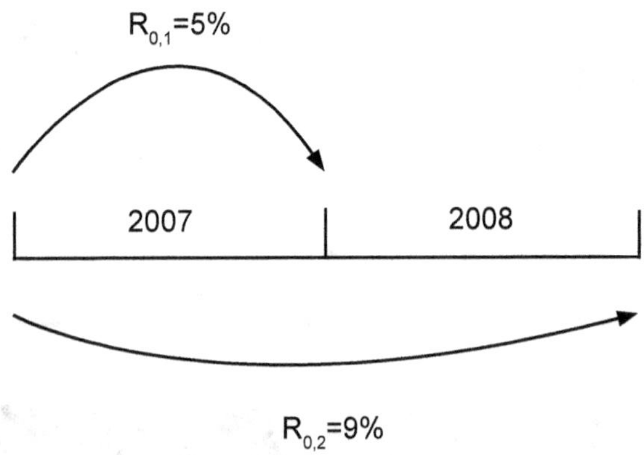

The interest rate expected to be earned in 2008 is 13.15%.

3.2 Theories of Term Structure

This section discusses the following theories of term structure:

- Liquidity preference theory.
- Preferred habitat theory.
- Market segmentation theory.

LOS. Describe the liquidity preference theory

This theory states that investors will hold longer-term maturities if they are offered a long-term rate higher than the average of expected future rates by a risk premium that is positively related to the term to maturity. Put differently, the forward rates should reflect both interest rate expectations and a liquidity premium (really a risk premium), and the premium should be higher for longer maturities.

According to the liquidity preference theory, forward rates will not be an unbiased estimate of the market's expectations of future interest rates because they contain a liquidity premium. Thus, an upward-sloping yield curve may reflect expectations that future interest rates will either rise, or will be unchanged or even fall, but with a liquidity premium increasing fast enough with maturity so as to produce an upward-sloping yield curve. That is, any shape for either the yield curve or the term structure of interest rates can be explained by the biased expectations theory.

LOS. Describe the preferred habitat theory

The preferred habitat theory indicates that investors prefer certain maturity ranges and they are determined to stay within them. What is meant by investors, in this instance, is borrowers and lenders. Lenders could have maturity ranges that they prefer to transact within and do not seem interested in investing in other instruments of different maturities. For instance, lenders could only be interested in five- to seven-year maturity bonds and unwilling to shift to shorter or longer maturities than that. These lenders could, however, shift to maturities other than their preference if they are induced to do so, i.e. if they are paid a higher premium.

For example, a lender who prefers five- to seven-year maturity bonds would agree to invest in a two-year bond if he is given a high premium that would induce him to move from his preference zone. Hence, he would get a higher interest rate in a two-year bond (because the higher the risk premium, the higher the nominal interest rate) than in five- to seven-year bonds.

This tells us that this theory states that investors do not make decisions based only on their expectation of the future but also on their preferences of investment time horizons. Thus, according to preferred habitat theory, the yield curve could be inverted, flat or normal. All of them are possible.

LOS. Describe the market segmentation theory

This theory suggests that the market for bonds is broken down into sectors or segments. Each segment is independent from other segments. In each segment there are investors who have certain preferences of maturity and yield. The interest rate in each segment is determined based on supply and demand forces. Preferred habitat theory is another form of market segmentation theory.

Chapter 4. Bond Markets And Contracts

In this chapter we will discuss:

1. Bond basics.
2. Pricing of bonds.
3. Analysis of the relationship between bond price and interest rate.
4. Types of bonds.
5. Features of bond markets.

4.1 Bond Basics

LOS. Define nominal (notional, face, par, maturity) value, maturity, term to maturity, coupon, coupon-rate, zero coupon and vanilla bond
LOS. Define and discuss the various characteristics of bond issues

Bonds are issued by institutions which have a shortage of funds to those who have a surplus of funds. So bonds are debt instruments used as a source of capital for the borrowers. Bonds are issued by the following types of parties:

- Corporations (including banks).
- Governmental bodies.
- Semi/quasi government bodies.

Face value is the amount written on the indenture, on the face of the contract. Face or par value is typically in multiples of $1000. It is customary to use a par value of $1000 if you are not given it in the exam question. If the par value is paid back to the lender in full on the maturity date it is called a bullet bond. Face value or the principal value could equal or differ from the amount the borrower has to pay to the lender at maturity. The amount paid at the maturity is called the redemption value. Redemption and face value are, however, used interchangeably in the PRM curriculum. Face value and par value are used interchangeably in this book.

When the bonds are issued it is not necessary that the issuance price is equal to the face value. The bond's price could be equal to, higher or lower than the face value. In exam questions, the price of the bond could be expressed in an absolute dollar amount or as a percentage of par value.

Maturity is the life of the bond, during which the borrower has to pay interest to the lender and on its last day the borrower has to pay the face value back to the lender. Not all bonds issued are held until the date of maturity. Some bonds are redeemed prior to maturity, either by the borrower or by the lender. In terms of maturity, bonds are classified as:

- Bills: bonds issued with maturity less than one year.
- Notes: bonds issued with maturity between one to ten years.
- Bonds: bonds issued with maturity exceeding ten years.

Coupon is the periodic interest payment paid by the borrower to the lender during the life of the bond. The coupon payment is determined by multiplying the coupon rate by the bond face value, like so:

$$\text{coupon periodic payment} = \text{face value} \times \text{coupon rate}$$

The frequency of coupon payments could be annual or semi-annual, but typically it is on a semi-annual basis.

Coupon rate is the rate of interest the borrower agrees to pay the lender during the life of the bond. The coupon rate is different from the market rate. The coupon rate could be equal to, more than or less than the market rate. The coupon rate could either be fixed, floating, or a mix of fixed and floating.

Zero coupon bond is a bond in which the borrower does not make any periodic interest payments to the lender. The return for the lender is the difference between the price of the zero-coupon bond and the face value. A zero-coupon bond is issued at a deep price discount relative to its face value.

Vanilla bond is a bond contract without any optionality, such as call, put or conversion.

Yield to maturity (YTM) is the interest rate that makes the present value of the bond's cash flows (coupon payments and the face value) equal to the price of bond. Thus, if you discount these cash flows and subtract them from the price of the bond you would get zero. This is identical to the internal rate of return (IRR) in a corporate finance context, in which it is defined as the interest rate that makes a project's net present value (NPV) equal to zero.

Embedded options are options that come with a bond that have a benefit for the issuer or investor. Examples of these options are call options, put options and sinking fund.

LOS. Describe a bond as a series of cash flows

As discussed above, in the case of coupon bonds, borrowers pay the lender periodic coupon payments during the life of the bond and a face value on the redemption date. Since there are no other cash flows received, the present value of these cash flows determines the price of the bond.

Example 4.1: Bond basics

Assume that John has lent $10,000 to his friend Nicole. Nicole has promised to pay back the $10,000 after three years. One risk that John would face in this transaction is that when Nicole pays back the $10,000 after three years, the purchasing power of $10,000 is lower than it was in the year in which he lent her the amount.

Another risk that John might be exposed to as a result of this lending is that he would lose earning an interest, say 1%, if he deposited the amount in his bank account instead of lending it to Nicole. (Opportunity cost.)

For these factors, Nicole should compensate John by paying him back more than the $10,000. The extra amount is paid to John in the form of periodic interest payments, called coupon payments.

4.2 Bond Pricing

The price of a bond is determined by discounting all the coupon payments and the face or redemption value, as illustrated in the formula below:

$$P = \left(\frac{C}{1+i} + \frac{C}{(1+i)^2} + \ldots + \frac{C}{(1+i)^N} \right) + \frac{M}{(1+i)^N}$$

$$= \left(\sum_{n=1}^{N} \frac{C}{(1+i)^n} \right) + \frac{M}{(1+i)^N}$$

$$= C\left(\frac{1-(1+i)^{-N}}{i} \right) + M(1+i)^{-N}$$

Where:

P = price of the bond, or the present value of the bond's future cash flows

C = coupon periodic payment paid by the issuer to the lender

M = par value, future value or the redemption value of the bond. (All these terms are used interchangeably throughout the text.)

N = bond's maturity

i = yield to maturity

Example 4.2: Bond pricing

Assume that you are asked to determine the current price of a bond with the following features: Par value = $1000, coupon rate = 9%, four years to maturity, coupon payments are paid on an annual basis and yield to maturity is at 5%. Calculate the current bond price.

a. $1,000

b. $870.411

c. $1,141.838

d. $780.411

e. None of the above

Solution

c.

LOS. Define discount and premium

A discount occurs when the coupon rate is lower than the yield to maturity. A premium occurs when the coupon rate is higher than the yield to maturity. If we denote yield to maturity as YTM and coupon rate as CR, then:

CR>YTM = premium bonds

CR<YTM = discount bonds

LOS. Define clean price, dirty price, accrued interest and bond yield
LOS. Calculate the clean and dirty price of a bond

The price of a bond is calculated as the present value (PV) of the coupon payment on the day immediately after a coupon payment. Investors, however, do not always buy bonds on the coupon payment dates. They might buy them between the coupon payments dates. Investors are entitled to full coupon payments when they buy a bond and hold from the last payment date until the immediate next payment. If an investor buys the bond between coupon payments he would be entitled to the coupon payment for the days he held the bond only.

For instance, in April an investor buys a semi-annual coupon payment bond that pays a coupon in January and July. The coupon in July is paid to those investors who bought the bond on 1 January and held until 1 July. For this investor, he is entitled to three months' coupon payment only. The other three months are the issuer's money. The coupon payments of January,

February and March are called accrued interest that should be paid from the investor to the issuer. The bond price that includes the accrued interest is called the dirty price, while the price net of accrued interest is called the clean price.

Example 4.3: Calculating clean and dirty price

Suppose you buy a five-year bond with a 4% semi-annual coupon exactly two months before a coupon payment date. You will receive the entire next coupon, but you are entitled only to 2/6 of it while the remaining 4/6 is owed to the party from whom you bought the bond.

The accrued interest in this case would therefore be equal to: (4/6) × (($100x4%)/2) = USD 1.33. The price that you would actually have to pay for the bond is the clean price plus accrued interest of USD 1.33.

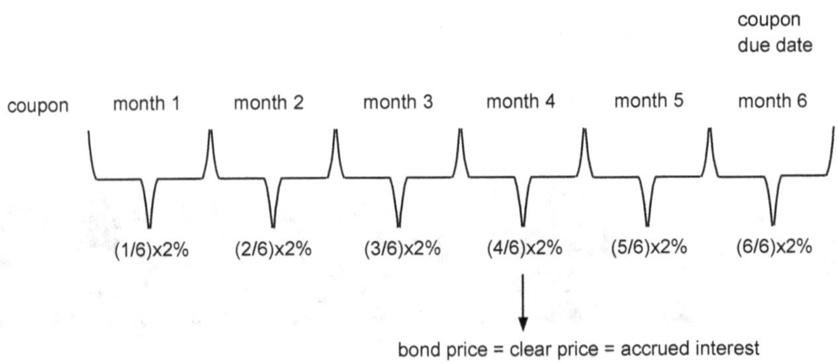

LOS. Calculate current yield and yield to maturity (YTM)

Current yield is the percentage of the annual coupon payment to the current market price of the bond. For example, if the annual coupon payment is $70 and the current market price of the bond is $980, the current yield will be equal to ($70/$980) = 7.14%. This is also known as *running yield* or *income yield*.

Example 4.4: Bond yield

The annual interest paid on a bond relative to its market price is:

a. Promised yield.

b. Yield to maturity.

c. Coupon rate.

d. Effective yield.

e. Current yield.

Solution

e.

Example 4.5: Calculating current yield

98.5%, four-year bond is traded with a coupon rate of 4.5% paid semi-annually, and face value of $1,000. Calculate the current yield on this bond.

a. 4%.

b. 4.50%.

c. 4.57%.

d. 2%.

e. 2.25%.

Solution

annual coupon payments = 4.5% × $1,000 = $45

bond market price = 98.5% × $1,000 = $985

current yield = $45/$985 = 4.57%

Example 4.6: Calculating the market price of a bond

Assume a 15% bond with a current yield of 10.5%. Calculate the market price of this bond.

a. \$1050.45

b. \$1,500.98

c. \$1350.56

d. \$1402.58

e. \$1,428.57

Solution

annual coupon payments = 15% × \$1,000 = \$150

current yield = \$150/price = 10.5%

bond market price = \$150/10.5% = \$1,428.57

Yield to maturity (YTM)

YTM is the interest rate which makes the present value of all the cash flows in a bond equal to zero. YTM can be calculated in three ways:

1. Trial and error.
2. Interpolation.
3. Financial calculator.

Since trial and error and use of a financial calculator are not viable alternatives in the PRM exam, we can *approximate* the YTM using the formula below:

$$\text{approximate YTM} = \frac{C + (F - P)/N}{(F + P)/2}$$

Where:

C = annual coupon payments

F = face value

P = bond price

N = years to maturity

We may also be asked to find an interest rate between two interest rates. For example, if you are given a three-year interest on a bond of 10%, a five-year interest on a bond of 14% and you are asked to estimate the interest rate on a four-year bond, you follow the below steps:

- Subtract the lower rate from the higher rate: 14% - 10% = 4%
- Multiply the difference by the fraction of the time:

$$4\% \times \left\{ \frac{\text{middle period} - \text{lower period}}{\text{higher period} - \text{lower period}} \right\}$$

$$4\% \times \left\{ \frac{4-3}{5-3} \right\} = 2\%$$

- Add the result to the lower rate: 2% + 10% = 12%

Exercise: Calculate the YTM

Calculate a YTM for an 11% bond traded at $750, with a face value of $1,000 and seven years to maturity.

a. 4.1%.

b. 17.45%.

c. 15%.

d. 12.5%.

Solution

b. 17.45%

For zero-coupon bonds, the formula to approximate the YTM is as follows:

zero-coupon bonds YTM = (maturity value/price)$^{1/n}$ - 1

4.3 Analysis of the relationship between bond price and interest rate

This section discusses the following:

1. Duration: Macaulay, modified and effective duration.
2. Key rate duration.
3. Convexity.

LOS. Describe the relationship between yield and price

The price of any instrument is equal to the present value of the cash flows generated from this asset during its life. For the present value, the cash flows have to be discounted using an appropriate rate of discount as applied in the basic present value formula in section 4.2.

From this formula we can see that the higher the interest rate, the lower the price. Thus, we can conclude that the price and interest rate of bonds are negatively related.

LOS. Discuss the pull to par of bond prices

When a bond sells at a premium, the present value (price) is higher than the face value. The premiums should be amortized over the life of the bond. This means that the price will eventually be amortized until it equals the face value at the expiry date. This is the pull to par, i.e. the bond's price moves towards the par value. The following example clearly illustrates this concept.

Example 4.7: Pull to par of bond prices

Assume that a bond has a face value of $1,000, a coupon rate of 8%, YTM of 6% and five years to maturity. Coupon payments are paid annually. The following table illustrates the price and premiums calculation.

Time	Payment	Present value
1	80	$80/(1.06)^1 = 75.47169811$
2	80	$80/(1.06)^2 = 71.1997152$
3	80	$80/(1.06)^3 = 67.16954264$
4	80	$80/(1.06)^4 = 63.36749306$
5	1,080	$1080/(1.06)^5 = 807.0388267$
Total	1,400	1084.247276
	Price	1084.247276

The amortization table of this bond is as follows:

Time	Payment	Interest	Premium	Carrying value
0				1084.247276
1	80	65.05484	-14.9452	1069.302112
2	80	64.15813	-15.8419	1053.460239
3	80	63.20761	-16.7924	1036.667853
4	80	62.20007	-17.7999	1018.867925
5	80	61.13208	-18.8679	1000
Total	**400**	**315.7527**	**-84.2473**	

The amortization table clearly indicates that the issuer has to pay only the $1,000 at maturity as the price has decreased since time (1).

Duration: Macaulay, modified and effective duration

LOS. Compare and contrast Macaulay duration and modified duration

In the previous LOSs we have seen that the price of the bond is sensitive to the change in interest rate. The higher the interest rate, the lower the price of the bond, and vice versa. If you have bonds in either side of your balance sheet you will be financially impacted when interest rates move in either direction.

Investors in bonds are exposed to an interest rate risk, which is a risk of decrease in the value of bond investments as a result of changes in interest rates. To manage this risk, investors need to measure the impact of this risk in the first place. A tool available to assess this risk called *duration*. Duration was developed as a concept in the 1930s by Fredric Macaulay.

In the past, investors would mostly use *Macaulay* and *modified duration*, but due to shortcomings in these methods investors have begun to rely more on the *effective duration* and *convexity*. We will discuss these tools shortly.

Macaulay duration is the total weighted average time for recovery of the payments and principal in relation to the current market price of the bond. Bond duration, therefore, is:

$$\text{duration} = \sum_{t=1}^{n} \frac{-t \times (PV)CF_t}{\text{market price}}$$

Where:

PV = Present value

CF_t = periodic coupon payments

T = time of paying the coupon

n = life of the bond

What is the economic reasoning behind Macaulay duration?

The price of any asset is equal to the present value of its future benefits. From the formula of present value, one can conclude that there is an inverse relationship between the price of the bond and interest rate, and between the price and the time to maturity. This means that the more you push the benefits from this asset further into the future, the lower the present value. The present value of benefits received in year 2 would be worth more than benefits in year 10. For an investor, the sooner she recovers her investment amount, the better. The longer she waits to recover some or all her investment, the riskier.

Also, for an investor in bonds (a lender), the coupons received are allocated in different time periods (mostly semi-annual). Thus, the higher the coupon rate the better. This is because with higher coupon payments your initial investment is recovered faster than with a lower coupon rate.

Macaulay wanted to measure the risk of bonds by taking into consideration these factors – the time and size of coupons compared to the market price. He wanted to answer this question: how many years does an investor need to recover his investment in any bond issue, given a certain maturity life and coupon rate? This explains why zero-coupon bonds have a Macaulay duration equal to their maturity life.

The impact, however, depends on the size of the move in interest rates. Investors would typically be interested to know how sensitive a bond is to the changes in interest rates. Market practitioners use duration as a measure of this sensitivity. Duration has these two definitions:

1. How long does it take the investor to get back his money that is invested in the bond?
2. How sensitive is the price of the bonds the investor holds to a change in interest rate?

Macaulay duration addresses the first definition while modified duration addresses the second one, as we shall see below. You should note that modified duration is conceptually identical to the concept of *price elasticity* in economics.

To calculate Macaulay duration, follow these steps:

1. Find the cash flows and timing of these cash flows.
2. Calculate the present values of these cash flows and the total of these present values. (Price of the bond.)
3. Multiply the timing of each cash flow by the present values of these cash flows, and total them.
4. Divide the total in Step 3 by the total in Step 2.
5. The result of the division in Step 4 is Macaulay duration.

Macaulay duration =

$$\frac{\frac{1C}{(1+y)^1}+\frac{2C}{(1+y)^2}+\ldots+\frac{nC}{(1+y)^n}+\frac{nM}{(1+y)^n}}{P}$$

Where:

P = price of the bond

C = semi-annual coupon interest (in dollars)

y = half the yield to maturity or required yield

n = number of semi-annual periods (number of years times 2)

M = maturity value (in dollars)

1. The duration of a single payment bond (zero-coupon bond) is equal to its life.
2. The duration of an ordinary annuity of coupon payments is calculated as shown in Example 4.8.

Example 4.8: Calculating Macaulay duration

Calculate Macaulay duration for the following bond: face value = \$100, coupon rate = 8%, maturity life = five years, YTM = 10%.

Answer:

Time	Cash flow	Present value	Time-weighted cash flow
1	100*8%=$8	7.27	7.273
2	$8	6.61	13.233
3	$8	6.01	18.03
4	$8	5.46	21.85
5	$108	67.06	335.298
Total		92.42	395.681

Macaulay duration (MD) = 395.681/92.42 = 4.28

LOS. Describe the shortcomings of Macaulay and modified durations

Macaulay duration assumes that the size of cash flows in the bond will not change during the bond's contract. This assumption is only realistic for straight bonds. Straight bonds are bonds which are issued with no optionality attached to them, such as a call, put or convertible option. For bonds with embedded options, cash flows will definitely change during the contract in relation to a change in the market interest rate. For example, in a callable bond (a bond with an embedded call option), as the interest rate declines, the price of the bond will increase and will reach a point at which the bond issuer would redeem the bond at the callable price. When this happens the cash flows received by the investor from the issuer would be interrupted. Hence, Macaulay and modified duration are not an accurate measure for such bonds.

Also, Macaulay duration assumes stable cash flows from the bond. This makes the application of such methods unsuitable for bonds with variable coupon payments or bonds embedded with options which might alter the size of the cash flows if they are exercised.

In addition to the above shortcomings, interpretation of Macaulay and modified duration in terms of the number of years to recover the investment is not very useful for investors. Investors prefer an accurate measure that answers this question: *by what percentage would the value of my bond investment decrease if the market interest rate decreases, or vice versa?* Macaulay and modified duration do not answer this question. Effective duration does, which we will discuss shortly.

Macaulay duration suffers from the following shortcomings:

- It assumes a small change in interest rate. If interest rates change significantly, it would not be as useful.
- Knowledge of future cash flows and their timings are needed for its calculation.
- It does not cater for a non-parallel shift in the yield curve.

LOS. Calculate modified duration of a bond

Modified Macaulay duration is calculated by the following formula:

$$\text{Modified duration} = \left[\frac{\text{Macaulay duration}}{\left(1 + \frac{\text{YTM}}{n}\right)} \right]$$

The interpretation of modified Macaulay duration is that when the interest rate (YTM) changes from Y1 to Y2, the duration of the bond would decline from duration X to duration Z.

LOS. Define dollar duration and key rate duration

Dollar duration

Duration gives a percentage change in price for a change in interest rate. If we want to know the size of the change in the price of the bond in dollar terms, we will have to calculate dollar duration, as follows:

> dollar duration = duration × dollar price of the bonds × change in interest rate

For example, for a bond priced at \$95 and with a duration of 3, when the interest rate increases by 1%, an investor will lose: 3 × \$95 × 1% = \$2.85 of its current price.

Key rate duration

As we discussed in the previous LOSs, duration is a measure of price sensitivity to a parallel small change in the yield curve, i.e. all the maturities along the yield curve change by the same size. If there is non-parallel change along the yield curve (i.e. a change in interest rate on some maturities while other maturities are unchanged, or changed by a different percentage) Macaulay duration as calculated above (page 74) would not give us a true measure of sensitivity.

We need to calculate the duration as a result of changing one rate and assess the impact, holding the rates of the other maturities unchanged. This is called *key rate duration*. The following example should clarify the concept.

Example 4.9: Key rate duration

Assume you have a portfolio of three bond positions with the following maturities: 2-year, 10-year and 25-year. Assume also that you are given the rate duration of each bond and their weights in the portfolio as follows:

Bond	Weight	D1	D2	D3
2-year bond	50%	2	0	0
10-year bond	25%	0	10	0
25-year bond	25%	0	0	25
Key rate duration, portfolio	100%	2 × 50% = 1	= 10 × 25% = 2.5	25 × 25% = 6.25

Portfolio effective key rate duration = 1 + 2.5 + 6.25 = 9.75

LOS. Discuss effective duration

$$\text{effective duration} = \frac{P_{-} - P_{+}}{2(P_{0)}(\Delta y)}$$

Effective duration is a measure of the approximate sensitivity of a bond's value to changes in interest rate. More specifically, it is the approximate percentage change in price for a 100 basis point change in rates. Consequently, a duration of, say, 9 means that the approximate change in price for this bond is 9% for a 100 basis point change in YTM.

LOS. Define basis point value (BPV)

The dollar value of basis point is also called the price value of a basis point (PVBP). A basis point is a unit that is equal to 1/100th or 1%.

PVBP is a measure that tells investors how much in dollars they would gain or lose as a result of a change in interest rate measured by basis points. Thus:

PVBP = | initial price – price if yield is changed by 1 basis point |

To calculate PVBP, you would begin with the initial situation in which you have the coupon rate, interest rate and bond price. Then you start to change the interest rate by, say, 50 basis points (i.e. 0.5%), in each direction, and add the new assumed interest rate into the formula for calculating the bond price. When you subtract the new price from the initial price you would get the PVBP.

LOS. Discuss the duration of a floating rate note (FRN)

A floating rate note is a debt instrument that pays a periodic interest rate to an investor during the life of the note. The difference between an FRN and a straight bond is that the periodic coupon payments are not fixed. Instead, they vary in each payment period. For instance, a two-year plain vanilla bond with $1,000 face value that pays a 5% coupon rate semi-annually would pay $25 every six months until the maturity date. A two-year FRN with $1,000 face value would have a different payment every six months, depending on the prevailing interest rate in the market.

Valuing a plain vanilla bond is straightforward by discounting the future cash flows using the YTM. Valuing an FRN is challenging, however, as the interest rate is not known. A solution to this problem is to value it retrospectively. This means that we start the valuation from the value on maturity, going backwards to today.

Example 4.10: Concept of FRN duration

Assume a two-year, $1,000 par value FRN that matures on 31 December 2011 and pays an interest payment on a semi-annual basis. To find the price of this FRN, we will start from the maturity date, 31 December 2011, going backwards to the immediate interest payment date before the maturity date, 1 July 2011. Thus, we will have only one unknown variable, the interest rate. We can solve for the present value of $1,000 to 1 July 2011:

$$\frac{1,000 + 1,000 \times i(1\text{ July }2011) \times d/360}{1 + i(1\text{ July }2011) \times d/360} = 1,000$$

Where:

$i(1\text{july }2011)$ = interest rate of the market on July 2011

$d/360$ = number of days between 1 July 2011 and 31 December 2011

We can conclude the following from this analysis:

- The price of the FRN on every coupon date is equal to its face value. This is an important conclusion that has an application in interest rate swap contracts, as we will see in Chapter 8.
- Essentially, the price of the FRN on every coupon payment date (also called settlement date) is determined irrespective of the cash flows in other periods of the contract.
- In duration context, if the cash flows in other periods are disregarded when calculating the present value, this is similar to the concept of zero-coupon bonds, for which the duration is equal to its life. Thus, duration of an FRN is equal to the time between the maturity date and the immediate previous coupon payment. In our above example, this is the time between 31 December 2011 and 1 July 2011.

LOS. Describe the impact of an embedded call or put on duration

In order to understand the impact of call and put options on bonds, we need to clarify some basic elements of callable and puttable bonds.

A bond with a call option (callable bond) gives the issuer or the borrower the right to call the bond – redeem it – prior to is maturity date. For example, in a three-year callable bond, the issuer can pay the bondholder a predetermined call price and cancel the bond's issue in year one, two or at any time prior to the maturity date in year three.

When will the issuer call the bond? To answer this question we have first to understand the motive of the issuer to call or redeem the bond. As a borrower paying periodic coupons to investors at a certain coupon rate, he would consider redeeming his current obligations and borrowing again if the market interest rate is considerably lower than what he currently pays. A callable bond gives an advantage to the issuer over the investor. To compensate the investor for this disadvantage, the interest rate on callable bonds is higher than the interest rate of bonds with similar characteristics but with no call option.

A bond with a put option (puttable bond), on the other hand, gives the investor, the lender, the right to put, or sell, the bond prior to its maturity date.

LOS. Calculate the hedge ratio for a bond using BPV

Bond futures are used for a variety of purposes. Much of a day's trading in futures will be speculative, that is, a punt on the direction of the market. Another main use of futures is to hedge bond positions.

In theory, if hedging a cash bond position with a bond futures contract, if cash and futures prices move together then any loss from one position will be offset by a gain from the other. When prices move exactly in lockstep, the hedge is considered perfect. In practice, the price of even the cheapest-to-deliver bond (which one can view as being the bond being traded – implicitly – when one is trading the bond future) and the bond future will not move exactly in line with each other over a period of time. The difference between the cash price and the futures price is called the *basis*. The risk that the basis will change in an unpredictable way is known as *basis risk*.

The modified duration hedge ratio may be used for all bonds, both deliverable and non-deliverable. In calculating this hedge ratio the modified duration is multiplied by the dirty price of the cash bond to obtain the basis point value (BPV). The BPV represents the actual impact of a change in the yield on the price of a specific bond. The BPV allows the trader to calculate the hedge ratio to reflect the different price sensitivity of the chosen bond (compared to the cheapest to deliver (CTD) bond) to interest rate movements. The hedge ratio calculated using the BPV must be constantly updated, because it will change if the price of the bond and/or the futures contract changes. This may necessitate periodic adjustments to the number of lots used in the hedge.

$$\text{hedge ratio} = \frac{\text{volatility of the bond to be hedged}}{\text{volatility of the hedging instrument}}$$

$$\text{number of contracts} = \frac{M_{bond}}{M_{Fut}} \times \frac{BPV_{bond}}{BPV_{Fut}}$$

Where:

M_{bond} = modified duration of the bonds portfolio

M_{Fut} = modified duration of the bond's futures.

Convexity

LOS. Define and discuss convexity

As discussed before, there is an inverse relationship between the price of a bond and the market prevailing interest rate. Theoretically, this inverse relationship may be depicted as a negatively sloped straight line. In reality, however, the relationship is not linear but curvilinear. As the interest rate increases, the price of the bond decreases slower than it increases when the interest rate decreases. The degree of curvature determines the size of sensitivity of the price to the change in interest rate.

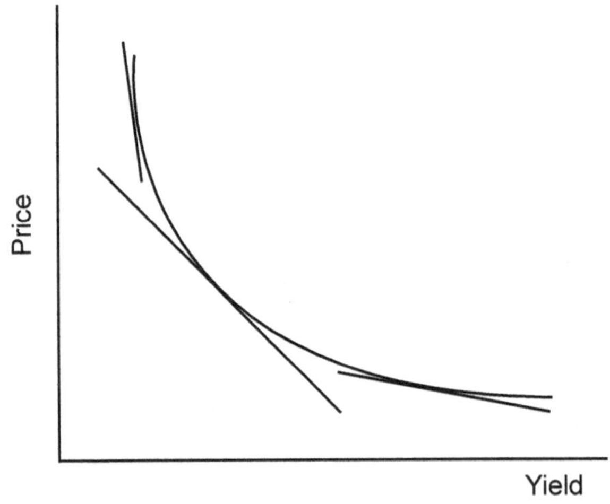

This graph indicates the following important features:

- The actual relationship between price and yield is not linear.
- The theoretical relationship between the price and yield is linear.
- The higher the change in the yield (increasing or decreasing) the wider the gap between the theoretical and actual yield curve (i.e. between the linear and curved line as in the graph).

As mentioned before, duration works well for a small change in yield as a result of a change in price. However, to calculate the price sensitivity of bonds to a big change in yield or interest we need to factor in the impact of convexity.

change in bond price = duration effect + convexity effect

LOS. Describe the impact of an embedded call or put on convexity

As discussed before, the relationship between the interest rate and price of a bond is convex, i.e. as the interest decreases, the price increases, and vice versa.

In callable bonds, as the interest rate decreases and prices increase, the prices cannot increase indefinitely or for a long time because the issuer at a certain point of time would have to call the bond at the call price.

The following diagram shows the relationship between the interest rate and the price of a callable bond. When the interest rate declines, the issuer would find other alternatives to raise funds by either directly borrowing from banks or issuing a new bond at a lower rate. In this case, the issuer would redeem the bond at the call price. The call price acts like a ceiling for the increase in the bond's price as the interest rate declines. Thus, a call price reduces the curvature of the price-yield curve.

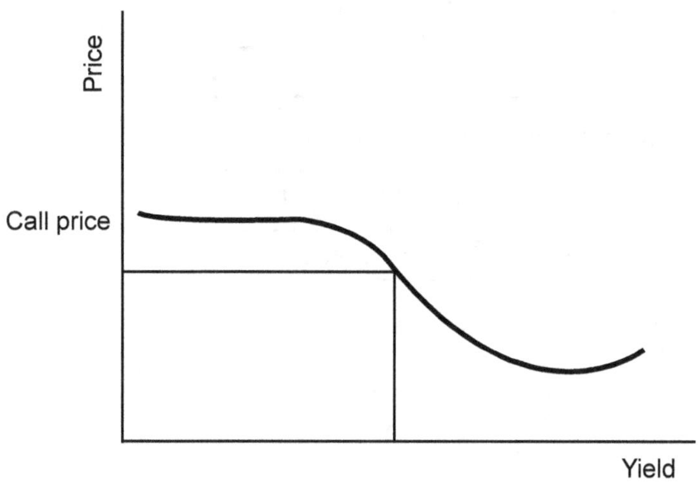

4.4 Types of bond

LOS. Compare and contrast sovereign, agency, corporate and municipal bonds
LOS. Compare and contrast general obligation and revenue bonds
LOS. Define types of foreign bonds (Yankee, Bulldog, Samurai, Alpine and Matador)
LOS. Define index-linked bonds, securitized bonds, amortizing bonds, callable bonds, puttable bonds and convertible bonds

The classification of the bond market is as follows:

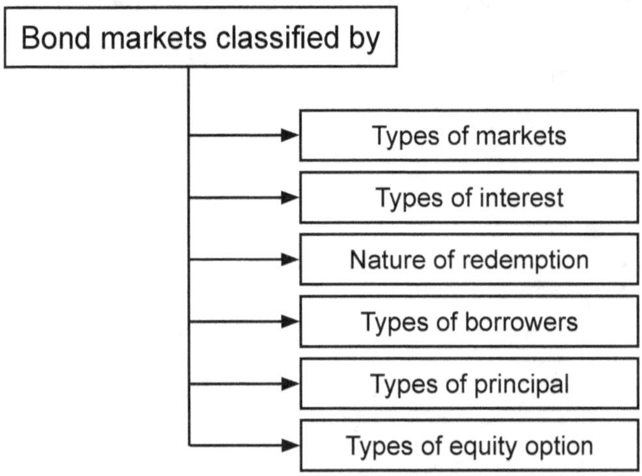

Each type/class is discussed in this section.

1. Bonds classified based on the type of market

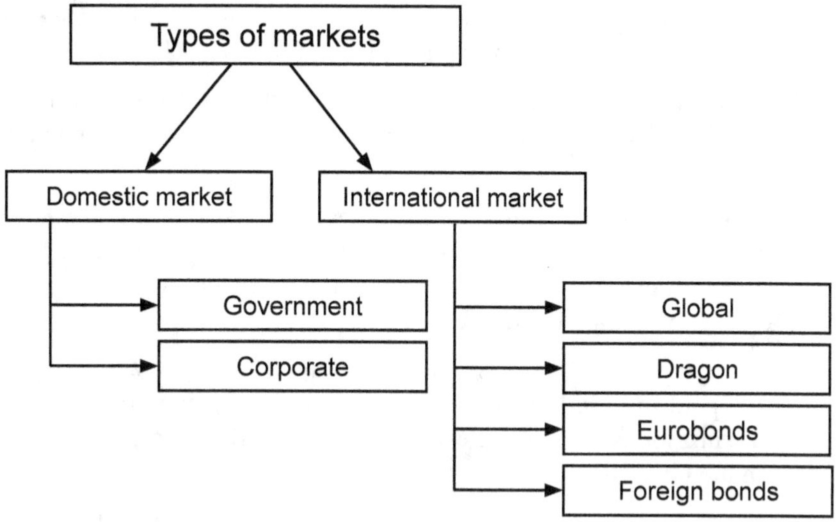

Bonds are traded either in domestic or international markets. In domestic markets, bonds are issued by governments or corporations (including banks). On the other hand, international bond markets include Global, Dragon, Eurobonds or Foreign bonds.

1. **Corporate bonds** are debt securities or instruments issued by corporations to bondholders in exchange for proceeds collected on the issuing date. Issuing corporations typically make periodic payments to the bondholders as a percentage of the face value of the issue. Corporate bonds are riskier than sovereign bonds as they are not backed by government support – hence, the interest rate on corporate bonds is higher than that on sovereign bonds. Bonds issued by public sector entities, banks, insurance companies, manufacturing and industrial entities, utility providers, telecommunications companies, etc., are all examples of corporate bonds.
2. **Government (or agency) bonds** are issued by bodies linked to governments, either through ownership or ultimate credit backing. For example, bonds issued by Fannie Mae or Freddie Mac are agency bonds. Such bonds are issued for a certain predetermined purpose to serve a public cause. Even though there is no explicit credit backing by the government for such bonds, they are generally considered *relatively* safe.

Investors would, however, expect a risk premium for holding such bonds to reflect this.

3. **Global bonds** are issued and traded on different markets at the same time. For example, bonds issued and registered in Japan but traded in the US, UK and Australian bond markets simultaneously.
4. **Dragon bonds** are issued to be traded in Asian markets, typically in either Hong Kong, Taiwan and Singapore. They are mostly denominated in US dollars.
5. **Foreign bonds** are issued in a domestic market in the domestic currency but by a foreign issuer. For example, bonds issued in Japan and denominated in Japanese yen but issued by an American issuer. Examples of foreign bonds are:
    - *Yankee bonds*: Bonds issued in dollars (principal and coupons are paid in USD) in the US but by non-American corporations or organizations. For example: a Japanese firm offering bonds in dollars in the US.
    - *Bulldog bonds*: Bonds issued in sterling (principal and coupons are paid in GBP) in the UK but by non- British corporations or organizations. For example: a Japanese firm offering bonds in GBP in the UK.
    - *Samurai bonds*: Bonds issued in Japanese yen (principal and coupons are paid in Yen) in Japan but by non-Japanese corporations or organizations. For example: a US firm offering bonds in yen in Japan.
    - *Alpine bonds*: Bonds issued in Swiss francs (principal and coupons are paid in francs) in Switzerland but by non-Swiss corporations or organizations. For example: a US firm offering bonds in francs in Switzerland.
    - *Matador bonds*: Bonds issued in euro (principal and coupons are paid in euro) in Spain but by non-Spanish corporations or organizations. For example: a US firm offering bonds in euro in Spain.
6. **Eurobonds** are issued in a currency other than the currency of the market in which the bond is issued. An example would be bonds issued in USD in the UK.

2. Types of Interest

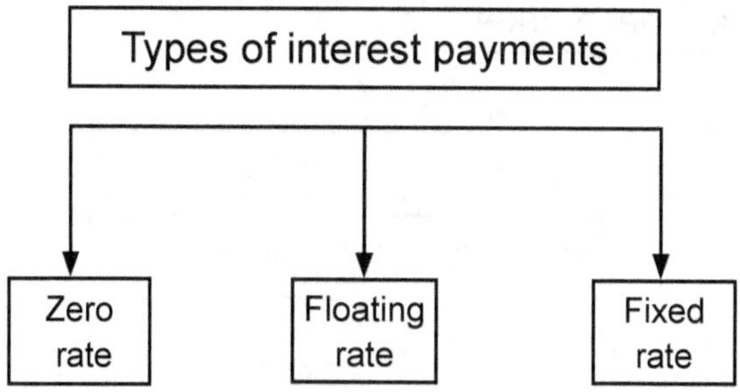

Bond issuers either pay periodic coupon payments to investors or they do not make interest payments at all. In the former case, the coupon payments could either be fixed or floating coupon payments. In the latter case, however, the issuer does not make periodic coupon payments to investors. In this case, the return on the investment is the difference between the price paid for the bond and the face value at the maturity date. The figure above illustrates these types of bond.

1. **Fixed rate bonds**: traditional bonds in which the issuer pays fixed coupon payments periodically while the principal is returned in one payment (called the bullet payment) at the maturity date. For example, the coupon rate is 5%.
2. **Floating rate bonds**: the coupon payments are benchmarked to an index or proxy so that the coupon changes from one period to another. For instance, the coupon rate may be quoted as LIBOR +45bps (45 basis points). The 45bps is called the adjustment margin. It can be positively correlated to the benchmark (LIBOR in this example), in the sense that it increases as the benchmark increases, hence it is written as LIBOR +45bps. The adjustment margin could also be negatively correlated to the benchmark, i.e. the quote is written as LIBOR -15bps, for instance. A bond with this relationship is called an **inverse floater**.

3. Nature of redemption

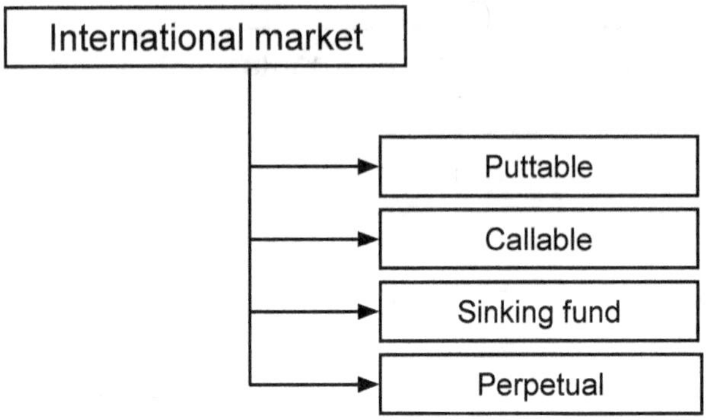

In the bond structure, the borrower pays the lender periodic coupon payments. For a bond with a five-year maturity and semi-annual coupon payments of 6%, for instance, the borrower will pay the lender ten future payments of 3% every six months. Since the life of the bond is five years, there is a chance that inflation will increase and when that happens the lender will be at a disadvantage because typically, with inflation, the purchasing power of money will decrease. So if after, say, two years of issuing the bond, inflation has increased to reach 5% annually, the lender is actually earning only 1% from this bond issue because the 6% annual coupon is wiped out by a 5% loss of purchasing power. To protect the bond investor from this inflation risk, the bond contract may be adjusted to give the lender a 6% *real* return, after deducting the impact of inflation. This type of bond is called an index-linked bond.

1. A **callable bond** is a normal (vanilla) bond contract that gives the borrower (issuer) an option to redeem (call) the bond prior to its maturity date. Typically the issuer would redeem the bond if he finds a better opportunity to issue another bond with a lower coupon rate than that which he is currently paying. This implies that the interest rate level in the market is low. Thus, the existing lender (investor) of the current bond issue will be at a disadvantage if the issuer calls the bond because they would receive their money earlier than they expected and they may have to reinvest at a lower interest rate elsewhere in the market. To compensate them for this disadvantage, callable bonds would have to be called at a price higher than the face value of the bond and a higher coupon rate would be paid than on bonds with no call option. Also, there would normally be a grace period from the date of investment until the bond can be called by the issuer.

2. A **puttable bond** is a bond contract with a put option. It is a bond with an option that allows the investor to sell (put) the bond back to the issuer. Investors would normally do that if the interest rate is increasing so that they can redeem this existing bond and invest their money into a higher interest rate issue. Since the put option is a disadvantage to the issuer, puttable bonds are issued with a lower coupon rate and face value than callable bonds or straight bonds.
3. **Convertible bonds** are bond contracts that give the lender the right to convert the outstanding amount of the bond to common stock of the issuer for a predetermined number of shares at a predetermined price.
4. A **securitized bond** is a bond with the principal and interest backed or sourced from cash flows from other assets. Mortgage-backed securities are examples of securitized bonds; the instalments collected by the bank from the mortgage loans are repackaged and channelled through to the holders of bonds issued by the bank.
5. **Sinking fund**: some bonds contracts (indentures) may include a requirement that asks the bond issuer to deposit a portion of the issue principal into a separate account in each specific period. The ultimate purpose of this procedure is to reduce the credit risk of the issuer by ensuring that the principal is available to the lenders at the bond maturity. The amount should be deposited in a separate account called a sinking fund. On certain agreed-upon dates, this amount accumulated in the sinking fund is used to redeem a portion of the principal to the lenders. A sinking fund is administered by a trust, which announces the number of bonds which are going to be redeemed/called at upcoming dates.
6. **Perpetual bonds** are bonds which are undated; these bonds have no maturity. Coupons on them are paid indefinitely.

4. Types of borrowers

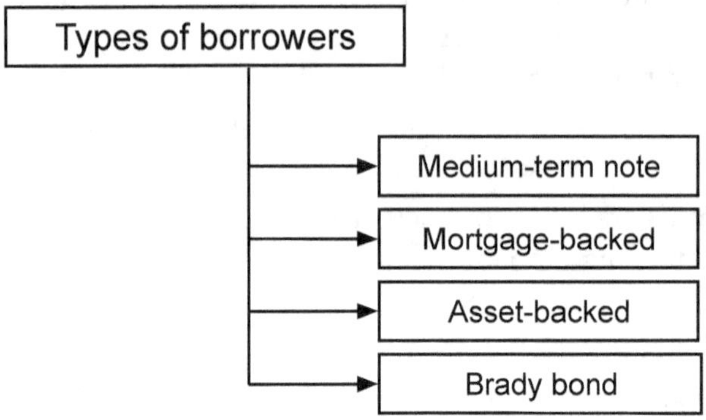

1. **Medium-term note**: bonds issued in maturities ranging from nine months to ten years and the coupons could either be floating or fixed.
2. **Mortgage-backed**: bonds whose coupons are paid to the investors from the cash flows generated from mortgage loans used as underlying assets.
3. **Asset-backed**: bonds whose coupons are paid to the investors from the cash flows generated from non-mortgage loans (such as leased properties, credit cards, car loans) as the underlying assets.
4. **Brady bond**: named after the US Treasury Secretary Nicholas Brady. In the 1980s, emerging countries such as Brazil, Argentina and Costa Rica took loans from US banks. These loans were non-performing due to economic problems in the debtor countries. Brady suggested restructuring these non-performing loans into bonds in which the outstanding amounts of the loans became the proceeds paid by the investor (the lender of the loan) to the borrower (the debtor countries). These bonds are tradable and guaranteed by the debtor countries' reserves of foreign currency. Furthermore, to give more creditworthiness of this issue of bonds, debtor countries sought finance from the International Monetary Fund and World Bank to buy US 30-year treasury zero-coupon bonds maintained in an escrow as collateral of the issue.

5. Types of principal

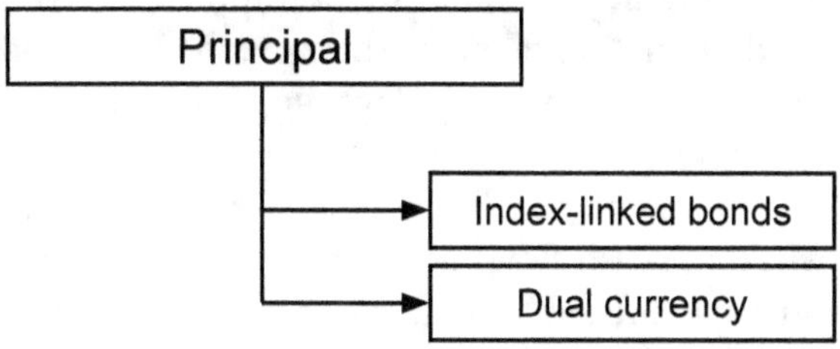

1. **Index-linked bonds:** bonds in which the interest or the principal paid on the redemption date is linked or benchmarked to an index that reflects the change in the purchasing power of the cash flows.
2. **Dual currency bond:** a bond for which the principal and coupon are paid in two different currencies. These types of bonds expose the bondholder to foreign exchange risk because if the coupon's currency appreciates against the bondholder's functional currency, the bondholder will suffer from a loss, and vice versa.

6. Types of equity options

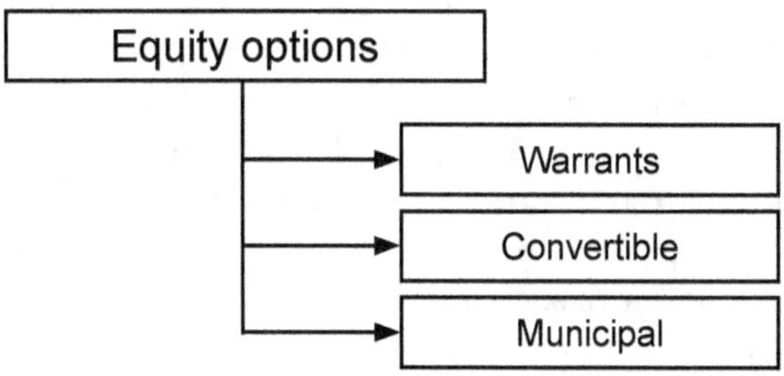

1. **Convertible bonds** give bondholders the right to exchange the outstanding amount of the bond to the equivalent in shares of the company that issued the bonds.
2. **Warrants** are sometimes included in a bond issue to encourage investors to subscribe to the bond issue. Bonds with warrants entitle bondholders to buy equity shares of the issuing company within a certain rage of prices within a certain period of time. Warrants, from this definition, are like options except that warrants are not exchanged and they are issued by the firm issuing the bonds and equity.

3. **Municipal bonds** are issued by non-central government bodies, i.e. local authorities. Such bonds are not backed by the credit merit of the government. Investors in municipal bonds are exempt from paying tax on the coupons received or any capital gain. There are, however, cases of municipal bonds that are not tax exempt. Revenue bonds are one type of municipal bonds – they are debt securities issued to finance projects. The proceeds collected from the bondholders are used to finance the underlying project while the cash flows generated from the project are used to make coupon payments, as well as pay back the face value to the bondholders. Examples of underlying projects could be universities, hospitals and schools. Principals and interest payments are secured by the revenues generated from these projects. General obligation bonds are another type of municipal bond, but in general obligation issues, the principal and interest are secured by the faith of the issuing bodies, not by the projects' revenues.

LOS. Discuss strips, floating rate notes and inflation-indexed bonds

In terms of features of coupon payments, bonds in general come in two forms: bonds which pay coupon payments and bonds which do not pay coupon payments (zero-coupon bonds).

Issuers of zero-coupon bonds do not pay coupon payments and make one payment on the maturity date. The difference between the amount borrowed and the amount paid back on the maturity date is effectively the interest/return the lender (investor) gets on his/her investment. Investors who are typically interested to invest in zero-coupon bonds are those with no immediate need for periodic cash flows, but are mostly interested in bullet payments in the long term, such as pension funds. These securities are called strips because they separate the payment of principal from the payment of coupons, i.e. the investor receives only the principal and the coupon payments are embedded implicitly in the structure, as reflected in the deep discount between the investment amount and the principal paid at the redemption date.

Floating rate notes (FRN) are bonds with maturity between one to ten years that pay coupon payments that are not fixed. The coupon payments in FRNs are linked or indexed to a certain index (such as three or six months LIBOR). The date on which the new rate becomes effective and the old rate ceases to be applied is call the *reset date*. LIBOR, in this example, is called the reference rate.

An FRN can be structured in such a way that the coupon rate in the FRN can be positively or negatively correlated to the reference rate.

- Positively related to the reference rate: fixed rate + reference rate. For example, 100bps + three-month LIBOR
- Negatively related to the reference rate: fixed rate - reference rate. For example, three-month rate LIBOR - 10bps.

Inflation-indexed bonds

A bond investment, since it extends for years, exposes the bondholder to the risk of changes in purchasing power. This means that the coupon and the principal received in the future might not have the same purchasing power of the money initially invested to purchase the bond. To protect the bondholder from such risks, inflation-indexed bonds index the future coupon payments and principal to the future inflation rate.

Coupon payments in such bonds are calculated as follows:

$$\text{inflation adjusted coupons} = FV \times \text{real coupon rate} \times (\text{daily inflation rate}_{(t)}/\text{daily inflation rate}_{(Base)})$$

4.5 Features of bond markets

LOS. Discuss the various risks associated with a bond

There are inherent risks in bond investment. These are as follows:

1. **Credit risk** is the loss incurred as a result of a borrower defaulting in paying back the obligations due to the lender. Thus, if the issuer of the bond defaults in its payment of coupon payments to the investor/lender then the lender is exposed to credit risk. There are some techniques that the lender could use to mitigate the credit risk, as we shall see in Chapter 10. Another form of credit risk is when the bond is rated by a rating agency at a certain level and after the issuance the bond is downgraded. Downgrading will negatively impact the tradability of the bond.
2. **Liquidity risk**: the aspect of the liquidity risk that is inherent in bond investment is the inability to sell the bond in the market in a short period of time with a minimum loss. There are several factors that might cause illiquidity of a bond, the most important of which are the type of issuer and currency of denomination. Bonds issued by high credit-rated organizations are typically liquid, i.e. in high demand with market participants. By the same token, bonds issued in major world currencies are generally more tradable than those issued in minor currencies.
3. **Interest rate risk**: the value of the bond investment when recorded on the balance sheet of the investor is impacted by changes in interest rate. There is a negative relationship between the value of a bond and the interest rate: the higher the interest rate, the lower the value, and the lower the interest rate, the higher the value of the bond. This risk is captured in duration and convexity.
4. **Foreign exchange risk**: in bond investing FX risk occurs with bonds denominated in currencies different to the domestic currency of the investor. Fluctuation in the FX rate between the domestic currency and the currency in which the bond is issued (the coupon and principal payments) will cause a loss to the investor. FX risk does not exist in the case of investing in bonds if the bond's currency is the investor's domestic currency.

LOS. Compare and contrast retail and investment banking

Retail banking is the offer of banking services to personal customers. Retail banking customers are numerous in volume but with lower transaction size compared to corporate or financial institution customers.

Investment banks offer banking investment activities to wholesale customers such as corporate and financial institutions and do not accept deposits from retail customers.

Listed below are some activities of investment banks:

- Mergers and acquisition: either the bank is directly involved in such deals or advises its customers in processing the transactions.
- Consultancy: there a wide range of consultancy services, such as wealth management, corporate finance and feasibility studies.
- Underwriting.
- Fund management.

LOS. Define market-making and origination
LOS. Define bid-price and offer-price
LOS. Compare and contrast a proprietary trader and an inter-dealer broker

Market making is the holding of an inventory of financial assets by a dealer or brokerage company. By holding the financial assets the dealer/broker quotes a buying and selling price for the assets (bid and ask prices, respectively) to interested buyers.

An investment bank may issue bonds on behalf of its customers. Proceeds from the bonds issue are then passed from the investment bank to its customer in exchange for fees for this process of **origination.**

The **bid price** is the price an investor is willing to pay for an asset and the **offer price** is the price at which she is willing to sell the asset.

Proprietary trading is when an investment bank or firm trades financial instruments using their own capital, for their own profit, instead of trading on behalf of their clients for fees and commission. An **inter-dealer,** on the other hand, is a brokerage house, in the bond market, facilitating trades between major dealers.

LOS. Describe the various market participants by group

As indicated at the beginning of the chapter, bonds are financial instruments transacted between those who have a shortage of funds and those who have surplus funds. Thus, the bond market participants are as follows:

1. **Issuers**: parties which seek capital by issuing bonds and collecting the proceeds. They are also called borrowers. Governments, banks and corporations can all be borrowers. In order to attract investors to subscribe to bonds they have issued, bond issuers in some issues seek to get the issue rated by rating agencies.
2. **Investors** invest their money in bonds expecting to generate a periodic coupon payment and a return on their investment. Financial institutions, corporations and pension funds could all be investors in the bond market.
3. **Financial institution**: due to the administration, legal and official procedural requirements, financial institutions facilitate bond transactions between the investor and issuer for a fee.

LOS. Describe on-the-run, off-the-run and benchmark securities

On-the-run securities are government securities issued recently into the market. Those securities which have been traded and transacted in the market over the long term are called off-the-run securities.

Benchmark securities are financial instruments that provide standards against which the performance of other financial instruments are measured. In the bond markets, for instance, bonds issued by governments are used as a benchmark for other bond issues.

LOS. Define property clauses and call provision

Some bonds are collateralized by physical assets such as plant and equipment. Such collateralization gives comfort to the lender that in the case of default the borrower (bond issuer) can sell the assets and recover part of the principal. Thus, the borrowers who pledged such assets would reflect this in the contract in a clause that stipulates that disposing of such assets is not allowed unless a portion of the proceeds generated from disposal of the assets is used to redeem part of the bond issue. Such a clause is called a **release of property clause**.

Corporate bonds, as in the US, are usually embedded with a call provision or option. This provision gives the issuer (i.e. the borrower) the right to redeem the bond at a predetermined price (call price). Bond issuers exercise this provision when interest rates decline and the bond price goes up. At a declined interest rate it becomes cheaper for the borrower to redeem the current issue of the bond and issue another bond, i.e. borrow at a lower rate. Investors (i.e. the lenders) would be forced to invest the proceeds received from the redemption of the bond at a prevailing lower interest rate. To compensate the investors for this loss, the call price is typically higher than the par value.

LOS. Compare gross and net interest payments

In some bond issues, such as agency or corporate bonds, the issuer pays the coupon payments after deducting the income tax or withholding tax due, i.e. it pays the coupon net of tax charges. These are net interest payments. Traditionally bonds pay coupon payments as gross interest payments, such as Eurobonds.

LOS. Compare and contrast the primary and secondary markets

The **primary market** is where *new* bonds are issued and traded for the first time. The issues are traded either directly between the sellers and the buyers or through an underwriter or agent on behalf of the issuer.

Bonds which are already issued can be traded again – bought or sold – in the **secondary market**. There are two methods by which bonds can change hands in the secondary market: over the counter (OTC) or on the stock exchange. In OTC, bonds are traded directly between the sellers and buyers without intermediaries and outside an organized exchange house. The majority of the bonds traded in the secondary market are traded OTC.

LOS. Define underwriter, lead manager and book-runner

An **underwriter** is a financial institution that helps the bond issuer set the pricing and volume of the bond issue. It also guarantees to the issuer that bonds will be fully subscribed or sold. If not, the underwriter will either sell the remaining bonds and incur a loss, or keep them. All these services are rendered for a fee called underwriting commission. The underwriter in this setup is also the **book runner** – the party that takes care of the sale of the issues, the bond owners, the legal aspect and the accounting.

The **lead manager** is the arranger of the underwriting process and syndication of investors into the bond issue.

LOS. Describe the characteristics of the Eurobond market

As opposed to bonds issued domestically in the local currency in any country, there are bonds which are issued across borders and in any currency. For example, bonds issued in Japan, denominated in US dollars, by a US company located outside the US. These bonds are called Eurobonds. Another name for Eurobonds is *international bonds*. So, Eurobonds are any bonds which are issued in a country's currency but not issued in that country. In order to attract investors to subscribe to/invest in these issues of bonds, they are typically issued with a low par value.

LOS. Define the different day-count conventions

An interest rate is quoted on a per annum basis. To calculate the interest due on a mortgage on a monthly-payment basis, for instance, we need to convert the annual quoted interest rate to the periods in question. For example, with a 5% annual coupon payment that is paid on 1 January every year, an investor would need how to know much interest he would earn if he bought the bond on 27 June, or any other date. Will he apply a rule of there being 30 calendar days in a month, or look at the actual days in the given month?

In interest rate markets, there are the following conventions:

- Actual/actual: as the name indicates, this convention takes the actual number of days between two dates. It is commonly used in Treasury bonds and notes. If the issuance date of a Treasury bond is 31 August, and the coupon payment is 11 September, then the investor is entitled to an accrued interest for 11 days only (the issuance date is counted but the settlement date, i.e. 11 September is not counted). So to calculate the accrued interest we multiply (11/365) by the amount of the coupon payment.
- Actual/360: specifies that each month has the same number of days as indicated by the calendar, regardless of the actual number of days,

divided by a 30-day month calendar. This convention is commonly used in financial instruments with less than one year to maturity such as commercial paper and Treasury bills. It divides the actual number of days between two settlement dates or periods by 360. Using the same example as in actual/actual above, the accrued interest would calculated by multiplying (11/360) by the amount of the coupon payment.

- 30/360: this convention disregards the actual number of days and assumes that all months of the year are 30 days. It is commonly used in corporate bonds, mortgage-backed securities and agency bonds.

The following table summarizes the days count convention in international markets.

Country	Number of intended annual payments	Day-count convention
Australia	2	actual/actual
Austria	1	actual/actual
US	2	actual/actual
Belgium	1	actual/actual
UK	2	actual/actual
Denmark	1	30E/360
France	1	actual/actual
Ireland	1	actual/actual
Italy	1	actual/actual
Canada	2	actual/actual
Norway	1	actual/365
New Zealand	2	actual/actual
Spain	1	actual/actual
Switzerland	1	30E/360
Sweden	1	30E/360
Germany	1	actual/actual

Source: Moorad, Choudry, *The Repo Handbook* (Oxford: Butterworth Heinemann, 2002).

30E/360 and 30/360 both assume a 30-day month. For example, "there are 30 days between 10 February and 10 March. Under the 30/360 convention, if the first date falls on the 31st, it is changed to the 30th of the month, and if the second date falls on the 31st and the first date is on the 30th or 31st, the second date is changed to the 30th. The difference under the 30E/360 method is that if the second date falls on the 31st of the month it is automatically changed to the 30th."[2]

LOS. Define default and recovery rates

Default is the issuer's failure to pay either the coupon payments or the face value of the bond to the investor. Defaults does not necessary mean, in all cases, that the investor has lost their entire investment. There are three cases of default, as follows:

1. The issuer defaults on some payments but it is still in business (it has not filed for bankruptcy), and has reached an agreement or negotiates with the investors to restructure the contract.
2. The issuer faces a financial problem. It is still in business but undergoes a restructuring of the organization, hence it cannot pay its dues.
3. Default as a result of bankruptcy. In this case the issuer firm's assets are liquidated and the investors as well as other creditors would receive portions of their investments from the sale of the assets. Whatever they receive is called the recovery, or **recovery rate**.

LOS. Define bond spread (yield spread) and bid-ask spread
LOS. Describe the impact of liquidity on spreads

A spread refers to the risk involved in an investment. The higher the risk, the higher the spread the investor would ask for. In bond context, and in terms of risks, we can classify bond issues as either risky bonds or non-risky bonds (also called zero-risk bonds). The risk being considered here is the ability of the issuer to pay back the coupon and the principal, i.e. the credit risk. So, zero-risk bonds mean zero or a very minimal risk that the issuer would not pay back his obligations.

---

2 Alexander, C. and Sheedy, E., *The Professional Risk Managers' Handbook, A Comprehensive Guide to Current Theory and Best Practices* (Professional Risk Managers' International Association, 2004).

Bonds issued by governments are considered zero-risk bonds (zero-credit risk). Non-government bonds, on the other hand, are prone to default. So, if a government bond pays an interest rate of 3%, an investor would expect bonds issued by a corporation to pay higher than 3% to account for the possible risks, say 2% more. The 2% is called the bond's spread or **yield spread**. It is important to note that the spread is not fixed during the life of the bonds – it changes based on variations in market participants' perceptions of the types of risks involved.

In addition to the credit risk, bond investors also consider liquidity risk. Liquidity risk is the investor's inability (or difficulty) to sell or liquidate its bond investments in the secondary market. This typically happens when the bond is issued in a small size so that it is traded in low volume. If bonds are issued and traded in high volume, hence they are liquid in the market, the risk is reduced and the spread required is reduced. So, high liquidity leads to small spreads and low liquidity leads to big spreads.

LOS. Describe how a bond's rating affects the yield spread
LOS. Describe the role of rating agencies
LOS. List and discuss Moody's and S&P ratings for bonds

As discussed in the previous sections, the bond issuer or borrower is obliged to repay either the redemption value and the coupons, or only the redemption value, to the bond investor or lender. In this case lenders are exposed to the risk that the bond issuer fails to honor this obligation; this exposure to a default risk is called credit risk.

Causes of credit risk might be internal or external to the issuer. An internal cause of default is a shortage of liquidity. For instance, the issuer's sales revenue has plummeted because of malpractices in operations and production, which reduce the cash flow available to settle the bond obligations. An external cause might be political uprising or economic instability in the country the issuer operates in, which in turn causes the clients and customers of the issuer to default on their obligations toward the issuer.

When a bond issuer defaults on the coupon or redemption value payment, the issuer negotiates restructured terms of contracts to cater for the financial difficulties. If the issuer's shares are publicly traded on an exchange market the issuer might offer the lenders the option to convert the outstanding amount of the bond to an equivalent number of the issuer's shares. In the worst-case scenario, the default would lead the issuer to bankruptcy.

Upon liquidation of the issuing firm, the lender might receive part of the outstanding amount of the bond as a recovered amount. The size of the recovered amount depends on the total debt size on the issuer's liability and the seniority of the defaulted bond.

Not all types of bonds are exposed to the same level of credit risk. The size of credit risk exposure depends on the type of issuer. Compared to government bonds, investment in corporate bonds is riskier.

We could infer from the above that a lender in a bond issue needs to know a lot of information about the issuer, such as information about the political and economic environments of the issuer, the size of debt on its balance sheet, the size and quality of sales revenues or its costs structure, in order to assess the size of credit risk she will be exposed to. Having access to all of this detailed information might not be possible for all lenders, but credit rating agencies such as Standard and Poor's (S&P) and Moody's offer this service of analysis for a fee.

The role of rating agencies is to assess the creditworthiness of corporations and analyze the likelihood of default of these corporations and the ability of an issuer to honor its obligations. Rating agencies also rate bond issues, which could have different ratings to the rating of the issuer. Criteria and methodologies for ratings vary amongst rating agencies, but these criteria are mostly around the quality of the issuer's profitability, liquidity, management and structure of cash flows in the bond issue. The final product of their analysis and assessment is a rating that indicates the level of creditworthiness. The table below gives examples of the ratings of S&P and Moody's. The highest quality rating means the lowest credit risk and the lowest spread the lenders will require.

Lenders in the bond market need this credit assessment service in order to determine the required return on their investment. Lenders require a high rate of return for a high possible credit risk. The difference in rate of return from different bond issues is called the spread. Taking an example – compared to a government bond, the spread on a corporate bond would be higher because, as already established, a corporate bond is riskier than a government bond.

The ratings of S&P and Moody's

Rating	S&P	Moody's
Highest quality, lowest credit risk, lowest spread	AAA	Aaa
High quality, low credit risk, low spread	AA	Aa
Upper medium quality, upper medium credit risk and spread	A	A
Medium quality, credit risk and spread	BBB	Baa
Speculative	BB	Ba
Low quality, low credit risk, high spread	B	B
Expected default	CCC	Caa
Partial recovery expected	CC	Ca
Default	C	C

Chapter 5. Options Markets And Contracts

This chapter discusses the following topics:

1. Basics of options.
2. Valuing options.
3. Pricing options.
4. Options strategies.
5. Options risks.

5.1 Basics of options

This section discusses options definitions and terminology as well as the types of options available in the market.

LOS. Define premium, underlying, strike (exercise) price, expiration date (expiry), in-the-money, at-the-money and out-of-the-money

An option is a contract that gives you the right to buy or sell an asset (the **underlying**) at a future exercise date at a price determined today. The future purchase or sale will take place in exchange for payment or receipt at the predetermined price, regardless of the market price at the time of exchange. If you buy the contract you are called the *long* party. The party which sells the options contract is called the *short* party or writer of the option contract. Theoretically, you can have options contracts on any asset.

This structure obviously results in one party gaining and another party losing. It is the movement of the asset's price that determines if an investor is gaining or losing in the option contract by comparing the price of this asset on the expiry date with the strike price.

- **Types:** options comes in two types: call options (right to buy) and put options (right to sell).
- **Strike** is the fixed price – predetermined at the date of inception – at which you either buy or sell the underlying asset at the expiration or exercise date.
- **Expiration date** is the last date of the contract on which you either buy or sell the underlying asset.

Let us look at a simplified example to illustrate the economic sense of an options contract.

Example 5.1: Options concept

Assume that you plan to buy a new house in three months' time because you do not have the whole amount of money ready to buy this house - which is offered for USD100,000 - at the moment. Obviously the concern here is that the price in three months will be more than USD100,000. To alleviate this concern, you can go and talk to the owner and inform him that you want to buy the house for USD100,000, but in three months' time. As prudent investors you both put this agreement in a form of contract that stipulates that you have the right to buy the house for USD100,000 in three months. Because of the contract, thw owner is obliged to sell you the house at the agreed price of $100,000.

In this exchange, one of you would incur a gain while the other would incur a loss. If after three months the price of the house is $130,000, while he sold it to you for only $100,000 as the contract says, the owner would incur a loss of $30,000, while you have saved $30,000.

How did we calculate the $30,000? It is the difference between the market price ($130,000) of the house and the pre-agreed price ($100,000). The $30,000 is called the payoff of the contract, or the intrinsic value of the contract. By making a profit of $30,000 the option contract is called **in-the-money** for the buyer of the house, while it is **out-of the-money** for the seller.

At any point in time during the life of a contract which has a profitable value, the contract is called in-the-money. On the other hand, at any point in time during the life of the contract which is carrying a loss, the contract is called out-of-the-money.

Finally, at any point in time where the buyer of the option contract finds herself indifferent whether to exercise the right in the contract or not because the prevailing market price and the pre-agreed price are identical, the contract is described as being **at-the-money**.

The last point in this example is that the owner does not give you the right of buying in three months for free. There is a price attached to this contract, paid from the buyer to the seller (owner).

In a call option, if the price of this asset on expiry is higher than the strike price, an investor will make a profit, and vice versa. In a put option, if the price of this asset is lower than the strike price the investor will make a profit, and vice versa.

The option contract's price is called its **premium**. The premium includes two parts: intrinsic value and time value. Intrinsic value is the difference between the underlying asset price at expiry or exercise date and the strike price.

LOS. Compare and contrast American, European and Bermudan options

- An **American** option is an option contract that gives the buyer the right – but not an obligation – to buy the underlying asset on any day during the life of the contract.
- A **European** option is an option contract that gives the buyer the right – but not an obligation – to buy the underlying asset *only* on the expiry date of the contract.
- A **Bermudan** option is an option contract that stands in the middle between the American and European call option in terms of timings of exercise. Bermudan option contracts give the buyer the right to buy or sell the underlying asset either on the expiry date or on *specific dates* only during the life of the contract.

The terms American and European do not refer to the place of trade or currency of transaction. They are just the particular terms used to denote the differences explained above.

Question 5.1

A European put option allows the holder to:

a. buy the underlying asset at the striking price on or before the expiration date.

b. sell the underlying asset at the striking price on or before the expiration date.

c. potentially benefit from a stock price decrease with less risk than short selling the stock.

d. sell the underlying asset at the striking price on the expiration date.

e. c and d.

Solution

e.

Question 5.2

An American call option allows the buyer to:

a. sell the underlying asset at the exercise price on or before the expiration date.

b. buy the underlying asset at the exercise price on or before the expiration date.

c. sell the option in the open market prior to expiration.

d. a and c.

e. b and c.

Solution

b.

Question 5.3

Relative to European puts, otherwise identical American put options:

a. are more valuable.

b. are less valuable.

c. are equal in value.

d. will always be exercised earlier.

e. none of the above.

Solution

a.

Question 5.4

A/An _______ gives the buyer the right, but not the obligation, to exercise the option at any time before the expiration or maturity date:

a. European option.

b. Complex option.

c. At-the-money option.

d. American option.

e. Asian option.

Solution

d.

5.2 Valuing options

LOS. Define intrinsic value and time value

When analyzing options, as well as other financial instruments, there is a distinction between pricing these instruments and valuing them. Pricing an option contract is determining its intrinsic value, i.e. the premium, by calculating the present value of its future cash flows – either by the Black-scholes or the binomial model (as we shall discuss later). Valuation of an option contract, on the other hand, is finding the contract's payoff at any point of time during the contract and on expiry date. The payoff is defined as the difference between the contract price and the prevailing market price at the time of valuation. In the following section, I provide the formulas to calculate an option's payoff and its value.

call option intrinsic value (option payoff) = **MAX{0, (prevailing underlying asset price at expiry - strike price)}**

call option payoff (intrinsic value) = **MAX{0,(S1-X)}**

in-the-money call option(ITM) intrinsic value = **MAX{0,(S1-X)}>0**

out-of-the-money call option(OTM) intrinsic value = **MAX{0,(S1-X)}<0**

at-the-money call option (ATM) intrinsic value = **MAX{0,(S1-X)}=0**

put option intrinsic value (option payoff) = **MAX{(0,(strike price - prevailing underlying asset price at expiry)}**

put option payoff (intrinsic value) = **MAX{0,(X-S1)}**

in-the-money put option intrinsic value = **MAX{0,(X-S1)}>0**

out-of-the-money put option intrinsic value = **MAX{0,(X-S1)}<0**

at-the-money call option (ATM) intrinsic value = **MAX{0,(X-S1)}=0**

Where:

S1 = prevailing underlying asset price at expiry

X = strike price

Using these rules, the intrinsic value of an option will have a different value from one day to another. For example, if it is a call option, and the underlying asset price is rapidly increasing, the intrinsic value will also be rapidly increasing.

The more days there are until the contract matures, the more intrinsic value will have room to increase. This means that the more days that are left until the contract expires, the more the asset's price will have a chance to volatilize, which might eventually change in your favor. This is called the *time value* of an option.

An in-the-money option is an option that has a positive intrinsic value, while an out-of-the-money option is an option with negative intrinsic value. The in-the-money option's price includes both intrinsic value and time value, while the out-of-the-money option's price, since it has zero intrinsic value, just includes time value.

Thus, the value of an options contract comprises two components, intrinsic value and time value:

option value = intrinsic value + time value

call option value = call option payoff + time value

= MAX [0, (S-X)] + remaining time to expiry

Example 5.2: Determine the moneyness of a call option

Assume that a stock currency is trading at $50 and there is a one-month call option issued on this stock with a strike price of $30. Determine the moneyness of the call option for the option buyer.

Solution

Call option payoff

= MAX{0,(50-30)}

= MAX{0,20} = $20

$20>0 so the call option is in-the-money. As a buyer of a call option, you would make a gain of $20, which also means that the seller of the option would have made a loss of $20. Options are a zero-sum game.

Question 5.5

What is the intrinsic value of an out-of-the-money call option equal to?

a. the call premium.

b. the stock price minus the exercise price.

c. zero.

d. the strike price.

e. none of the above.

Solution

c.

Question 5.6

The maximum loss the writer of a stock put option can suffer is equal to:

a. the strike price minus the put premium.

b. the strike price.

c. the stock price minus the put premium.

d. the put premium.

e. none of the above.

Solution

a.

Question 5.7

Which of the following statements is false?

a. Out-of-the-money for a call means that the stock price is less than the exercise price.

b. European options are traded in Europe as well as in America.

c. The intrinsic value reflects the option's potential appreciation.

d. Option prices almost always exceed intrinsic values.

e. An option's premium cannot decline below intrinsic value.

Solution

e.

LOS. Draw the expiration payoff diagram of a put and a call
LOS. Identify and discuss the graphic representations of a put and a call

Example 5.3: Call and put options

1. Call option

Assume a call option is written with a strike price of $30, sold for $2.4 on ABC stock. The following tables and diagrams illustrate the payoff for long and short positions.

Long call payoff and profit is illustrated in the table below.

Stock price	Call payoff	Premium	Net profit
0	0	$2.40	($2.40)
10	0	$2.40	($2.40)
20	0	$2.40	($2.40)
30	0	$2.40	($2.40)
40	10	$2.40	$7.60
50	20	$2.40	$17.60
60	30	$2.40	$27.60
70	40	$2.40	$37.60

The following diagram depicts the long call payoff:

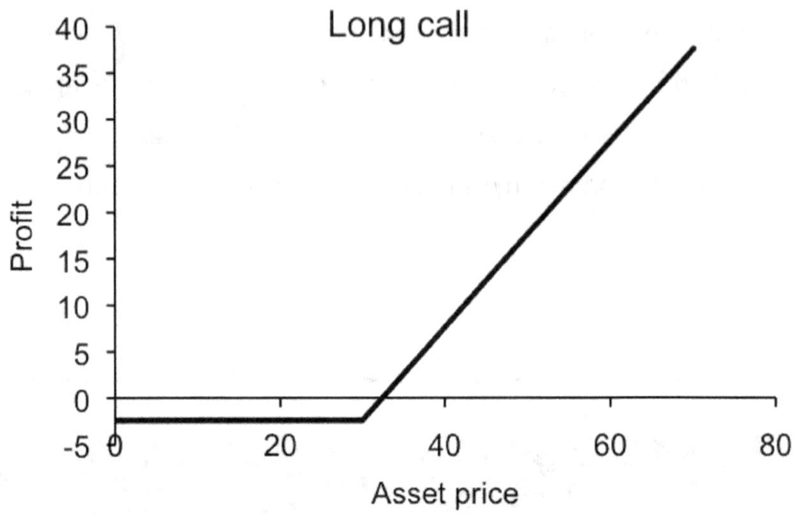

For the short position, the opposite position would be like this:

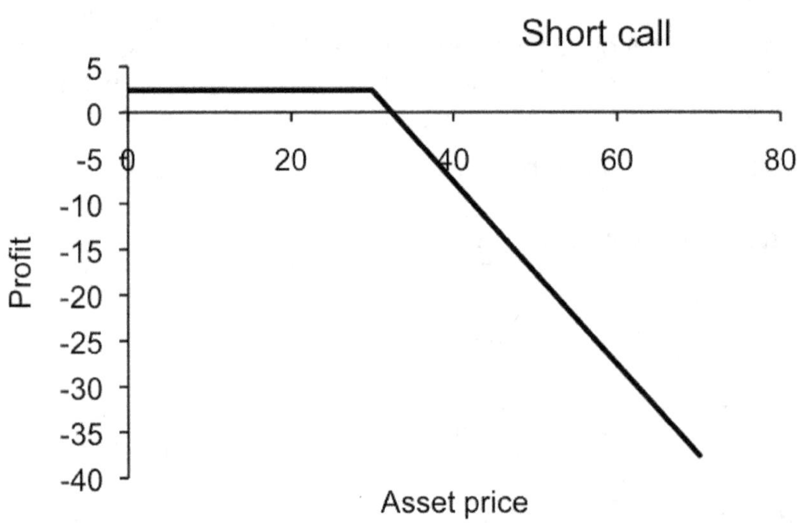

2. Put option

Assume a put option is written with a strike price of $30, sold for $1.9 on ABC Stock. The following table and diagrams illustrate the payoff for long and short positions.

Long put payoff and profit is illustrated in the table below.

Stock price	Long put payoff	Premium	Net profit
0	30	$1.90	**$28.10**
10	20	$1.90	**$18.10**
20	10	$1.90	**$8.10**
30	0	$1.90	($1.90)
40	0	$1.90	($1.90)
50	0	$1.90	($1.90)
60	0	$1.90	($1.90)
70	0	$1.90	($1.90)

The following diagram depicts the long put payoff:

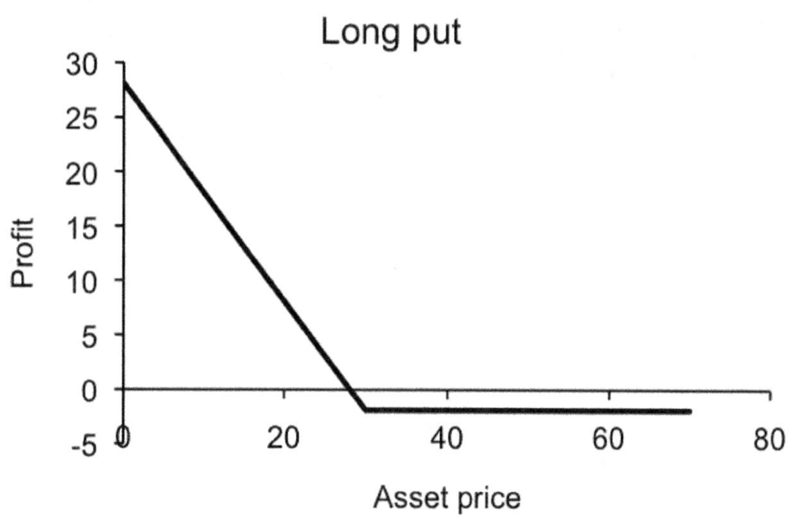

For the short position, the opposite position would be like this:

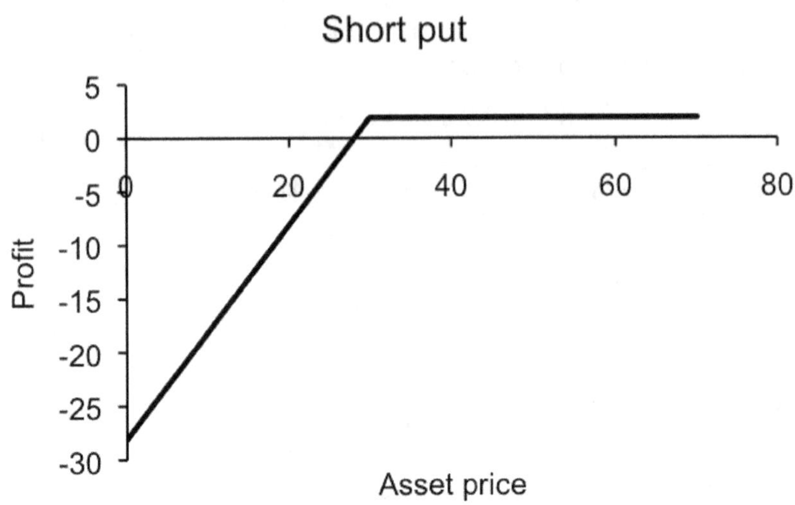

5.3 Pricing options

This section discusses the following two methods of pricing options:

1. Binomial model.
2. Black-Scholes-Merton model.

1. Binomial model

LOS. Discuss the basic principles of the binomial option model
LOS. Calculate an option price using a one-step binomial model
LOS. Define the symbols and letters of inputs into the binomial model

What does binomial mean? Binomial means the sum or difference of two terms.

A binomial options pricing model breaks down the asset's price into two directions: up and down, or increase and decrease. The size of the movement in either direction is estimated by the probability of occurrence. The movement in the asset's price could be for a single-period or multiple periods. For example, we can work out estimated changes in the price of an asset over a six-month period, and conduct the exercise on the six-month period thereafter (i.e. multiple six-month periods of time).

The following figures depict the single and multiple binomial model:

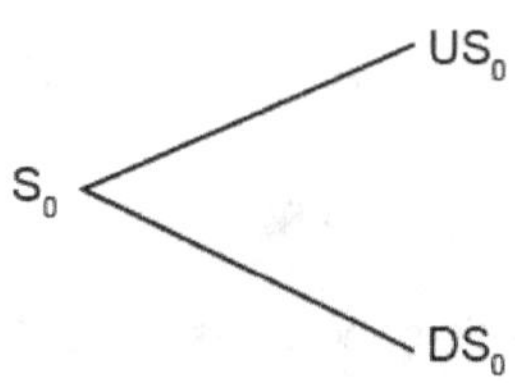

Single period
binomial model

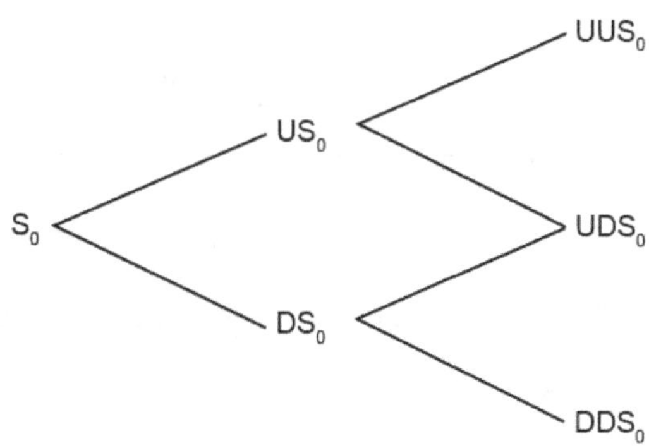

Multiple-period
binomial model

Where[3]:

S_0 = current asset price

U = size of anticipated upward move of the price

D = size of the anticipated downward move of the price

UU = size of two consecutive increases in price over the period

UD = size of an increase followed by decrease in price of the asset over the period

DD = size of two consecutive decreases in price over the period

Once we determine the expected move in the asset price, we can determine the expected price of an option (call or put) on this asset using the same techniques of the binomial pricing model, as illustrated in the following diagram:

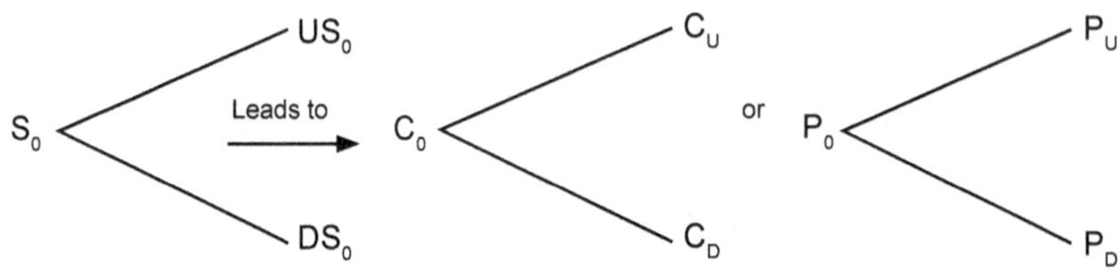

Where:

C_u = call option payoff when the underlying asset's price goes up

C_D = call option payoff when the underlying asset's price goes down

P_u = put option payoff when the underlying asset's price goes up

P_D = put option payoff when the underlying asset's price goes down

3 Different texts use some different forms of these letters, such as lower case. The principle is the same irrespective of the letters and symbols.

Since the up move and down move is expected in the future, we would need to factor in the probability of these movements in the calculation of options pricing. To calculate the:

risk-neutral probability of an upward move =

$$\frac{1 + \text{risk-free rate} - \text{size of downward move}}{\text{size of upward move} - \text{size of downward move}}$$

risk-neutral probability of an upward move =

$$\frac{1 + RF - D}{U - D}$$

risk-neutral probability of a downward move (Π_d) = 1 - risk-neutral probability of upward move (Π_u)

If we are given the size of one move in either direction, we can calculate the size of the move in the other direction using the following equation:

$$\text{size of downward move} = \frac{1}{U}$$

After determining the probability of the movement in either direction, we can then calculate the price of the option by calculating the present value of the option's payoffs. The following example illustrates these techniques.

Example 5.4: Binomial option pricing

Assume that a stock is currently priced at $30. Calculate the price of a six-month call option on this stock if its strike price is $30, and the stock price is expected to increase by 30%. The risk-free rate is 5%.

Solution

Size of up move = 1+30% = 1.30

Size of down move = 1/1.30 = 0.77

$$\Pi_u = \frac{1+RF-D}{U-D} = \frac{1+0.05-0.77}{1.3-0.77} = 0.53$$

$$\Pi_d = 1-0.53 = 0.47$$

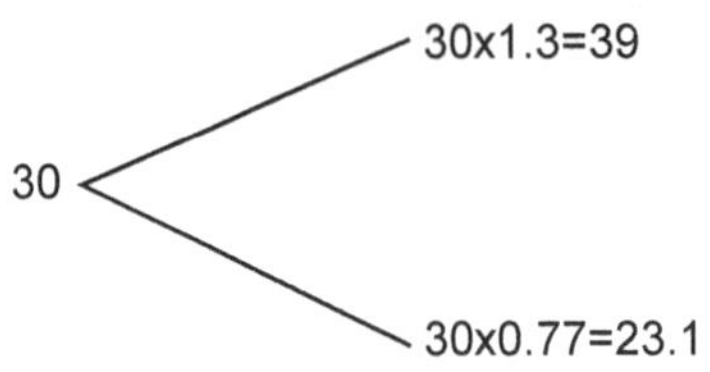

Stock (underlying asset)

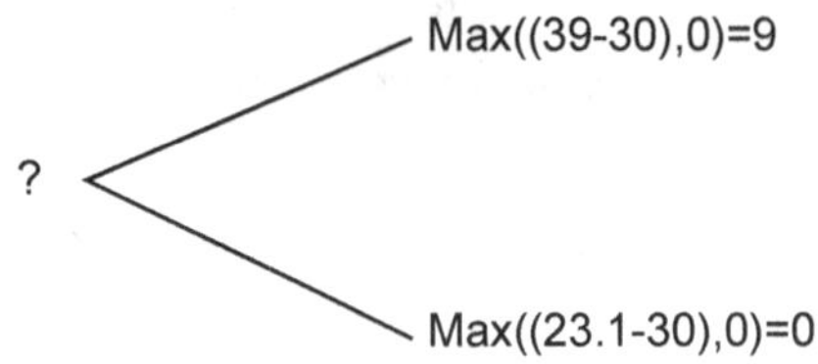

Call option on the stock

Since we are seeking to find the price of the call option, we will have to follow the same principle as in finance, so that is to find the present value of its future cash flows ($9 and $0).

$$\frac{(9\times 0.53)+(0\times 0.47)}{1.05} = \$4.54$$

So, a six-month call option's fair price should be at $4.54, using a one-period binomial option pricing model.

LOS. Compare and contrast the risk of long and short option positions

The diagrams in the above LOSs show the following:

- A long call option has an unlimited profit and the maximum loss is the premium paid.
- A short call option has an unlimited loss and the maximum profit is the premium received.
- A long put option has limited profit equal to the put payoff less the premium paid. The maximum loss is the premium paid.

- A short put option has limited loss equal to put payoff less the premium received. The maximum profit is the premium received.

In summary:

Position	Maximum profit	Maximum loss
Long call	Unlimited	Premium
Short call (call writer)	Premium	Unlimited
Long put	Strike-premium	Premium
Short put (put writer)	Premium	-Strike + premium

Question 5.8

The maximum loss the writer of a stock put option can suffer is equal to:

a. the striking price minus the put premium.

b. the striking price.

c. the stock price minus the put premium.

d. the put premium.

e. none of the above

Solution

a.

LOS. Describe put-call parity

Put-call parity is a relationship between call and put options on the same underlying asset, with the same strike price and expiry date. The relationship is that if a call option on Asset A is combined with a cash position, it would give the same payoff at expiration as the combination of holding Asset A and a put option on the same asset. This relationship must exist because if these two combinations do not hold, an arbitrage opportunity would exist.

Put-call parity only holds with European options, i.e. it cannot be applied to American options.

Put-call parity: cash position + call option on Asset A = fiduciary call = protective put

$C_T + Xe^{-rt} = P_T + S_0$

Where:

C_T = price of call option at time T

X = strike price

r = risk-free rate

P_T = price of put option at time T

S_0 = current market price of the underlying asset

From this equation, we can find the value of any of the four variables if the other three are given. For example:

call option = put option on Asset A + Asset A - cash position

This means that you can have a similar payoff to a call by owning the assets, owning a put option and lending an amount equal to the strike price. **This is called having a synthetic call position.**

So, a synthetic put option = $C_T + Xe^{-rt} - S_0$

synthetic asset position = $C_T + Xe^{-rt} - P_T$

2. Black-Scholes-Merton Model

LOS. Describe the basic principles of the Black-Scholes-Merton (BSM) model
LOS. State the Black-Scholes-Merton formula for pricing a call option
LOS. Calculate an option price using the Black-Scholes-Merton model

In analyzing movements in any asset's pricing, we either observe and/or assume discrete[4] or continuous movements. The binomial model is used to price options under an assumption of discrete movements, while the Black-Scholes-Merton model (BSM) is used under an assumption of continuous price movements.

The (BSM) holds the following assumptions:

1. The options are European. So, BSM cannot be used to price American or Bermuda options.
2. Risk-free rate is known and constant.
3. Volatility of the underlying assets' prices is known and constant.
4. The underlying assets' prices follow the geometric lognormal diffusion process.
5. There are no cash flows in the underlying assets, i.e. stocks do not pay dividends and bonds do not pay coupons. If you want to price call options on stocks that pay dividends, you should use the adjusted formula, as we shall see shortly.
6. There are no transactions costs or taxes.

The BSM is calculated using the following formulas:

---

4 Discrete movements mean changes with identifiable, whole time intervals, such as years, months, days, hours. But when asset prices change over time intervals which become smaller and smaller, to a fraction of a measure of time, such movements are called continuous. It is assumed in the BSM model that the prices of underlying assets in the options contract follow continuous movement.

$$c = S_0\ N(d_1) - K\ e^{-rT} N(d_2)$$
$$p = K\ e^{-rT}\ N(-d_2) - S_0\ N(-d_1)$$
$$\text{where}\ \ d_1 = \frac{\ln(S_0 / K) + (r + s^2/2)T}{s\sqrt{T}}$$
$$d_2 = \frac{\ln(S_0 / K) + (r - s^2/2)T}{s\sqrt{T}} = d_1 - s\sqrt{T}$$

Where:

c = call option price (premium)

P = put option price

K = strike price

r = risk-free rate

T = time to expiry of the option contract

S_0 = current price of the underlying assets

N = cumulative standard normal distribution

e = exponential terms equal to 2.7183

σ = standard deviation of stock returns

σ^2 = variance of stock returns

Example 5.5: Calculation of an option's price using BSM

Calculate the price of European call and put options given the following: underlying asset price is \$54, continuous risk-free rate is 7%, time to expiry is nine months, exercise price of \$50 and volatility of 30%.

Solution

We firstly calculate d_1 and d_2

$$d_1 = \frac{\text{IN}\left(\frac{54}{50}\right) + \left(\frac{0.07 + (0.3)^2}{2}\right)\left(\frac{9}{12}\right)}{0.30\sqrt{\left(\frac{9}{12}\right)}} = 0.6284$$

$$d_2 = 1 - 0.6284 = 0.3716$$

From the cumulative probabilities for a standard normal distribution, we get the values for N(d1) and N(d2) as follows: 0.7357 and 0.6443 respectively.

call option price = 54 × 0.7357 -50.$e^{(-0.75x0.07)}$ × (0.6443) = $9.16

put option price = 50.$e^{(-0.75x0.07)}$ × (1 - 0.6443) - 54 × (1 - 0.7357) = $2.62

LOS. Discuss the factors influencing option price

The factors affecting option price are:

1. Interest rate (Rho): If you look again at the call option lower bound formula – $\mathbf{S_0 - X(1+i)^{-T}}$ – you can see that the higher the interest rate, the lower the $\mathbf{X(1+i)^{-T}}$ part of the formula, which results in a higher price. Thus, the higher the interest rate, the higher the value of the call option. Exactly the opposite is true for a put option – the higher the interest rate, the lower the price of the put option.
2. Maturity: Maturity affects both call and put options. The longer the maturity, the higher the probability of getting a positive payoff.
3. Volatility: Volatility affects both call and put options. Volatility is the level of fluctuation of the underlying asset's price. The higher the volatility, the higher the probability of getting a positive payoff.
4. Strike price: From the payoff formulas for both call and put, we can conclude that the higher the strike price, the lower the call value and the higher the put option value.

The following table summarizes the impact of the factors affecting option price. For each factor, except for the exercise of strike, there is a formula to quantify its impact in light of the options pricing models. Also, each of these factors has its unique terminology in the options market context, which is called a Greek.

Factor	Greek	Call	Put
Exercise price		Negatively related	Positively related
Interest rate	Rho	Positively related	Negatively related
Volatility	Vega	Positively related	Positively related
Asset price	Delta	Positively related	Negatively related
Time to expiry	Theta	The closer the date to expiry, the lower the value	The closer the date to expiry, the lower the value

5.4 Option Strategies

LOS. Draw and discuss the expiration payoff diagrams of a covered call, protective put, call spread, put spread, straddle, strangle, collar, butterfly and condor
LOS. Discuss uses of straddles, strangles, risk reversals, collars, butterflies and condors

1. Straddle

A straddle is a volatility option strategy instrument. It involves buying calls and puts with the same strike price and expiration date to benefit from movement of the underlying asset's price moves in either direction. A straddle is typically purchased near the date when a firm announces earnings information. This information is material enough to lead market players to cause volatility, but the direction of the move cannot be determined in advance.

By combining put and call, the profit is theoretically unlimited in a straddle and the loss is limited to the premiums paid for the two options.

long straddle = long call option + long put option

short straddle = short call option + short put option

straddle payoff (long) = $\text{Max}[(S_t\text{-}X),0] + \text{Max}[(X\text{-}S_t),0]$ - premiums

straddle payoff (short) = $-\ \text{Max}[(S_t\text{-}X),0] - \text{Max}[(X\text{-}S_t),0]$ + premiums

A straddle is traded by market makers who think the price is going to move explosively, i.e. a trader or market maker who is looking for high volatility and with no concern for the direction of the movement because he is going to benefit from any movement. Hence, a straddle is called a directionally neutral strategy.

What do you get from buying a straddle?

- Generates a profit if the underlying asset price moves up or down.
- Theoretically unlimited profit potential.
- Limited loss, around the strike price when asset prices do not move materially.

A straddle, however, is an expensive instrument because the call and put are bought at the money.

Let us look at an example.

Example 5.6: Long straddle

Assume that a call and put option both have a $50 strike price, three months to expiration and the underlying asset has a current market price of $50, i.e. call and put are at-the-money, and premiums are assumed to be $3 for the call option and $2.50 for the put.

Stock price	Long call payoff	Long put payoff	Premiums paid	Total payoff
35	0	15	5.5	9.5
40	0	10	5.5	4.5
45	0	5	5.5	-0.5
50	0	0	5.5	-5.5
55	5	0	5.5	-0.5
60	10	0	5.5	4.5
65	15	0	5.5	9.5

The following diagram depicts the position payoff:

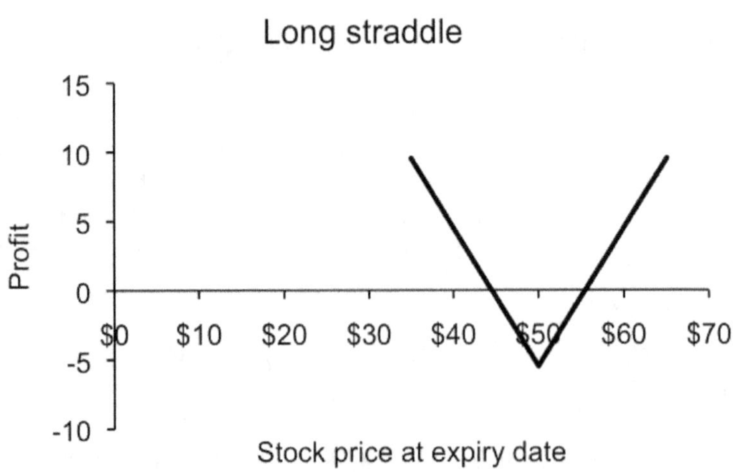

Exercise: Short straddle

Using the information in the example above, prepare the table for the short straddle payoff and draw its profit line across the asset's price.

Solution

Stock price	Long call payoff	Long put payoff	Premiums paid	Total payoff
35	0	-15	5.5	-9.5
40	0	-10	5.5	-4.5
45	0	-5	5.5	0.5
50	0	0	5.5	5.5
55	-5	0	5.5	0.5
60	-10	0	5.5	-4.5
65	-15	0	5.5	-9.5

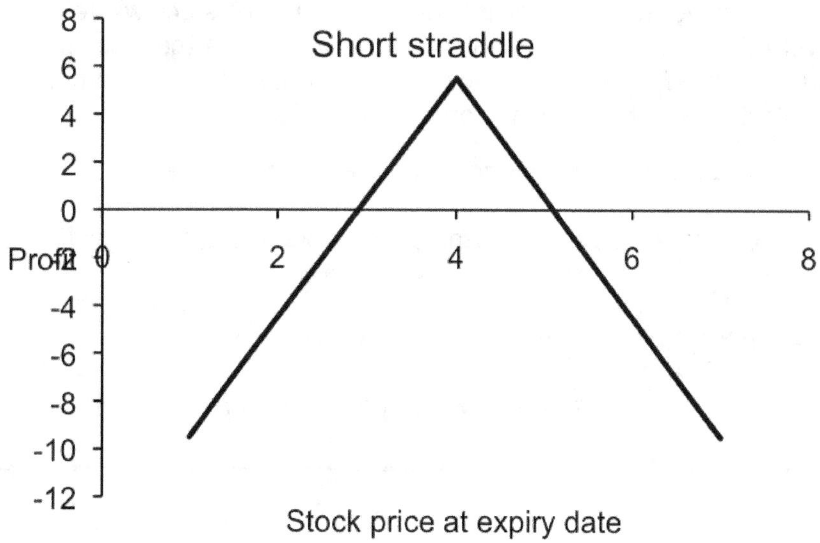

2. Covered call

A covered call strategy involves having a short position in a call option and a long position in the underlying asset of this call. The purpose of having a long position in the underlying asset is to cap the loss when the call option is exercised. This is why a covered call is categorized as an *income option strategy*. This basically means that a dealer wants to reap the benefit of owning the stock and enjoy the premiums from writing call options. In order to ensure that this is able to run for quite a good span of time, the dealer writes out-of-money call options and keeps selling call options as long as the strike is above the share price.

A dealer in a covered call is considered bullish about the market. He expects the price to increase, although not as far as to reach the level of the strike price he sold the call options at.

This is how a covered call works.

When the stock price increases and reaches higher than the strike, the buyer of the call option will exercise his right and the dealer will have to sell the stock to the buyer. The dealer will be losing the advantage of owning the increasing stock, but he has already collected a considerable cushion in the form of the option's premiums. On the other hand, when the stock price decreases, the option buyer will not exercise the option and the stock will remain with the dealer, but the dealer will incur a loss as the stock price decreases. This will be mitigated, once again, by the premiums collected and the dividends on the stock, if any.

covered call = buy underlying asset + sell OTM call option

total payoff = call payoff + assets payoff + premiums from writing the call

$= -\text{MAX}\ \{(S_1\text{-strike price}), 0\} + \{S_1 - S_0\} + \text{premiums}$

The table and diagrams below show how a covered call works.

Example 5.7: Covered call

Assume that you own shares of ABC Company and would like to write call options on these shares. The current share price is $50. Call options can be written for $2.60 with an exercise price of $50.

The table below illustrates the total payoff according to the equation on the previous page.

Stock price	Short call payoff	Long stock payoff	Premium	Call payoff	Covered call payoff
0	0	-50	2.6	2.6	-47.4
10	0	-40	2.6	2.6	-37.4
20	0	-30	2.6	2.6	-27.4
30	0	-20	2.6	2.6	-17.4
40	0	-10	2.6	2.6	-7.4
50	0	0	2.6	2.6	2.6
60	-10	10	2.6	-7.4	2.6
70	-20	20	2.6	-17.4	2.6

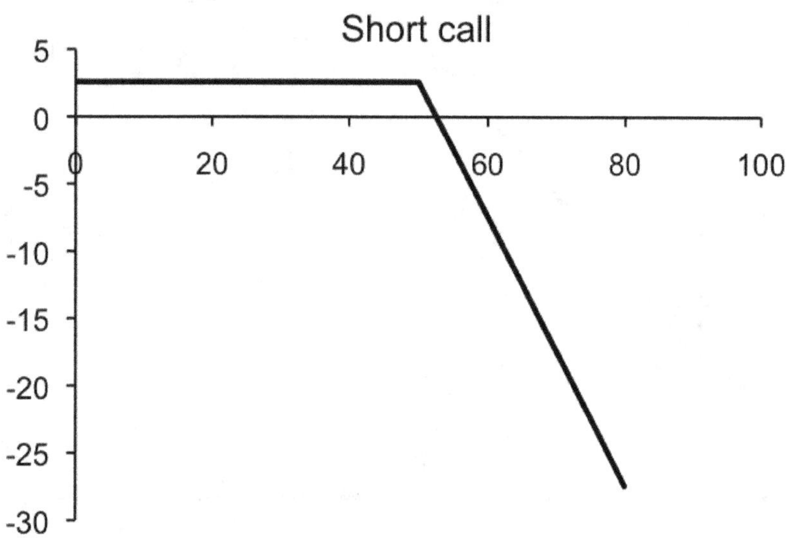

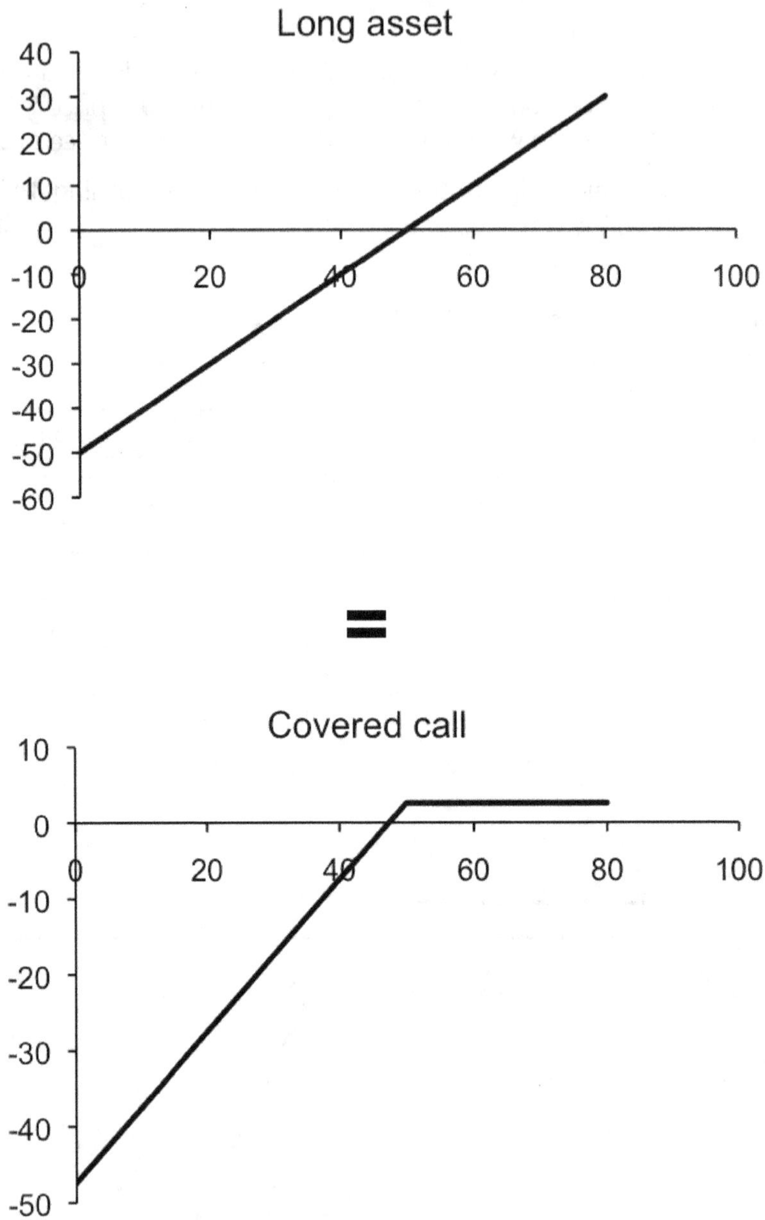

The short call option payoff diagram shows that when the asset's price is below the strike price, $50, the buyer will not exercise the call and the writer will not incur any loss and would enjoy the premiums. Above $50, the buyer will exercise and the writer will incur a loss.

The stock option diagram depicts the investor's gain and loss from owning the stock. The gain and loss is calculated by comparing the price of acquiring the asset to the price at expiration date.

The covered call payoff diagram combines a short call with a long asset. The diagram clearly shows that when the call option is not exercised, the writer's maximum profit is the premium. And if the option is exercised then the maximum loss is $47.40. The loss and gain in a covered call is capped.

In summary, with a covered call:

- maximum risk = price paid to buy the stock - premium
- maximum profit = stock price - strike price + premium
- break-even point = price paid to buy the stock - premium
- It is bull strategy, i.e. a bet on an increasing price

The astute reader will notice that the covered call payoff is identical to the short put option payoff illustrated above. An explanation of why this is the case was given in the discussion of put-call parity.

3. Protective put

The name protective put implies that a put is used in this strategy to protect the dealer from the negative impact of another asset's price movement. A dealer that has 100 shares, for instance, that are worth $10 each today and which he anticipates selling at some time in the future, say in one month, may be concerned about how much these 100 shares will lose from their value in the next month.

By buying put option contracts on these shares, the dealer can limit the loss that might be incurred from decreasing prices. This can be done by buying, for example, 100 option contracts with an exercise price of $10 and one month to expiry.

protective put = buy or own a stock + buy put option

total protective put payoff = stock payoff + long put payoff - put premium

$= \{S_1-S_0\} + \text{MAX}\ \{(\text{Strike} - S_1), 0\} - \text{premium}$

The table and diagrams below illustrate how this strategy works.

Example 5.8: Protective put

Assume a dealer is long ABC Stock, which is currently trading for $50. To hedge against a drop in price in the future, the dealer decides to go long put options, which are selling for $1.90 with a strike price of $50. Show the payoff of the stock, the long put option and the combined payoff of this strategy, against different market prices of the stock.

Solution

Stock price	Long put payoff	Long asset	Premium paid	Protection put payoff
0	48.05	-50	-1.95	-1.95
10	38.05	-40	-1.95	-1.95
20	28.05	-30	-1.95	-1.95
30	18.05	-20	-1.95	-1.95
40	8.05	-10	-1.95	-1.95
50	-1.95	0	-1.95	-1.95
60	-1.95	10	-1.95	8.05
70	-1.95	20	-1.95	18.05
80	-1.95	30	-1.95	28.05

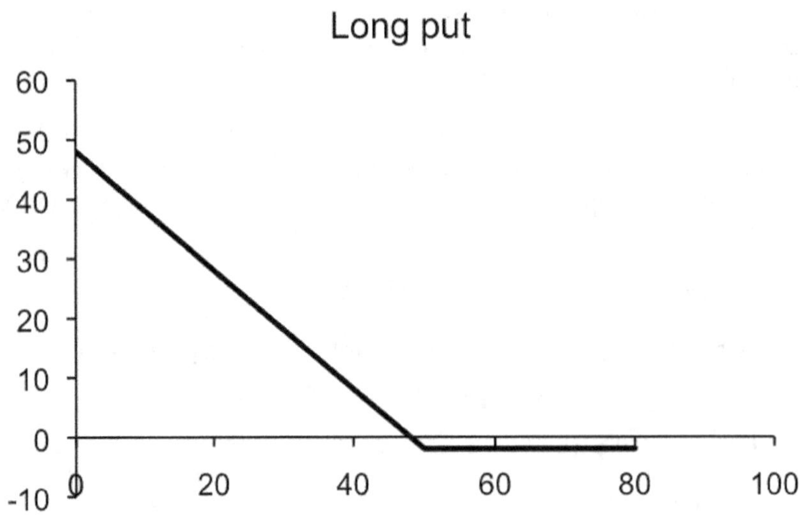

+

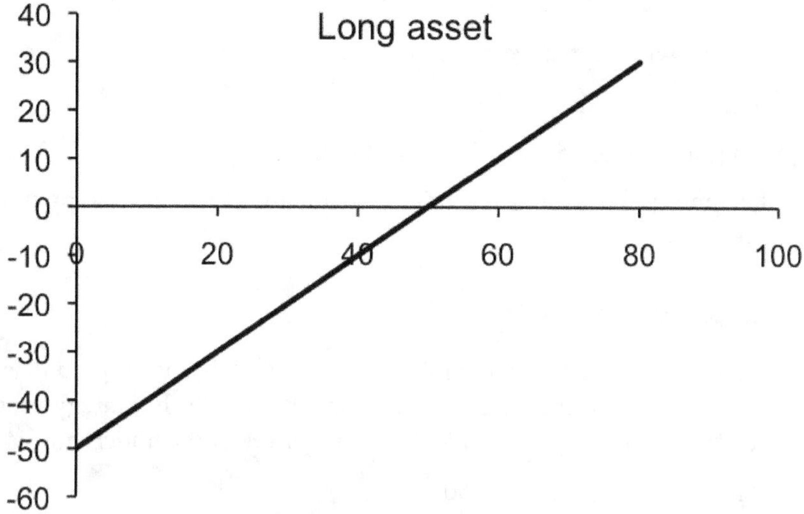
Long asset
40
30
20
10
0
-10
-20
-30
-40
-50
-60
0
20
40
60
80
100

=

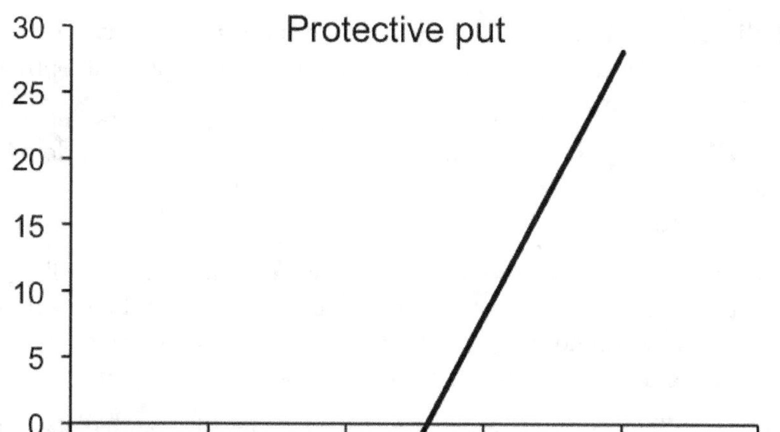
Protective put
30
25
20
15
10
5
0
-5
0
20
40
60
80
100

The protective put payoff is identical to the long call option payoff illustrated above.

long assets + long put = long call option

In summary, with protective put contracts:

1. Profit is unlimited.
2. Loss is limited to the premiums paid to buy the put option.
3. Maximum risk is losing the price paid for the stock and the premium paid.

4. Call spread

A spread is a strategy of combining options of the same type but with different strikes, maturities, etc. A call spread is a bullish strategy that is adopted by dealers who anticipate increasing prices of the underlying asset.

There are two types of call spread:

1. bull call spread.
2. bear call spread.

1. Bull call spread

A **bull call spread** involves buying an at-the-money or near at-the-money call option and at the same time selling an out-of-the-money call option on the same underlying asset.

Why sell a call option? You sell a call option because when you do so you collect premiums and you use these premiums to finance the premiums you paid to buy the call option.

Why sell an out-of-the-money call option? You are basically selling the call option just to collect the premiums to reduce the cost of buying the call options and you do not want the option to be exercised so that you would be obliged to deliver the asset to those who bought it from you.

Why is it called a bull call spread? A bullish strategy is one that is adopted based in anticipation of price increases. You buy a call when you think the price is going to increase and, on the other hand, you sell the call option.

bull call spread payoff = long ATM call + short OTM call + short premium - long premium

= MAX {(S_2 - strike), 0} + [-MAX {(S_2 - strike), 0} + sold call premium – bought call premium

Example 5.9: Bull call spread

Assume that you are bullish on the market and plan to buy a call option with a strike price of $50 on shares in Company A. The price of the call option is $2.76 per contract. To finance these premiums you sell an OTM call option with a strike price of $70 and a premium of $1.00. Draw and calculate the payoff of this strategy at expiry.

Solution

The table below illustrates the possible payoff value of this strategy. The diagrams depict the payoff for the long position in the bull call spread.

Stock price	Net premium	Long call profit	Short call profit	Total payoff
0	-1.76	-2.76	1	-1.76
10	-1.76	-2.76	1	-1.76
20	-1.76	-2.76	1	-1.76
30	-1.76	-2.76	1	-1.76
40	-1.76	-2.76	1	-1.76
50	-1.76	-2.76	1	-1.76
60	-1.76	7.24	1	8.24
70	-1.76	17.24	1	18.24
80	-1.76	27.24	-9	18.24
90	-1.76	37.24	-19	18.24

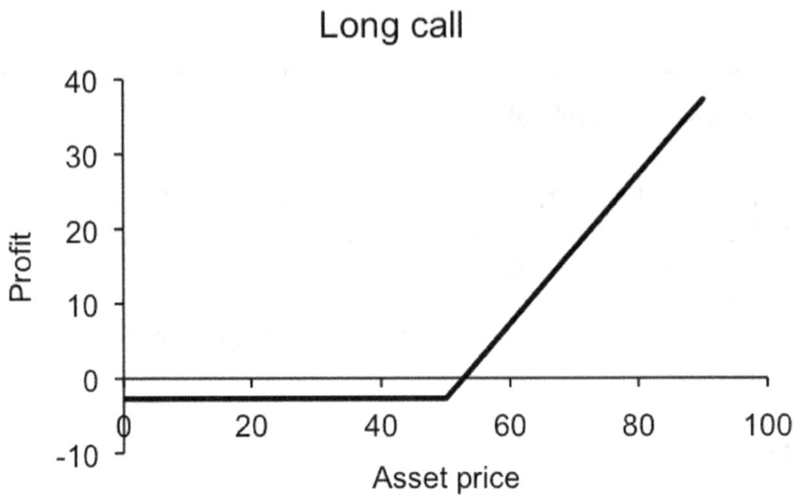
Long call
Profit
40
30
20
10
0
-10
0
20
40
60
80
100
Asset price

+

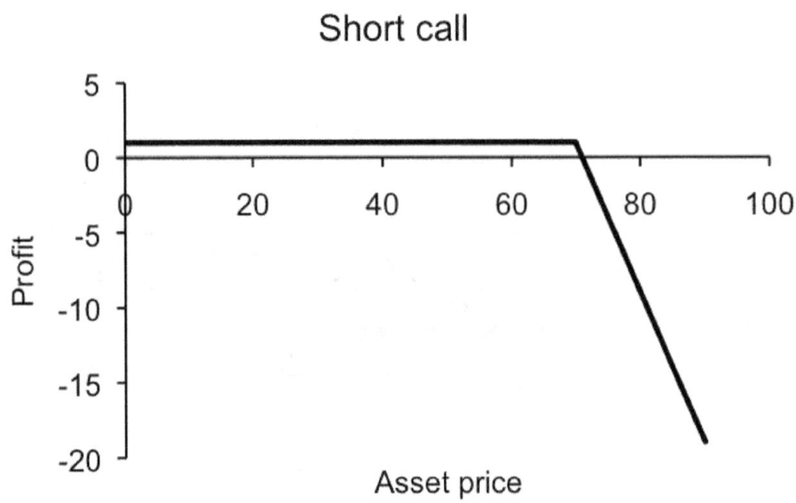
Short call
Profit
5
0
-5
-10
-15
-20
0
20
40
60
80
100
Asset price

=

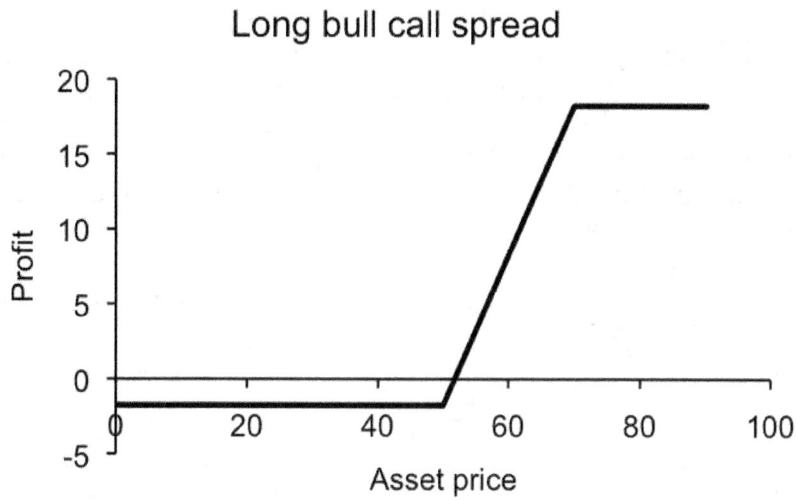

With a bull call spread:

1. Risk is limited to the net premiums. In the example above: premium paid for ATM call - premium collected from OTM call = 2.76-1 = $1.76.
2. Profit is limited (capped) to the difference between the strikes, less the net premiums. In the example above: ($70 - $50) - $1.76 = $18.24.
3. Break-even point on the x-axis is equal to the lower strike + net premiums. In the example above: 50 + 1.76 = $51.76.

(ii) Bear call spread

This is a strategy adopted by a trader who is bearish on the market, i.e. anticipates declining prices, but still wishes to limit the loss when prices increase. Thus, he would buy a call option as insurance against an increasing price (which he considers to have a remote chance of occurring). As he expects a slim chance of increasing prices, he would need to buy an out-of-the-money call option. Although inexpensive compared to an ATM call option, the trader wants to finance the premium paid for the OTM call by issuing an OTM call option. The issued call option would have a lower strike price.

Example 5.10: Bear call spread

Assume that you are buying an OTM call option on Company B's shares with a strike price of $70 and a premium of $1.10. To finance this premium you issue an OTM call option with a strike price of $60 and a premium of $1.80. The Company's shares are currently trading at $50. Draw this strategy and show its payoff under different share prices.

Stock price	Net premium	Long call profit	Short call profit	Total payoff
0	0.7	-1.1	1.8	0.7
10	0.7	-1.1	1.8	0.7
20	0.7	-1.1	1.8	0.7
30	0.7	-1.1	1.8	0.7
40	0.7	-1.1	1.8	0.7
50	0.7	-1.1	1.8	0.7
60	0.7	-1.1	1.8	0.7
70	0.7	-1.1	-8.2	-9.3
80	0.7	8.9	-18.2	-9.3
90	0.7	18.9	-28.2	-9.3

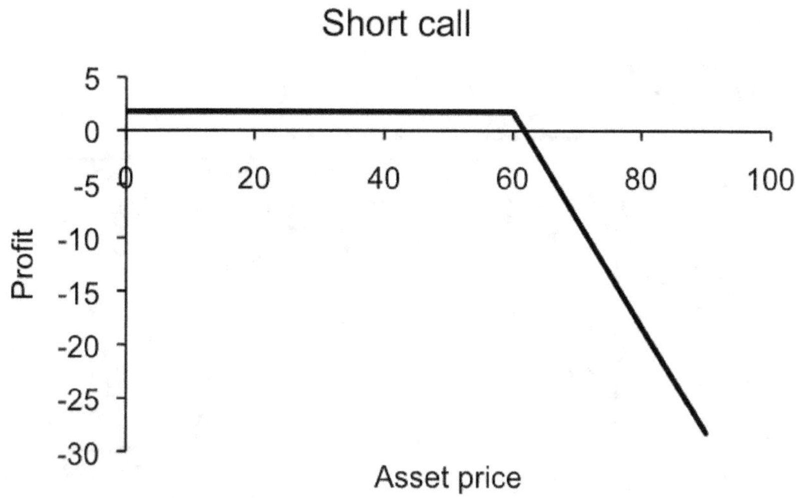
Short call
5
0
-5
-10
-15
-20
-25
-30
Profit
0
20
40
60
80
100
Asset price

+

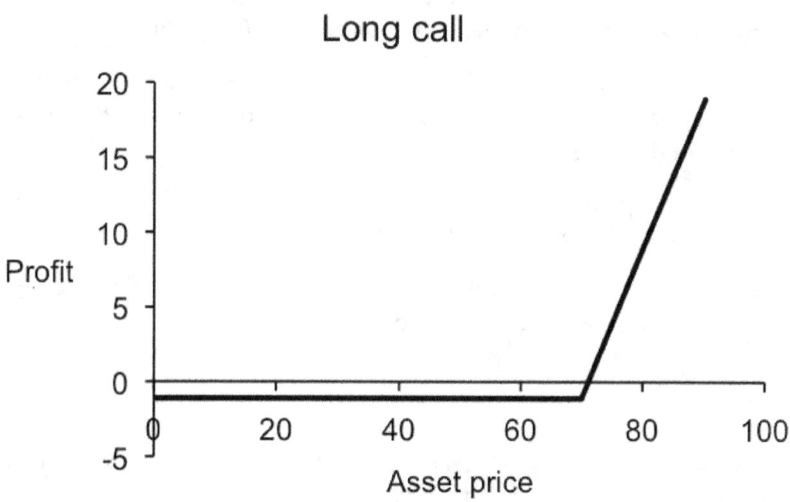
Long call
20
15
10
5
0
-5
Profit
0
20
40
60
80
100
Asset price

=

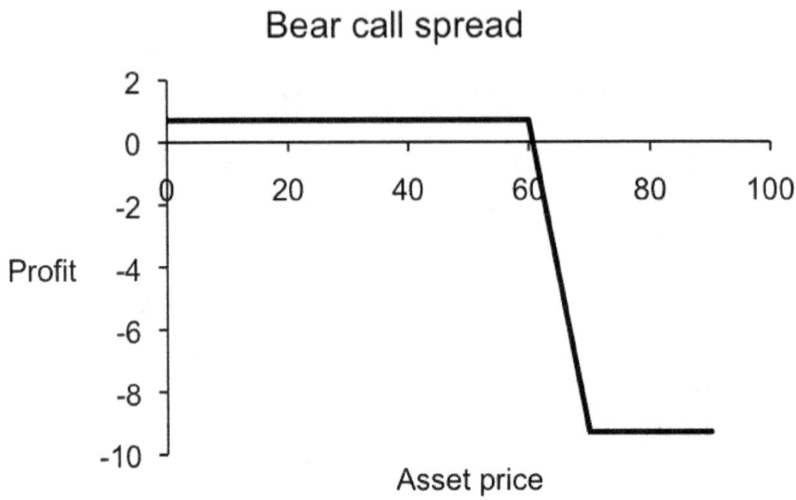

With a bear call spread:

- Maximum risk is the difference between the two strikes, less net premiums. In this example: (\$70 - \$60) - \$0.70 = \$9.30.
- Maximum profit is the difference between the premium to buy the call and the premium collected from issuing another call. In this example: \$1.8 - \$1.1 = \$0.70.
- Break-even point on the x-axis is equal to lower strike + net premiums. In this example: \$60 + \$0.60 = \$60.70.
- A long position in a bear call spread has the same risk and reward features as a short bull call spread.

5. Put spread

Similar to a call spread strategy, there are two types of put spread strategy: a bull put spread and a bearish put spread.

A dealer anticipating increasing prices can use put options to generate income and limit losses if the increase expected does not occur. He would sell a put option with a strike price lower than the current market price, i.e. an OTM put option. This is because he wants to generate income from premiums and if his expectation is right that the price is going to increase the put option will not be exercised, thus leaving him to enjoy the premiums.

On the other hand, for security, a dealer has to think of the possibility that the price may decrease rather than increase. If that happens, the put option he sold would be exercised and the buyer would sell the share to the dealer at the lower price. To hedge this risk, the dealer would buy an OTM put option. Remember, it is OTM because it is cheaper and he is just buying it *just in case*, so it does not make sense to buy an expensive ITM or ATM put option.

Example 5.11: Put spread

Assume that a dealer is bullish on Company C shares and adopts a put spread as a strategy to make a profit based on his price expectation. Show how can he implement this strategy with the following given data and show the risk and return profile of this strategy.

1. Current Company C share price is $50.
2. Put option on Company C with strike of $40 costs $1.70.
3. Put option on Company C with strike of $30 costs $0.90.

Solution

1. Go long on the lower strike put, i.e. $30.
2. Go short on the higher strike put, i.e. $40.
3. The maximum reward is the difference between the premiums paid and collected: $1.70 - $0.90 = $0.80.
4. The break-even point on the x-axis = higher strike - net premiums = $40 - $0.80 = $39.20.
5. Maximum risk = difference between the two strikes - net premiums = ($40 - $30) - $0.80 = $9.20.

Stock price	Net premium	Long put profit	Short put profit	Total payoff
0		29.1	-38.3	-9.2
10	-1.7	19.1	-28.3	-9.2
20	-1.7	9.1	-18.3	-9.2
30	-1.7	-0.9	-8.3	-9.2
40	-1.7	-0.9	1.7	0.8
50	-1.7	-0.9	1.7	0.8
60	-1.7	-0.9	1.7	0.8
70	-1.7	-0.9	1.7	0.8
80	-1.7	-0.9	1.7	0.8
90	-1.7	-0.9	1.7	0.8

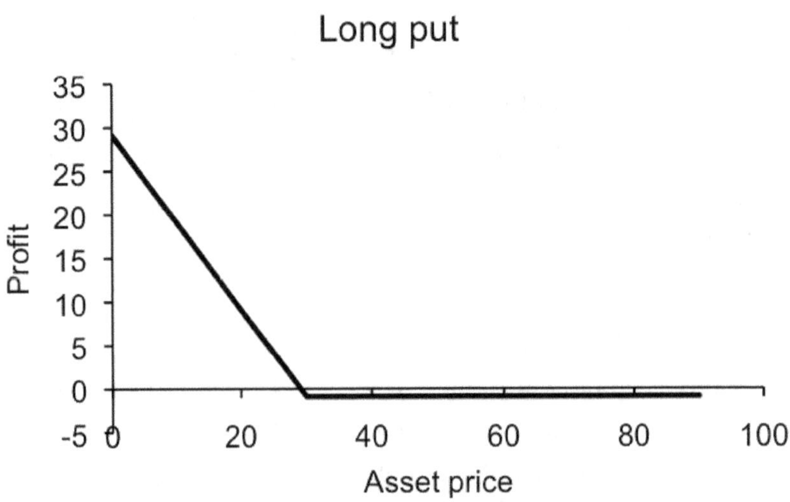

+

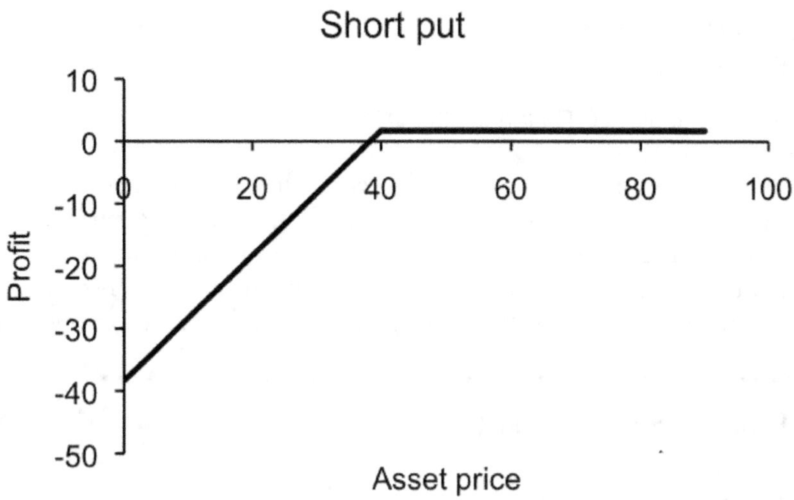
Short put
10
0
-10
-20
-30
-40
-50
0
20
40
60
80
100
Profit
Asset price

=

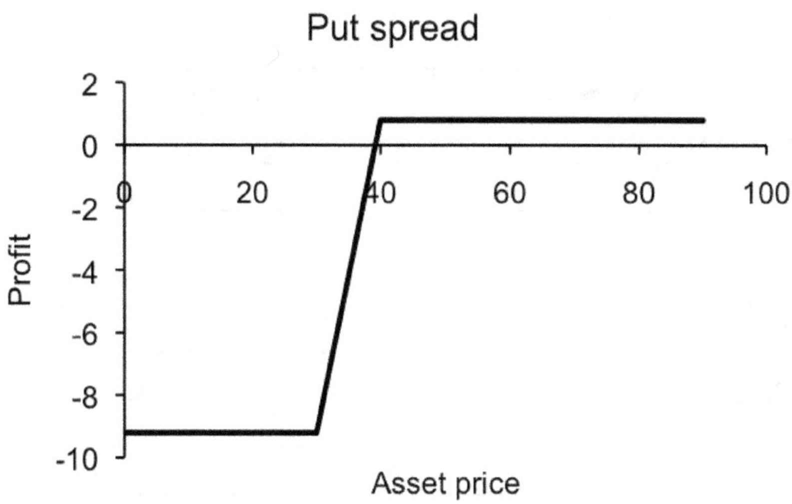
Put spread
2
0
-2
-4
-6
-8
-10
0
20
40
60
80
100
Profit
Asset price

6. Strangle

A strangle is identical to a straddle, but involves a long call and put with a different strike price.

long strangle = OTM long call + OTM long put

The reason behind buying an OTM call and put is to create a strategy similar to a straddle but at a lower cost than a straddle, as a straddle involves buying an ATM call and put, which are more expensive. Buying an OTM call and put with different strike prices results in the break-even point of the strategy payoff being pushed apart, as we shall see in the example below.

Example 5.12: Long strangle

Assume a call and put option with a $60 call strike and $40 put strike and three months to expiration and the underlying asset has a current market price of $50 (i.e. call and put are at-the-money), and premiums are assumed to be $1.67 for call option and $1.9 for put.

Solution

Stock price	Net premium	Long call profit	Long put profit	Total payoff
0	-3.57	-1.67	38.1	36.43
10	-3.57	-1.67	28.1	26.43
20	-3.57	-1.67	18.1	16.43
30	-3.57	-1.67	8.1	6.43
40	-3.57	-1.67	-1.9	-3.57
50	-3.57	-1.67	-1.9	-3.57
60	-3.57	-1.67	-1.9	-3.57
70	-3.57	8.33	-1.9	6.43
80	-3.57	18.33	-1.9	16.43
90	-3.57	28.33	-1.9	26.43

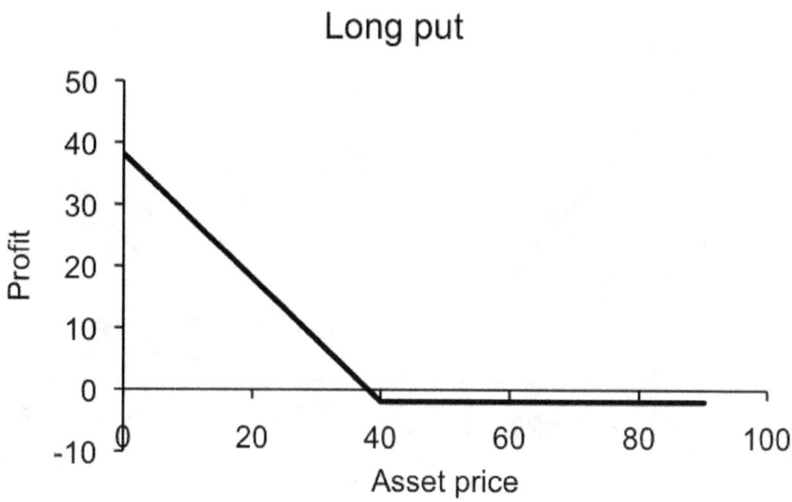
Long put
Profit
50
40
30
20
10
0
-10
0
20
40
60
80
100
Asset price

+

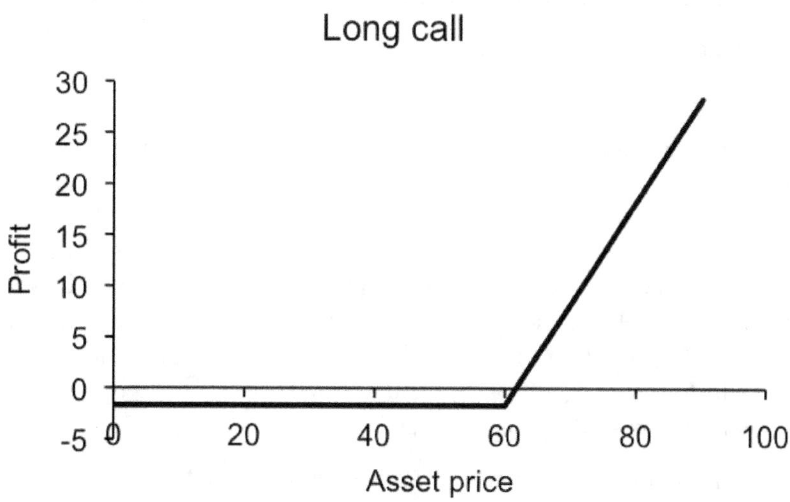
Long call
Profit
30
25
20
15
10
5
0
-5
0
20
40
60
80
100
Asset price

=

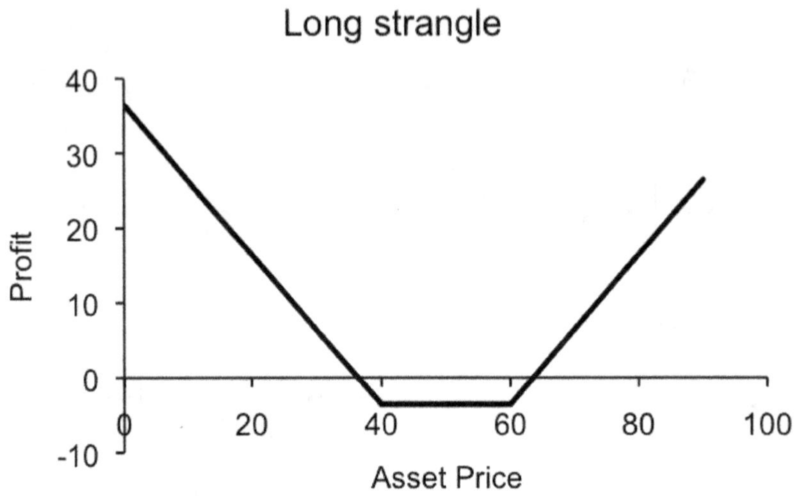

From the above table and diagrams we can conclude that in the strangle:

- Maximum loss is the premiums paid for the call and put.
- Maximum profit is unlimited.
- First break-even point = lower strike - net premiums.
- Second break-even point = higher strike + net premiums.

7. Collar

A collar strategy involves buying the underlying asset, selling an OTM call and buying an ATM put. So, a collar is similar to a covered call strategy with the exception that in a collar the put option is bought. The put option is bought to insure against a decrease in stock prices. The OTM call is sold to finance the cost of buying the put.

collar = long asset + short OTM call + long ATM put

Example 5.13: Collar

Assume an investor buys a stock currently trading at $20 in the market. To hedge against a drop in the stock price, he considers buying a put option with a strike price of $20 and six months to expiry for $0.870. To reduce the cost of this premium, he also considers selling a $13 call option with six months to expiry for $0.450. Tabulate the payoff of this strategy and draw its diagrams.

Solution

Stock price	Net premium	Long put	Short call	Total payoff
0	-0.42	9.13	0.45	9.58
10	-0.42	-0.87	0.45	9.58
20	-0.42	-0.87	-6.55	12.58
30	-0.42	-0.87	-16.55	12.58
40	-0.42	-0.87	-26.55	12.58
50	-0.42	-0.87	-36.55	12.58
60	-0.42	-0.87	-46.55	12.58
70	-0.42	-0.87	-56.55	12.58
80	-0.42	-0.87	-66.55	12.58

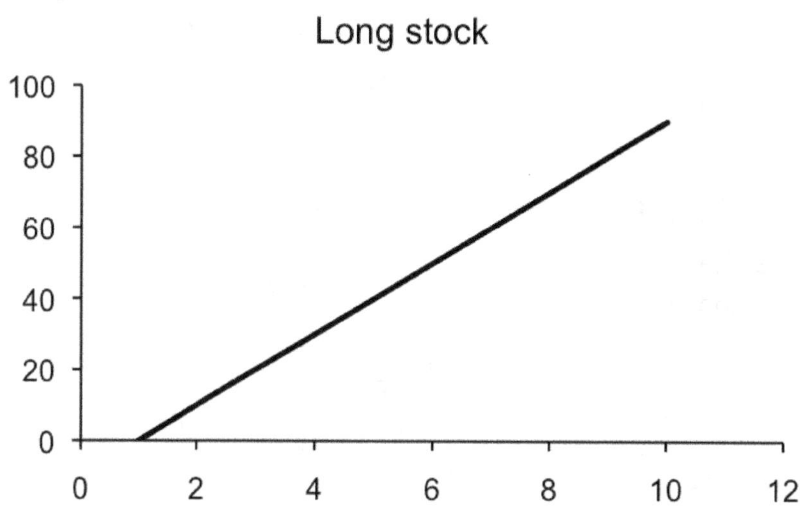

+

Long ATM put

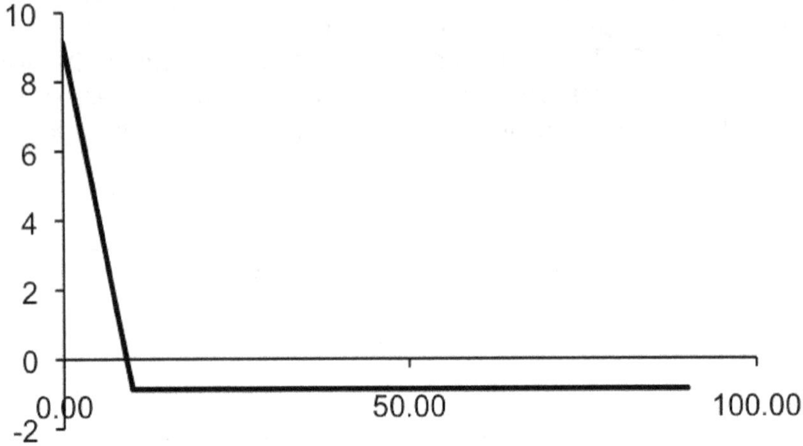

+

Short OTM call

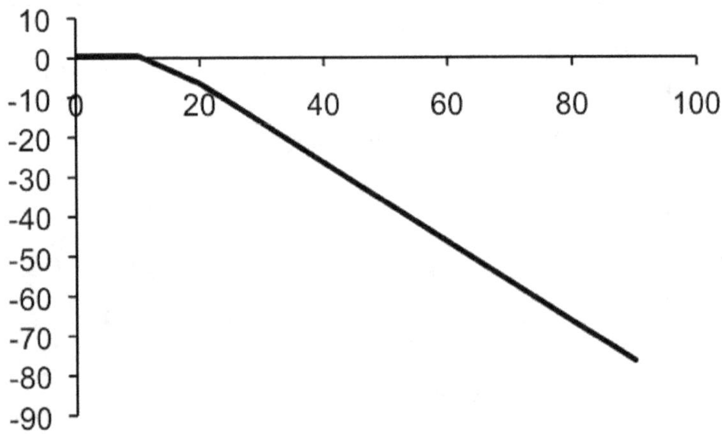

=

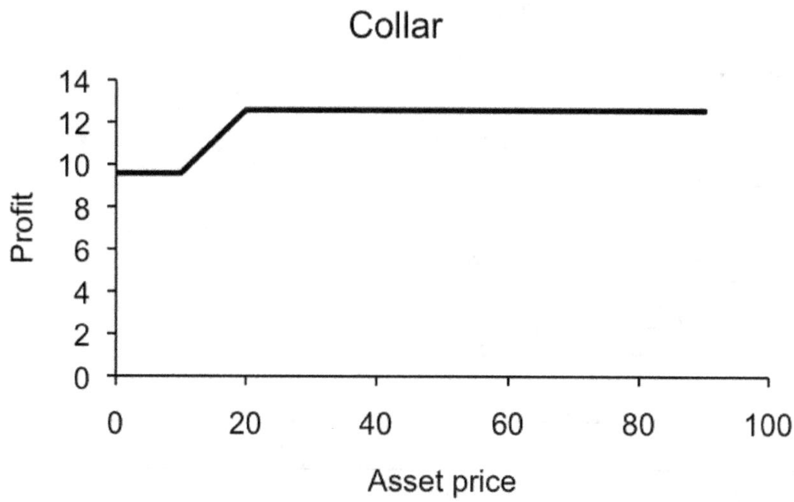

From the above we can notice that the risk profile of the investor in a collar is conservative, with a low risk appetite. The maximum loss of the collar is = (stock price + put premium) - (put strike - call premium)

The merit of the collar strategy is that it insures the investor against a decrease in the underlying asset price.

8. Butterfly

A butterfly involves buying a low strike call and one high strike call, and selling two OTM call options to reduce the cost.

> butterfly = long lower strike call + long higher strike call + short two ATM calls

Example 5.14: Long butterfly

Assume an investor buys two call options on ABC Stock that is currently trading at $100: one with a strike of $50, and another with strike of $150. The price of the low strike call is $22, while the $150-call costs $20. To reduce the costs of these two positions, the investor sells two call options with a strike of $100, at a premium of $20. Show the payoff table and diagram, the break-even points (BEPs), and the maximum profit and loss of this strategy.

Solution

Stock price	High strike call	Low strike calls	Short two ATM calls	Total payoff
0	-20	-22	40	-2
10	-20	-22	40	-2
20	-20	-22	40	-2
100	-20	28	40	48
150	-20	78	-60	-2
200	30	128	-160	-2
250	80	178	-260	-2
300	130	228	-360	-2

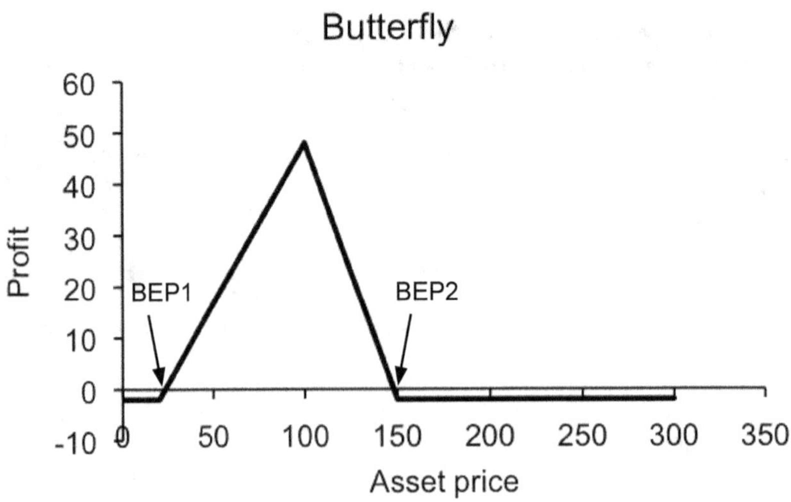

BEP1 = lower strike + net premium

BEP2 = higher strike - net premium

maximum loss = net premiums

9. Condor

A condor is similar to a butterfly except that the two short calls will have different strikes, i.e. a condor will have four strikes, while the butterfly has only three.

Example 5.15: Condor

Assume an investor buys two call options on ABC Stock that is currently trading at $50: one with a strike of $30, and another with a strike of $70. The price of the low strike call is $3, while the $70-call costs $4. To reduce the costs of these two positions, the investor sells two call options: one ITM call with a strike of $40, sold for $2.50, and another OTM call with a strike of $60, sold for $3.50. Show the payoff table and diagram, the break-even points (BEPs), and the maximum profit and loss of this strategy.

Solution

The following table and diagrams illustrate the payoff of the condor.

Stock price	Long ITM Call	Short ITM call	Long OTM call	Short OTM call
0	-3	-4	2.5	3.5
10	-3	-4	2.5	3.5
20	-3	-4	2.5	3.5
30	-3	-4	2.5	3.5
40	7	-4	2.5	3.5
50	17	-4	-7.5	3.5
60	27	-4	-17.5	3.5
70	37	-4	-27.5	-6.5

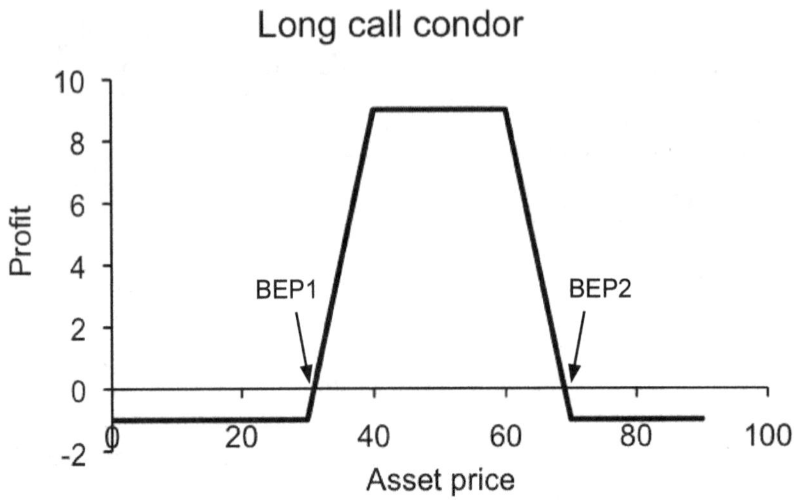

maximum risk = net premium paid

maximum profit = difference between adjacent strikes – net premium

BEP1 = lower strike + net premium

BEP2 = higher strike – net premium

A condor is a low-volatility option strategy in which an investor does not expect high volatility in the underlying asset. It is also implemented with a very low cost, as can be seen in the above example.

LOS. Describe a calendar spread

A **calendar spread** is an option strategy that combines one call option and one put option with the same strike price but different times to expiry. An investor uses this strategy if he has a view on the timing and direction of the move of the underlying assets against which the option is bought or sold.

5.5 Option Risks

This section discusses:

1. Option Greeks: delta, gamma, vega, theta and rho.
2. Implied volatility.
3. Volatility smile.

LOS. Define and discuss delta-hedging
LOS. Explain risk neutral valuation

Delta is defined as a percentage change in option price as a result of a change in underlying asset price.

$$\text{delta} = \frac{\Delta\text{option price}}{\Delta\text{underlying asset price}}$$

We calculate delta to tell us how many options contracts we need to have against a certain amount of the underlying asset in order to hedge our position. As expounded earlier in the chapter, and from the above example, the price of a call and put are derived in relation to the price of the underlying asset. Hence, there is a correlation between the asset and option prices. Exploiting the correlation between two securities in a manner that reduces cost or risk is called **hedging**.

For instance, if you own the underlying asset and would like to hedge this position against a decrease in the asset price, you would buy a put option. But how many option contracts would you need to buy to approximately hedge the risk? Delta gives this approximation. So, a delta of 0.566 of call option, for instance is interpreted as: for each one unit of an asset we own, we need to sell 0.566 call option contracts.

$$\text{delta} = \frac{9-0}{39-23.1} = 0.566$$

Regarding **risk neutral valuation**, we will start with the definition of risk neutral. There are three types of people in financial markets, at least theoretically, in the context of return and risk: risk neutral, risk averse and risk taker. If we pose the question: which decision will an individual choose if given a 100% chance to win $1000 today, or a 50% chance to win $2000 tomorrow, each one of the three will opt for a different option.

The risk averse, as the name implies, when faced with a certain or probable event, will opt for the certain return if it is lower. The risk seeker will opt for the 50% chance of winning $2000. The risk neutral will be indifferent because to him the outcome of the two decisions is the same, $1000 (50% × 2000 = $1000). To the risk neutral, the $1000 is the present value of the expected return adjusted for probability terms as risk-neutral probability.

Risk neutral is a theoretical concept. It does not exist in reality because no lender or borrower is indifferent to risk. Every one of them is either risk averse or a risk taker. The concept is used in asset pricing, in particular the derivatives contracts such as options, based on the complete market assumption. Since this assumption does not hold in practice, quite often there is a difference between the risk-neutral probability of a change in an asset price and the *real* probability. For the exam, you just need to know that the probability used in options pricing is the risk-neutral probability. You are not required to technically contrast the different probabilities.

Example 5.16: Calculating delta for call option using the binomial model

Calculate the delta of a $50, three-month call option on a stock currently trading at $65. The stock can either go up by 25%, or down by 15%.

Solution

If the price can go up by 25%, the underlying asset price could increase by 1.25: 50 × 1.25 = $62.50.

If the price can go down by 15%, the underlying asset price could decrease by 0.85: 50 × 0.85 = $42.50.

So the change in the underlying asset's price = 62.5 - 42.50 = $20.

Having the strike price of the call option at $50, we can calculate the call option payoff in the case of an upward and downward move as follows:

If the price goes up by 25%, call options = MAX [0, (S-X)] = MAX [0, (62.5-50)] = 12.50

If the price goes down by 15%, call options = MAX [0, (S-X)]

= MAX [0, (42.5-50)] = MAX[0,-7.5] = 0

So the change in the call option payoff as a result of the change in the price of the underlying asset is = 12.5-0 = 12.50.

Having defined delta as a measure of the sensitivity of the option's price to the change in the asset's price, delta is calculated by dividing 12.5/20 = 0.625.

Example 5.17: Calculating delta for a put option using the binomial model

Calculate the delta of a $50, three-month put option on a stock currently trading at $65. Its price can either go up by 25%, or down by 15%.

Solution

If the price can go up by 25%, the underlying asset's price could increase by 1.25 = 50 × 1.25 = $62.50.

If the price can go down by 15%, the underlying asset's price could decrease by 0.85 = 50 × 0.85 = $42.50.

So the change in the underlying asset's price = 62.5 - 42.5 = $20.

Having the strike price of the call option at $50, we can calculate the put option payoff in the case of an upward and downward move as follows:

If the price goes up by 25%, call options = MAX [0, (X-S)] = MAX [0, (50-62.5)] = 0.

If the price goes down by 15%, call options = MAX [0, (X-S)] = MAX [0, (50-42.5)] = 12.50

So the change in the call option payoff as a result of the change in the prices of the underlying assets is = 0-12.5 = -12.50.

Having defined delta as a measure of the sensitivity of the option's price to a change in the asset's price, delta is calculated by dividing -12.5/20 = -0.625.

From the above examples, please note these important relationships:

1. Delta ranges from 0 to 1 for call options.
2. Delta for call options will always be positive, because the payoff of a call is MAX[0, (S-X)], so as the asset's price increases, the call option payoff increases.
3. Delta for put options ranges from -1 to 0.
4. Delta for put options will always be negative, because the payoff of a put is MAX[0,(X-S)], so as the asset's price increases, the put option payoff decreases.
5. Delta of the in-the-money call option will approach +1.
6. Delta of the in-the-money put option will approach -1.
7. Delta of the at-the-money call option is +0.5.
8. Delta of the at-the-money put option is -0.5.
9. Delta of out-of-the-money call and put options approaches zero.

LOS. Define delta, gamma, vega, theta and rho

1. **Delta**: measure of the option price's sensitivity to changes in the price of the underlying asset.
2. **Gamma**: measure of the sensitivity of delta to changes in the price of the underlying asset.
3. **Vega**: measure of the sensitivity of the option's price to the volatility of the underlying asset's price.
4. **Theta**: measure of the option price's sensitivity to changes in the time to expiry of the option contract (i.e. time decay).
5. **Rho**: measure of the option price's sensitivity to changes in the risk-free rate.

LOS. Define and discuss implied volatility

Volatility is a change, in either direction, of an option's price (or change in the price of any asset). Volatility is measured by standard deviation, variance, range, etc. In the context of option pricing, it is measured by variance and standard deviation. There are two ways to calculate volatility:

1. **Historical method**: This involves collecting observed asset prices over a certain historical period and then calculating the mean and standard deviation on this set of data. You will need to know the following important formula in the exam:

   $$\text{annualized volatility} = \text{daily volatility} \times \sqrt[2]{252}$$

2. **Prospective method**: It is difficult to estimate the asset's price and its movements over an extended period of time into the future. So, investors approximate the level of volatility in the market, implicitly (hence the name **implied volatility**), using the option's price. An investor observes the current price of a European non-dividend paying stock in the market, then he would take this price and insert it into the BSM formulas that we stated in the above LOS, and log in all the other variables, having volatility as the unknown variable. He would then solve for the volatility from the formulas, to give the implied volatility. Please note that this can also be done by trial-and-error.

LOS. Define a volatility smile

If we have a group of options with different strike prices and implied volatilities, but with the same expiry date, and plot them in a diagram, we would get a result like the one shown in the diagram below.

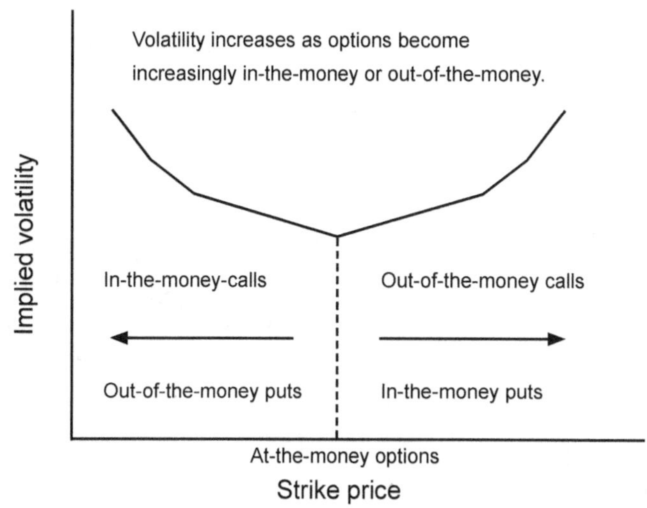

This diagram, which depicts the relationship between the strike price and volatility, is called the **volatility smile**. It indicates that the volatility of any option is at its minimum level when it is at-the-money and increases when the option turns out to be deep in-the-money or out-of-the-money.

Chapter 6. Forward Markets And Contracts

Upon completion of this chapter you will have learnt:

1. Forward contract terminology and features.
2. Pricing and valuing of forward contracts.

6.1 Forward Contract Terminology and Features

LOS. Define spot price and forward price

1. **Spot price** is the market price of the underlying asset on the date of initiating the forward contract, denoted as (S_0).
2. **Forward price** is the market price of the underlying asset on the expiry or settlement date. Forward price is determined in light of the spot price.

6.2 Pricing and Valuing Forward Contracts

This section explains pricing and valuing forward contracts of:

1. Stocks.
2. Bonds.
3. Commodities.
4. Currency.
5. Interest rate.

LOS. Calculate the forward price of a bond, stock, currency and commodity

The formula for determining the forward price is as follows:

$$\text{forward price} = \text{spot price}\ (1+ \text{interest rate})^{\text{maturity of the contract}}$$

$$F = S_0\ (1 + i)^T$$

Example 6.1: Pricing of a forward contract

Consider Asset A that is currently trading in the market for \$200. A three-month forward contract is written on this asset. Calculate the price of the forward contract if the risk-free rate is at 5%.

Solution

$$T = 3/12 = 0.25$$

$$F = \$200(1+5\%)^{0.25} = \$202.4544$$

We can apply the formula shown above for pricing forward contracts on stocks, bonds, currencies and commodities.

Example 6.2: Price of forward contract on stocks

Assume that you currently own ABC Stock and it is trading at $150. You plan to sell it in six months and to cater for the risk of its price declining below $150, you enter into a forward contract. If the risk-free rate is 5%, calculate the forward price on this contract.

Solution

T = 6/12 = 0.50

F = $150(1+5%)0.50 = $153.7043

Example 6.3: Price of forward contract on bonds

Assume an investor has just purchased a four-year, 7% semi-annual corporate bond. YTM is at 6.5%, the risk-free rate is at 3%, and the face value of the bond is $1,000. The investor plans to sell the bond after 270 days and enters into a forward contract to hedge against a decline in the bond's price. Calculate the forward price on this contract.

Solution

We have to find the spot price of the bond, as the underlying asset of the forward contract.

N = 4 × 2 = 8, I = 6.5%/2 = 3.25%, FV = $1,000, PMT = (7%/2) × $1,000 = $35

Price of the bond is equal to (S_0) = $ 1,017.366

Now we calculate the forward price:

T = 270/365 = 0.753

F = $1,017.366$(1 + 3\%)^{0.753}$ = $1,040.277

LOS. Calculate the value of a forward contract at expiration and prior to expiration

The value of a forward contract at expiration and prior to expiration is different from the price of the forward contract. The price is the amount determined at the inception of the contract to be paid on the expiry date in exchange for the underlying assets. The value of the contract, on the other hand, determines whether the buyer or the seller has made a gain or loss as a result of getting into the forward contract on any specific date during the contract.

For example, an investor has bought a long forward contract in which he will have to pay \$100 per kg on 30 June in exchange for 10kg of wheat. The contract was initiated on 1 March. If on 20 May the prevailing market price of 1kg of wheat is \$101, the value of the contract to the buyer is (101-100) × 10 = \$10. This does not mean he has actually cashed in the \$10, it just means that so far, the benefit of getting into the contract is \$10. If he had not got into the contract, he would be required to pay \$101 per kg, while currently he will have to only pay \$100 per kg. Thus, the value of the contract is essentially the benefit or loss the contract holder might have incurred as a result of striking the contract.

Thus, the value of the forward contract to the long position prior to the expiry date is calculated as follows:

value of the forward to the long at time(t) = prevailing market price at time(t) - (forward price/(1+interest rate)$^{\text{remaining maturity}}$)

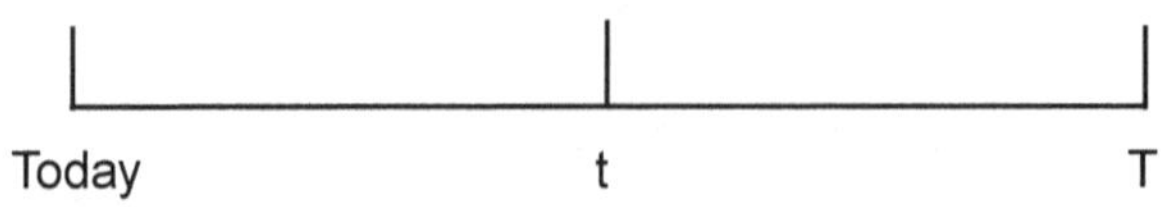

value of the forward to the long at time(t) = S_t - $FP/(1+i)^{T-t}$

value of the forward to the short at time(t) = $-(S_t - FP/(1+i)^{T-t})$

Where:

i = risk-free rate

FP = forward contract price

S_t = asset market price at time(t)

T-t = remaining days in the contract

On expiry date, the (T-t) would be zero as there are no remaining days to maturity. Thus, on expiry, the S_T - $FP/(1+i)^{T-t}$ will be equal to S_T - $FP/(1+i)^0$, which means only S_T - FP.

value of the forward to the long on expiry date = ST - FP

value of the forward to the short on expiry date = - (ST - FP)

Example 6.4: Value of forward contract prior to maturity

Assume that a speculator entered a three-month forward contract on 1 April 2012 to buy an asset. The forward price is $500 and the risk-free rate is 5%. Calculate the value of the contract to the speculator on 1 May 2012 when the prevailing market price is $509. Calculate the value of the forward contract on the expiry date.

Solution

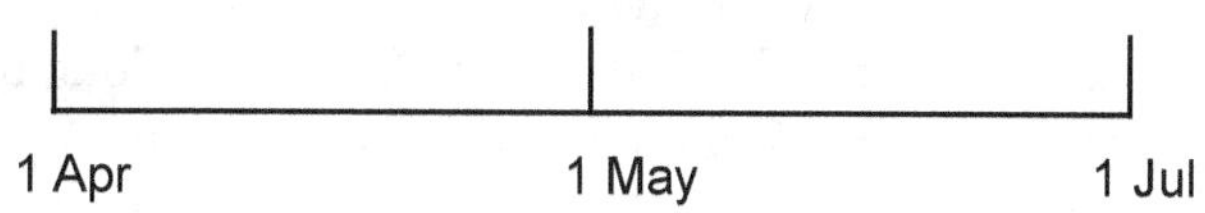

The contract maturity is three months. On 1 May T-t = 3 - 1 = 2

2/12 = 0.1667

V (long) = ST - $FP/(1+i)^{T-t}$

= $509 - 500/(1.05)0.1667

= $4.918

V (short) = -(\$509 - 500/(1.05)$^{0.1667}$)

= -\$4.918

On the expiry date, 1 July, T-t = 0

Thus:

V (long) = S_T - FP/(1+i)$^{T-t}$

= \$509 - 500/(1.05)^0

= \$9

V (short) = -(\$509 - 500/(1.05)^0)

= -\$9

LOS. Describe the impact of intermediate cash flows on the value of a forward contract

Intermediate cash flows are in dividends for equity forward contracts or coupons for bond forward contracts. If you go long an equity forward contract and the underlying stock will pay dividends before the expiry date, you are not entitled to receive these dividends because the ownership of the stock will be transferred from the seller to you after the expiry date. Since you are not entitled to receive the dividends because you do not own the stock now, the value of the forward contract to you as a long position at any time during the contract should reflect this fact by deducting the dividends from the forward contract price. Forward contracts on bonds are valued in the same way.

Example 6.5: Valuing forward contracts with dividends

Assume that you own a share of ABC Company that is currently priced at \$100. You plan to sell the share in three months' time and you are concerned about a fall in the price of the share. To hedge your position against a fall in the share price, you enter a short position in a forward contract with three months to maturity. The risk-free rate is 5.5%.

The price of the forward contract at the beginning is:

a. $105.500

b. $125.000

c. $101.348

d. $101.550

Solution

c.

Assume that, during the next 30 and 60 days, ABC Company will distribute 0.95% and 1% as dividends, respectively. Calculate the price of the contract at the beginning:

a. $99.384

b. $103.443

c. $98.050

d. $101.550

Solution

a.

present value of the first dividends = PV = $0.95/(1.05530/365) = $0.946

present value of the second dividends = PV = $1/(1.05560/365) = $0.991

total present value of dividends = 0.946 + 0.991 = $1.937

FP = (100-1.937)(1.055)0.25 = $99.384

LOS. Describe the impact of storage costs on the value of a forward contract

Storage cost is the cost incurred to keep the underlying asset in warehouses until the date of delivery to the buyer of the forward contract. It is only applicable to underlying physical commodities, such as oil, wheat or corn. Forward contracts on financial assets such as stocks, currencies or bonds do not incur such costs.

Storage cost would have to be reflected in the price the buyer of the forward contract has to pay on the delivery date upon receiving the assets. It typically works like this: we buy the underlying asset, enter into a short forward contract, store the assets and incur the resultant costs until maturity. On the maturity date, we deliver the assets and receive the forward price. This clearly says that we have to include the costs incurred to store the asset during the life of the contract. Thus, we have to add the storage cost to the formula shown in Example 6.1, as follows:

forward contract price = future value of the spot price + future value of the storage costs

$FP = S_0 (1+i)^T + SC(1+i)^T$

Where:

SC = storage costs

Example 6.6: Pricing forward contracts with storage costs

Consider a 60-day forward contract with an underlying asset that is currently priced at \$500. Storage cost at t_0 is \$35. Calculate the forward price at t_0 if the risk-free rate is at 6%.

Solution

future value of the storage cost = $\$35(1.06)^{60/365} = \$35.337$

forward price at $t_0 = \$500(1.06)^{60/365} + 35.337$

$= 504.812 + 35.337 = \$540.149$

LOS. Describe the impact of convenience yield on the value of a forward contract

Certain assets are in short supply due to several reasons related to their nature, types of usage, prices, and customer demand. Due to short supply the prices of such assets are mostly on the high side and possessing them is considered an advantage for the holder/owner.

Thus, holding these assets gives the holder the benefit of not being susceptible to an increasing price or running out of such an asset. These benefits are non-monetary as they provide *convenience* to the holder and are called **convenience yield.**

The impact of the convenience yield on the forward price is identical to the impact of dividends with stocks or coupons with bonds. The following formula reflects this impact:

$$FP = (S_0 - \text{convenience yield})\ (1+i)^T$$

In the case of incurring storage costs and the existence of convenience yield, the overall impact on the forward price will be as follows:

$$FP = S_0\ (1+i)^T + (\text{storage cost} - \text{convenience yield})(1+i)^T$$

Example 6.7: Pricing forward contracts with convenience yield

Consider a 60-day forward contract with an underlying asset that is currently priced at $500. Calculate the forward price at t0 if the risk-free rate is at 6%, where:

a) Storage cost at t0 is $35 and convenience yield is estimated to be at $3.50.

b) Storage cost is zero and convenience yield is estimated to be at $3.50.

Solution

a) future value of the storage cost = $\$35(1.06)^{60/365} = \$35.337$

future value of the convenience yield = $\$3.5(1.06)^{60/365} = \$3.534$

net future value = \$35.337 - \$3.534 = \$31.803

forward price at t_0 = $\$500(1.06)^{60/365}$ + 31.803 = \$536.615

b) future value of the storage cost = 0

future value of the convenience yield = $-\$3.5(1.06)^{60/365}$ = \$3.534

net future value = 0 - \$3.534 = \$-3.534

forward price at t_0 = $\$500(1.06)^{60/365}$ - 3.534 = \$501.279

Alternatively:

$FP = (500 - 3.5)(1.06)^{60/365} = \$501.279$

LOS. Define and discuss a forward rate agreement (FRA)
LOS. Discuss the nomenclature, uses and settlement of an FRA
LOS. Calculate the value and price of an FRA

So far, we have been discussing forward contracts on either fixed or financial assets. In this section we will discuss forward contracts on interest rates – that is, an interest rate payment is the underlying asset.

Similar to the case of physical or financial assets, **forward rate agreements (FRAs)** are used to hedge against increasing interest rates for those market participants planning to borrow or concerned about the return on their investments.

Since the underlying asset is an interest rate, there must be an amount indicated in the contract against which the rate is applied. The amount is called the *notional principal.* This amount typically represents a Eurodollar time deposit instrument. Eurodollars are the lending and borrowing of US dollars by banks outside the United States. Banks in London lend each other US dollars on a short-term basis and the interest rate quoted amongst them is called London Interbank Offered Rate (LIBOR).

How does the FRA work to protect a borrower or an investor from an increasing or decreasing rate, respectively?

Assume that you will receive $10,000,000 in two months' time and you plan to keep this amount for six months. Only after that time will you inject it into one of your short-term investment projects. So, your concern is an interest rate decrease after two months. To hedge yourself against this possible loss, you approach me to quote you a fixed rate today on this amount that you plan to keep for six months, after you have received it in two months' time. Assume that I quoted you a fixed rate of 5%.

Thus, we strike a 2x8 FRA contract with a fixed rate of 5%. The 2x8 means: a forward contract that starts today and expires in two months, with an underlying asset maturing in six months (2 + 6 = 8). After two months, you would receive the amount and the first day of your investment horizon starts and would last for six months.

If immediately after the two months, the six-month LIBOR is 4%, I would compensate you the reduction in interest rate compared to the fixed rate I agreed with you on the first day of the FRA, i.e. I would compensate you the 1% (5% - 4%). If, however, the six-month LIBOR rate is 5.5%, then you would have to compensate me the 0.5% (5% - 5.5%).

Example 6.8: FRA in borrowing

Assume that a bank treasurer would like to hedge against an increasing borrowing rate on an amount to be borrowed in three months, for six months. The treasurer determines that buying (long FRA) 3x9 FRA could hedge against the possibly of an increasing rate. Assume that the seller of the FRA quoted 4.4% as a fixed rate, starting three months from now.

After three months the FRA will expire. The six-month LIBOR has to be observed. If the six-month LIBOR is below 4.4%, the buyer of the contract would have to pay the difference to the seller.

1 January: Treasurer agrees with the seller a 3x9 FRA with a fixed rate of 4.4%.

1 April: The FRA expires. Now both the treasurer and the seller observe the six-month LIBOR. If the six-month LIBOR is more than 4.4%, the buyer has to receive the difference from the seller. So, if the six-month LIBOR is 5%, the buyer will receive 0.6% from the seller. The difference is to be paid over the six-month period, i.e. until 1 October.

1 October: At this date the difference between the fixed rate and six-month LIBOR should be settled. In practice, buyers and sellers do not wait until the last day. They prefer to settle the payment on 1 April. This means that if they want to settle the amount that should be paid on 1 October on 1 April, this amount has to be discounted:

$$\text{value of the FRA contract} = \frac{(\text{reference rate} - \text{FRA fixed rate})}{1 + \text{interest rate}(t)}$$

Where:

reference rate = the benchmarked LIBOR rate (in this example it is the six-month LIBOR)

Example 6.9: Valuing FRA on expiry date

Suppose that a treasurer needs to enter into an FRA that expires in 45 days and is based on 140-day LIBOR. The dealer quoted a rate of 4.50% on this FRA. Assume that at expiration, the 140-day LIBOR is 3.75% and the notional principal is $20,000,000. Calculate the FRA payoff on a long position at the end of 45 days (the expiry of the FRA).

Solution

$$\left[\frac{(3.75\% - 4.5\%)(140/360)}{1 + 0.0375(140/360)}\right] \times 20{,}000{,}000 = -\$57{,}494.00$$

This means that the treasurer would have to make this payment to the dealer.

Until now we have assumed that the FRA fixed rate is given to you in the question. The FRA fixed rate is not arbitrarily chosen by the long and short parties, it is determined taking into consideration the maturity of the FRA and a Eurodollar deposit's maturity, and the respective interest rate for each of these maturities.

To illustrate how to calculate the FRA rate, suppose that a treasurer needs to enter into a 3x9 FRA that expires in 90 days and is based on 180-day LIBOR. Assume that 90-day LIBOR is 3.5% and the 270-day LIBOR is 4.2%. Calculate the FRA fixed rate.

To calculate the FRA rate, draw the FRA structure as follows:

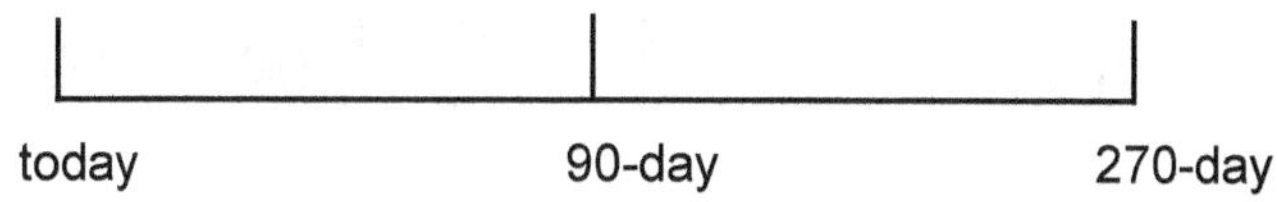

Where:

today = the date of entering into the FRA

90-day = the last day of the FRA and on which both the long and the short party observe the LIBOR for the coming period, between 90-day and 270-day, to compare it to the fixed rate and settle accordingly.

270-day = the maturity day of the Eurodollar deposit, i.e. the underlying asset of the FRA.

Thus, the settlement between the long and the short depends on the prevailing interest rate for the 180-day maturity (between 90-day and 270-day) on day 90 and comparing it to the FRA rate determined today.

Today you can calculate the 180-day rate by dividing the interest rate for the 270-day by the interest rate for the 90-day.

In the PRM exams, any interest rate quoted is annualized unless stated otherwise, so you need to adjust it for the maturity in question as follows:

$$\text{180-day FRA rate} = \left[\frac{1+0.042(270/360)}{1+0.035(90/360)} - 1\right] = 2.26\%$$

This is a result of un-annualized rates, so we need to annualize the 2.26%:

$$2.26\% \times (360/180) = 4.51\%$$

As a general rule, for FRA:

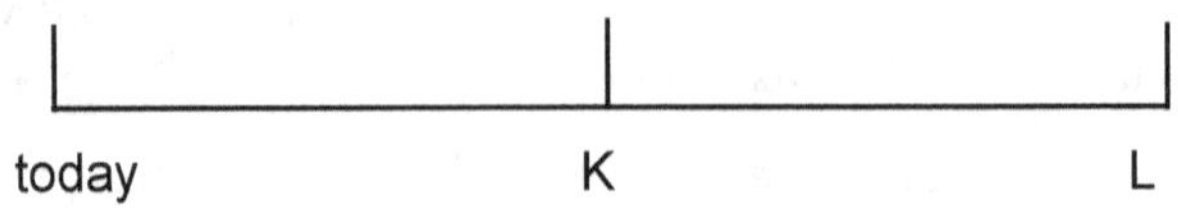

$$(L-K)\text{FRA fixed rate} = \left[\frac{1+i_L(M_L/360)}{1+i_K(M_K/360)} - 1\right] \times (360/L-K)$$

Where:

i_L:= interest rate for the maturity between today and L

i_K = interest rate for the maturity between today and K

M_K = number of days between today and K

M_L = number of days between today and L

L-K = number of days between L and K

today = the day of entering into the FRA contract

K = the expiry day of the FRA contract, i.e. the settlement date

---

Example 6.10: Pricing an FRA

Calculate the price of a 1x4 FRA if 30-day LIBOR is 7% and 120-day LIBOR is 9%.

Solution

LIBOR rates are annualized. So the first step is to convert the annualized interest rates to the periodic interest rate as follows:

$$R_{30} = 7\% \times \frac{30}{360} = 0.00583$$

$$R_{120} = 9\% \times \frac{120}{360} = 0.03$$

Where:

R_{30} = interest rate for a 30-day contract

R_{120} = interest rate for a 120-day contract

So, the price of 1×4 FRA is $= \frac{1+R120}{1+R30} - 1 = \frac{1+0.03}{1+0.0075} - 1 = 0.0240$

And the annualized FRA rate $= 0.0240 \times \frac{360}{90} = 9.611\%$

The price of an FRA that ensures zero arbitrage on the inception date of the contract is 9.611%.

Chapter 7. Futures Markets And Contracts

Upon completion of this chapter you will have learnt:

1. Futures market definitions and terminology.
2. Futures market and contract nomenclature.
3. Hedging using futures contracts.

7.1 Futures Market Definitions and Terminology

LOS. Define a futures contact

A **futures contract** is a standardized agreement between two parties: the buyer (the long) and the seller (the short) in which the short delivers a specified asset to the long at a specified date in the future. In exchange, the long pays to the seller a specified amount agreed on the date of the agreement. The asset delivered is called the *underlying asset* of the contract and the price paid to the short is the *future price*. A standardized contract means the futures contract is traded through an exchange and a clearing house is between the short and long to reduce the counterparty risk.

LOS. Define open outcry, contract size, tick size, limit up, limit down, expanded limit, delivery month, offsetting transaction, volume and open interest

- **Contract size**: In the futures market, contract sizes are standardized by the clearing house. There are standard sizes for the amount of dollars, weights, dimensions and other descriptions of the underlying physical assets. For example, the standard contract size of the soybeans futures contract is 5000 bushels, and equity options contracts are 100 shares.

- **Delivery month**: The clearing house specifies the months and days of the physical delivery of the futures contract's underlying asset.
- **Offsetting transactions**: Those who hold long and short positions in futures contracts can terminate (i.e. offset) their positions in the contracts independently (i.e. without informing each other) by taking short and long positions, respectively, of the same contracts.
- **Expanded limit**: Prices in the futures market are allowed to move within set daily limits. Deviation from these limits is allowed in certain circumstances. In these circumstances the futures exchange expands the daily trading limit.
- **Tick size**: The minimum price movement, or minimum increment, in which the price of a financial contract can change during a trading day.
- **Limit up and limit down**: Exchange markets put limits on the size of movements of the price of futures contracts to restrain arbitrage and speculation. If in one trading day the price of the futures contract has gone down by an amount equal to the limit, it is said that is a **limit down** contract and if it rises by an amount equal to the limit, it is **limit up**.
- **Transaction volume**: The number of shares, bonds or any financial instruments traded in the exchange market in a trading day.
- **Open interest**: At the end of a trading day, open interest refers to the outstanding futures contracts that have not yet been delivered or cash settled.
- **Open outcry**: An arrangement in an exchange market in which traders on the trading floor shout their orders and negotiate prices by shouting and using hand signals.

7.2 Futures Market and Contract Nomenclature

LOS. Discuss types of orders in futures markets

- **Market order**: An order to use the current prevailing market price to buy or sell an asset immediately.
- **Limit order**: Limits given to the trader to buy a security if the price is not more than the limit you give, or sell an asset at a price not less than the limit given.
- **Market on close order:** An order that would be executed at the prevailing market price at the closing time of the market.
- **Market on open order:** An order that would be executed at the prevailing market price at the opening time of the market.
- **Good till cancelled order:** An order that stays live until it is executed or cancelled by the client. For example, a trader is given an order to buy a stock when the price is $15 on Monday. The order will stay alive until the market price reaches $15 or is cancelled by the client. If the order was placed to buy the stock at $15 without the *good till cancelled* element, the order will expire at the end of trading on Monday if the market price has not reached $15.
- **Stop order**: An order given to the trader to buy or sell an asset at the prevailing market price if the asset price reaches a certain level.
- **Market if touched order:** Assume the prevailing market price is $10. An order is given to the trader to immediately sell when it reaches $12. Or, a buy order is placed to buy immediately when it reaches $8.
- **Fill or kill order:** An order that is sent to the trader to execute immediately. If it cannot be executed immediately at the set price it is cancelled.

LOS. Discuss the role of the clearing house

In the futures exchange market, a **clearing house** stands between the buyer and seller in every transaction. The clearing house acts as the short to every long position and long to every short position. With the clearing house between them, neither the buyer nor the seller has to worry about counterparty risk because the clearing house will honor all obligations.

Immediately after initiation and agreeing on the terms of the futures contract between the buyer and seller, the clearing house steps in. The seller does not have an obligation to deliver the asset to the buyer but to the clearing house, and the buyer has no obligation to receive an asset and pay to the seller, but to the clearing house.

With this role in place, counterparty risk for the buyer and the seller is considered null because the buyer and the seller would each have a counterparty risk to the clearing house, but not to each other. The clearing house uses the tool of initial and maintenance margin to guarantee the transactions. The clearing house would also ensure that settlement or physical delivery is performed smoothly between the buyer and seller. The clearing house is not, however, responsible for making up any differences or disputes between the buyer and seller on the specifications of the assets physically delivered.

For example, in futures contracts with physical delivery, the clearing house would ensure that the delivery is handled smoothly between the two parties, but if after accepting the delivery notice the buyer found out that the products delivered were not according to the specification, the buyer should handle this dispute outside the clearing house with the seller. The clearing house is not legally obliged to assist in this dispute.

LOS. Compare and contrast physical delivery and cash-settlement
LOS. Discuss the process of physical settlement

Futures contracts are either settled by: cash settlement, delivery of the asset, or offsetting the position.

- **Settlement by cash**: The asset is not physically delivered from the seller to the buyer. The counterparty who has a negative position at the expiry date pays the amount to the other counterparty. The loss or gain in either position is determined by the difference between the futures price and the last settlement price (marked to market price).
- **Settlement by delivery**: Theoretically, this implies physical delivery of the underlying asset from the seller to the buyer. Practically, the buyer receives a warehouse receipt that indicates the address of the warehouse, the quantity and all other specifications of the asset. This receipt is tradable. The following steps explain the process of settlement by delivery:

- It is the responsibility of the short position to initiate the delivery process.
- Each futures contract has a delivery period. The delivery period is toward the last days of the month prior to the delivery month in the futures contract.
- A buyer who does not wish to receive delivery of the physical asset and is interested only in the cash settlement should offset the contract prior to the delivery period. If the offsetting does not take place the asset is delivered. Delivery would not be of the physical asset; instead, delivery would be through a warehouse receipt advising of the asset's delivery.
- If the buyer does not advise of the offsetting intention, the seller would inform the clearing house of the intention to deliver and the clearing house would give the buyer the delivery notice.
- On the delivery day the buyer has to make the payment of the futures price to the seller.

LOS. Define flex option

An option offered by the Chicago Board Options Exchange in which investors have flexibility to customize the options contract's expiry dates, types, exercise price, etc.

LOS. Discuss the exercise of an option on a futures contract

Assume an investor anticipates an increase in the price of Asset A. An investor chooses to buy an option on futures contracts. In this arrangement, if he thinks it is profitable to exercise the option, he would exercise the option and take a long position in a futures contract on Asset A, in which he could receive Asset A and pay the futures price (the exercise price). The maximum loss for the long position on a futures contract is limited to the premium, while the seller's risk is theoretically unlimited. So, it is the seller only (the writer of the option on the futures) who is requested to deposit a margin with the clearing house.

LOS. Discuss the various participants in futures markets: hedgers, speculators, managed futures investors
LOS. Define calendar spread and basis

Hedgers are market participants who take futures contracts to protect them from adverse price movements. An investor could either have a futures contract to protect her from a drop in price or increase in price (long hedge as buyer of the asset).

Example 7.1: Short hedge using futures contracts

Assume an investor has bought 100 shares for $9 each and is considering selling the 100 shares after three months. As a long position in shares his concern is a drop in price. To protect against this risk, he sells futures contracts according to which he could sell the shares for $10 each after three months. If after three months the price of each share in the market is $8, his financial position would be:

Value of the long position in shares: the 100 shares were bought for $9 and would have been sold for $8 if no futures contract was entered into, so the investor would incur a loss of 100 × ($8-$9) = -$100

Value of short futures contract: the shares would be either delivered or cash settled to the buyer for the futures price of $10. So the gain for the investor is:

100 × ($10 - $8) = $200

So the loss on the long position of shares is covered by the short position in futures contracts and making a net profit from this hedge of $200 - $100 = $100.

Speculators in futures markets are categorized in four types, as follows:

1. Locals: As the name indicates, locals refers to the traders on the floor of the exchange house. Taking benefits from being on the floor of trading amidst the buy and sell orders, they act based on their knowledge and experience to take advantage of mispriced securities. The time horizon of these speculators is very short – it could be less than a day, less than an hour, or even just a few minutes.

2. Spreaders: Speculators who take a long position in a futures contract and a short position in another contract in which the underlying asset is interrelated. An underpriced asset would be bought and an overpriced asset would be sold. The anticipation is that asset prices have deviated from their norm and will revert to norm in the future. A spreader's position is classified into four classes:
   - *Calendar spread:* buying and selling futures contracts on the same underlying asset but with a different maturity life.
   - *Inter-commodity spread:* buying and selling futures contracts with different underlying assets but these assets are related to each other: either as complement or substitute.
   - *Inter-market spread*: buying and selling futures contracts with the same underlying asset but on a different exchange market.
3. Day traders: Arbitragers who benefit from mispriced securities, but with a time horizon of one day only.
4. Position traders: Speculators who benefit from mispriced securities and who are able to wait for days, weeks or months until they can foreclose the position with the targeted profit. Position traders have the financial capacity to withstand losses during this extended period until they reach the target, in contrast to locals or day traders.

LOS. Discuss some uses of stock index futures

Stock index futures are futures contracts, the underlying asset of which is a market index, such as the FTSE 100 or S&P 500. As a type of futures contract, stock index futures are used for hedging, speculation and arbitrage. Since the underlying asset is the whole market index, it is used mainly to hedge the market risk of stocks.

LOS. Define index point and the value of an index point

The underlying asset of index futures is the market index; the market index is an absolute number and does not represent a dollar amount. To determine the futures price of the index future we need to translate the index into a dollar amount. The fixed *multiple* given by each exchange market to multiply by the index to get the dollar amount is referred to as the **index point**. The index point for the S&P 500, for instance, is 250. This means that if the current S&P 500 index is 1350, then the futures price for the S&P 500 contract would be determined as follows:

$$FP_0 = (\$250 \times 1350) \times (1+i)^t$$

LOS. Describe index arbitrage and program trading

A non-arbitrage futures price is determined as follows:

$$\text{futures price} = \text{spot price } (1+i)^t$$

If this relationship does not hold, an arbitrage opportunity accrues. This opportunity is called cash-and-carry arbitrage; it means that an arbitrageur buys the asset at a lower price, stores or holds the asset until the delivery date as per the futures contract, and on the expiry date delivers the asset and receives the futures price. The following example shows how this works.

Example 7.2: Index future price arbitrage

Assume an index has a current value of 1250 and the one-year future price is 1370. If the investor can borrow at 8%, determine if there is an opportunity for arbitrage. (Assume 250 index point.)

$$\text{non-arbitrage future} = (1250 \times 250) \times (1.08) = \$337,500$$

$$\text{future price quoted} = 1370 \times 250 = \$342,500$$

So the quoted future price is overpriced and an arbitrage opportunity could accrue by following the steps below:

1. Borrow at 8%.
2. Buy the index.
3. Sell index future.
4. At expiration, deliver the index and receive the future price.
5. Repay the loan and its interest and keep the remainder!

7.3 Hedging Using Futures Contracts

LOS. Calculate a minimum variance hedge ratio for a portfolio of stocks, using futures, given beta

As discussed earlier in this chapter, futures contracts are used either in a *long hedge* or *short hedge*. In a short hedge an investor owns the security but is worried about a fall in the price. The risk of a decrease in the security's price can either be attributed to idiosyncratic risk (specific or unsystematic), or systematic risk. To eliminate the idiosyncratic risk, an investor can hedge the position using a futures contract that mirrors the performance of the spot/cash position. But that will not eliminate the systematic risk. Another alternative is using the index futures contract; since its underlying asset is the *market* index, it can eliminate the risk of an adverse movement in the market. Hence, it theoretically eliminates the market, or systematic, risk.

The next step – after realizing the convenience of using the index futures contract to hedge the spot/cash position in either a single asset or a portfolio – is to determine the number of futures contracts needed for the hedge. To determine the number of the contracts, an investor needs to know the value of the spot (hedged) and the futures price (hedging tool). By dividing the value of the hedged by the value of the hedging we can determine the number of contracts as follows:

$$\text{number of futures contracts needed for the hedge} = \frac{\text{spot}}{\text{future price }(t0)}(\beta)$$

The (β) in the above formula is a measure of correlation between the portfolio we are trying to hedge against the market movement and the market itself. If the portfolio is perfectly positively correlated with the market (β) would be +1 in the above formula. This makes intuitive sense because the size and nature of the hedge depends on the correlation and the relationship between the hedged and the hedging instrument.

In practice, since futures are standardized contracts, there might be cases in which a firm needs to hedge its risk using futures contracts but there are no standard futures contracts in the futures exchange for the particular underlying asset for which the firm seeks to hedge its risk. If a firm faces such a situation it might still use futures contracts to hedge the risk, but by using futures contracts on an underlying asset with similar features to that asset the firm seeks to hedge.

Assume, for instance, an airline seeks to hedge the risk of rising jet fuel prices. There are no futures contracts on jet fuel. The airline can still use the futures market to hedge the fuel price by finding a futures contracts on an asset that is close in nature to jet fuel. The closest contract, for example, is found to be the heating oil futures contract traded in size of 10,000 gallons.

After that the airline company needs to know how many contracts it needs to hedge its 15,000,000 gallons of jet oil. The ratio that gives the optimum number of contracts to hedge this kind of position is called the **minimum variance hedge ratio**. It is calculated as in the formula below.

It is called the minimum variance because we take into consideration the correlation between the futures contract and the spot position. In our example, this is the correlation between the jet fuel price and the futures contract price for heating oil. The stronger the relationship, the higher the number of contracts to be bought for a hedge, and vice versa.

This makes intuitive sense because if there is no linear correlation between the jet oil price and the futures contract on heating oil, it means that heating oil does not have the same features as an asset as jet oil. We have to calculate the variance for the jet oil price and for the futures contract price.

$$\text{optimal contracts} = \left(\frac{\text{size of desired underlying portfolio}}{\text{contract size of one futures contract}} \right) \times \rho \frac{\sigma_S}{\sigma_F}$$

Where:

ρ = correlation between the underlying asset of the future and the assets desired to be hedged

σ_F = standard deviation of the future price

σ_S = standard deviation of the spot position.

Example 7.3: Hedge using index future

Assume an investor has a stock portfolio worth $1,000,000 in the spot market. To hedge the portfolio against a drop in price, she considers selling S&P 500 futures contracts of 1350 (F_0 = 1350). If the correlation between the portfolio and S&P 500 is 0.45, calculate how many futures contracts she needs to hedge this portfolio.

Answer

spot value = \$1,000,000

future value = 1350 × 250 = \$337,500

$$N \text{ (number of futures contracts for the hedge)} = \frac{1{,}000{,}000}{337{,}500} \times 0.45$$

$$= 1.33 \text{ contracts}$$

LOS. Describe the risks in index hedging

As you have seen in the hedge ratio, beta can affect the calculation of how many futures contracts are needed to hedge the risk. So the major risk of index hedging is whether an investor can correctly calculate beta. Another risk is whether the investor's model for calculating beta is dynamic, to cater for the daily volatility of beta. The more volatile beta, the more the number of futures contracts would need to be adjusted.

LOS. Discuss tailing the hedge

If an investor buys or sells a futures contract, she would have to deposit a margin with the clearing house for the life of the futures contract. As the position of the futures contract (short or buy) would be marked to market on a daily basis, the investor's margin account would change as well. If the investor's position is of positive value, the account would increase above the margin requirements and vice versa. Interest is paid (charged) to the investor's margin account when the account increases (decreases) in relation to the margin requirement. The interest expenses or receipts can be utilized by the investor to dynamically hedge her positions using the futures contract. An investor is **tailing the hedge** when she takes into consideration the interest receipts or expenses in the calculation of the hedge ratio.

LOS. Compare and contrast currency forwards and futures contracts

Forward contracts are not standard. They can be transacted in any currency for any period of time and for any amount, with no money required at the inception of the contract from the short or the long. Futures contracts, on the other hand, are *standardized*. They can be traded for a limited number of currencies as per the exchange market. Delivery dates and the size of the contracts that can be sold or bought are all fixed and set by the exchange. This indicates that the forward contract gives more flexibility to the investor to exactly fit the forward contract to his spot position/needs.

Since forward contracts are OTC, both parties in the contract are exposed to counterparty risk, while performance in futures contracts is guaranteed by the clearing house. So, the counterparty risk in currency forward contracts is greater than the risk in futures contracts.

LOS. Calculate a forward exchange rate

A current quote of one currency relative to another currency is a spot exchange rate: a rate that is transacted and settled between traders within two business days. The exchange rate for the same currencies to be settled beyond these two days is the forward exchange rate. The forward exchange rate is calculated as follows:

$$\text{forward exchange rate} = \text{spot rate} \pm \text{forward premium or discount}$$

A forward premium is a case when one currency is quoted at a premium on the spot price relative to the other currency; on the other hand, a forward discount is a case when one currency is quoted at a discount on the spot price relative to other currency. Premiums and discounts are applied to the *base currency* of the quote.

For instance, if the spot price is MXN/USD 0.630 while the forward price is MXN/USD 0.640 we say that USD is trading at forward premium relative to MXN. (Conversely, MXN is trading at discount relative to USD.)

Example 7.4: Forward exchange rate

Assume you are given the following quotes for USD/BHD. Calculate the 60-day bid and offer forward rate.

Spot: 0.3750/0.3780

60-day: +10.6/+11.0

Solution

60-day bid = 0.3750 + (10.6/10,000) = 0.3761

60-day offer = 0.3780 + (11.0/10,000) = 0.3791

So, the forward rate between the USD/BHD is 0.3761/0.3791.

LOS. Calculate a hedge ratio using foreign exchange futures

Example 7.5: Hedging using foreign exchange futures

Assume that an English importer has to pay USD 1,000,000 to an American exporter for agricultural products in three months. The importer has a concern that GBP will have weakened relative to USD in three months' time and that he will end up paying more GBP to settle for the amount of the imported products. One tool of hedging this risk is to buy USD futures contracts with a maturity of three months.

Assume that:

- Spot rate = GBP/USD 0.667.
- Futures price = GBP/USD 0.6730.
- Contract size = USD 125,000.

Calculate the number of contracts needed for the hedge and determine the profit/loss from the hedge if the spot price after three months is GBP/USD 0.7321.

Solution

Number of futures contracts needed for the hedge is = 1,000,000/125,000 = 8 contracts

After three months:

- Cash market: 0.7321 × 1,000,000 = GBP 732,100
- Gain (loss) = (0.667-0.7321) × 1,000,000 = (65,100)

In the futures market:

The importer is not interested in the delivery of the USD. He is interested in hedging the risk, so he would offset his position by taking a short futures contract (because he is currently in a long position). Assume the future price (F1) is 0.7401, the gain (loss) from the future market is (0.7401 - 0.6730) × 1,000,000 = 67,100. The gain in futures market covers the loss in the cash or spot market with a gain of 2,000 (67,100 - 65,100).

LOS. Discuss the relative basis risks with commodity futures

Basis is the difference between the spot price (cash market) and the futures price. A futures contract's basis is calculated as follows:

basis = cash price of underlying asset – future price of the underlying asset

$$\text{basis} = S_T - FP_T$$

Basis risk is the opportunity that the difference between the S_T and FP_T widens or shortens. Positive basis reflects a situation where the cash price for the underlying asset is higher than the futures price of the same asset. This is called *backwardation*. Backwardation is attributed mostly to the convenience yield. Investors, merchants or producers would, in some situations, prefer to have storage of the assets in the present time as compared to needing to go out and buy them in the future.

On the other hand, there are producers who wish to acquire ownership of assets in the future as opposed to having them in the present time; hence the futures price would be higher than the spot price. This latter case is called *contango*, i.e. negative basis. Negative basis results from the cost-of-carry. This is the cost of storage of the underlying asset and maintaining it until the futures contract expires and this cost is added to the spot price, resulting in a futures price higher than the spot price.

LOS. Calculate T-bill and Eurodollar futures prices

Before addressing the calculation of T-bill futures contracts, I will first give a brief introduction to this contract. T-Bill futures contracts are traded by the International Monetary Market (IMM) of the Chicago Mercantile Exchange (CME). The face value of these contracts is USD 1,000,000, with a 90-day maturity. T-Bill futures contracts are discounted contracts: they are quoted at a price discounted from its face value.

According to IMM, the price of T-Bills is quoted as follows:

IMM index = 100 - discount yield

And the spot price of the T-Bill is calculated as:

$$\text{bill price} = \$1{,}000{,}000 - \frac{DY(\$1{,}000{,}000)(DTM)}{360}$$

Where:

DTM = days until maturity

DY = discount yield

The price of T-Bills futures contracts is quoted in DY; if the futures price of the T-Bills futures contracts is a DY of 7.5%, for instance, then the cash that must be delivered to the short from the long on the expiry date of the futures contracts, assuming 90 days to maturity, is:

delivery price for the bill on expiry date =

$$\$1{,}000{,}000 - \frac{0.075(\$1{,}000{,}000)(90)}{360} =$$

$\$981{,}250$

It is important to note that in T-Bills futures contracts, daily price fluctuation is not smaller than one basis point. That is, for a 90-day $1,000,000 T-Bills futures contract, the minimum fluctuation point is $25, or 0.0025% of $1,000,000.

With regard to Eurodollars futures contracts, the underlying asset is US dollars deposited with commercial banks outside the boarders of the US. With this nature of underlying asset, Eurodollars futures contracts do not allow physical delivery, but only cash settlement. Similar to T-Bills futures contracts, Eurodollars futures contracts are discounted contracts and trade for a maturity of 90 days and at $1,000,000 face value.

Since it is a discounted contract, the futures price is the discount rate from the face value and it is calculated as follows:

$$\text{add-on yield} = \frac{\text{discount from the face value in dollars}}{\text{price}} \times \frac{360}{\text{DTM}}$$

Where price is calculated as follows:

$$\text{price} = \$1{,}000{,}000 - \frac{\text{DY}(1{,}000{,}000)(\text{DTM})}{360}$$

For example, calculate the Eurodollar futures contract price if the discount yield is 8%.

$$\text{price} = \$1{,}000{,}000 - \frac{0.08(\$1{,}000{,}000)(90)}{360} = \$980{,}000$$

So the discount = $1,000,000 - 980,000 = $20,000

$$\text{add-on yield} = \frac{\$20{,}000}{\$980{,}000} \times \frac{360}{90} = 8.16\%$$

LOS. Construct a hedge using Eurodollar or T-bill futures
LOS. Define cheapest-to-deliver and conversion factor
LOS. Construct a hedge using T-bond futures

In bonds futures contracts, the underlying asset is a Treasury bond. Treasury bonds are issued with different maturities and coupon rates; hence, there are a wide pool of bonds that can be delivered at the expiry date of the futures contracts. The choice of which bonds are delivered resides with the seller of the Treasury bond futures contracts. T-bond futures are traded with a face value of $100,000 and a minimum price fluctuation of $31.25 (1/32 × 1% basis point × 100,000).

T-bond futures have a special quotation; a future quotation of 93-00 refers to 93% of the $100,000 face value, i.e. $93,000. When the future declines by 21/32, this refers to the reduction in futures price by $31.25(-21) = -$656.25 (futures price is equal to $93,000 - 656.25 = $92,343.75).

It is the rule of the exchange that bonds delivered in T-bonds futures are those bonds with a face value of $100,000 and 15 years' residual maturity for redemption.

There are various T-bonds issued that fit these criteria, with different coupon rates. This means some of the bonds which fit the criteria are expensive and some are cheap. Since the decision of which bonds to deliver from various bonds that fit the criteria resides with the seller, one would initially think the seller would always choose the bonds that are cheapest to deliver to the buyer at the expiry date of the futures contracts. That would be detrimental to the buyer's interest. The exchange, however, adopts a conversion factor mechanism, as a formula factoring in the coupon rate and residual maturity. The purpose of this mechanism is to cater for the interest of both the buyer and the seller.

Thus the price that would be paid from the buyer to the seller at the time of delivery of the T-bonds is calculated as follows:

invoice price = DSP($100,000)CF + AI

Where:

CF = conversion factor, determined by the exchange (CBOT)

DSP = decimal settlement price

AI = accrued interest in the bonds

Alternatively:

invoice price = (future price × bond conversion factor) + bond accrued interest

---

Example 7.6: Cheapest to deliver T-bond

Assume you are given the following bond prices and the conversion factor is 9, as given by the exchange market.

If the future price is 95.0364, determine the cheapest to deliver bond.

Bond	Bond price	Conversion factor
A	95.00	1.0543
B	125.25	1.5949
C	150.25	1.6348

Gain for the seller from delivering the T-bond is:

future price × conversion factor - bond price

So:

Bond A gain from delivery = 95.0364 × 1.0543 - 95.00 = 5.197

Bond B gain from delivery = 95.0364 × 1.5949 - 125.25 = 26.323

Bond C gain from delivery = 95.0364 × 1.6348 - 150.25 = 5.11

Bond B is the cheapest to deliver.

An investor who is long a bond investment and fears a reduction in the value of the bond as the interest rate increases can hedge his long position by going short on T-bonds futures contracts. With this contract, when interest rates increase, the value of the bond investment would drop. The loss from this reduction would be offset by the gain generated from the short futures contracts position.

Example 7.7: Hedging using T-bond futures

Assume an investor has a long position in a bond. She fears that an increase in the interest rate would decrease the value of her bond investment. To hedge this risk, she is considering selling T-bonds futures contracts. She would sell the contracts because she has a long position in the asset. If she was short the bonds she would need to go long the futures contracts to hedge.

Information about her long position in the bonds that needs to be hedged and the hedging instrument (T-bonds futures contracts) is illustrated in the following table. Determine the number of futures contracts needed to hedge the position and calculate the gain (loss) from this hedge.

Long position: spot
Bond nominal value: 1,400,000
Bond market value: $1.5 million
Bond duration: 3.9
Coupon rate: 9%
YTM: 9.7%

Short position: T-bond futures contracts
Size of the contract: $100,000
Bond duration: 5.8
Future contract value: $120,000
Conversion Factor (CF): 1.15

Number of contracts needed for the hedge =

$$\frac{\text{value of the bond in spot position}}{\text{value of the futures contracts}} \times \frac{\text{duration of the bond in spot position}}{\text{duration of bonds in the futures}} \times \text{CF}$$

Number of contracts =

$$-\frac{1,500,000}{120,000} \times \frac{3.9}{5.9} \times 1.15 = -12.5 \text{ contracts}$$

Assume after two months, the value of the long bond position has reduced as a result of an increase of 2.5% in the interest rate. At the same time, the value of the futures contract position has reduced by 2%, so the gain and loss in each position is determined as follows:

loss in spot position = S1 - S = -2.5% × 1,400,000 = -35,000

gain in futures contract position = (2%) × $100,000 × 12.5 contracts = + 25,000

net loss = -10,000. So, the T-bond futures contracts reduced the loss by $25,000.

LOS. Compare and contrast stack and strip hedges

I will compare stack and strip hedges through a worked example.

Example 7.8: Stack and strip hedges

Assume a manufacturing company needs to expand one of its factories and is seeking to finance this expansion with a 360-day loan from a bank for $100,000,000. The bank charges a floating interest rate at 1.5% above 90-day LIBOR.

The risk the company is exposed to is an interest rate rise. Since this a USD loan, to hedge this risk the company chooses to use Eurodollars futures contracts.

Today is 15 September 2XX1 and the 90-LIBOR for Eurodollars are as follows. Eurodollars futures contracts mature in March, June, September and December.

90-day LIBOR = 5%

DEC Eurodollar = 5.5%

MAR Eurodollar = 5.8%

JUN Eurodollar = 6.1%

Stack hedge

Cash market	Futures market
On 15 Sep borrow the 100,000,000 at 6.5%.	Short 300 Eurodollar futures contracts at discount yield 7%
On 15 Dec pay the quarterly interest of \$100 million × 6.5% × (3/12) = 1,625,000. Assume 90-day LIBOR on this day is 5.9%, borrow the 100,000,000 at this rate.	Offset the 300 Eurodollar futures contracts at 7.4% (1.5% + 5.9%) discount yield. This generates a profit of: 40 basis points × 300 × \$25 tick size = \$300,000
March, pay the interest of 7.4% × \$100 million × (3/12) = \$1,850,000. Assume 90-day LIBOR is now 6.2%.	
June, pay interest of 7.7% × \$100 million × (3/12) = \$1,925,000. Assume 90-day LIBOR is now 6.5%.	
September, pay interest of 8% × \$100 million × (3/12) = 2,000,000	
Total interest actually paid = \$7,400,000	
Total interest that would have been paid if 90-day LIBOR did not change, on average (6.5% + 7% +7.3% +7.6%)/4 = 7.1%, \$7,100,000.	
So the loss due to an increase in LIBOR is \$300,000.	
So, the company reduced the cost of increasing LIBOR with the gain produced from the hedge. Net interest expenses: \$300,000 - \$300,000 = \$0.	

Strip hedge

A strip hedge allocates a bulk of the required futures contracts to hedge the position evenly across the maturity of the underlying exposure for which the hedging tool (Eurodollars futures contracts in our example) is acquired. So, a strip hedge is a series of futures contracts.

<table>
<tr><th>Cash market</th><th>Futures market</th></tr>
<tr><td>On 15 Sep borrow the 100,000,000 at 6.5%.

On 15 Dec. pay the quarterly interest of $100 million × 6.5% × (3/12) = 1,625,000. Assume 90-day LIBOR on this day is 5.9%, borrow the 100,000,000 at this rate.

March, pay the interest of 7.4% × $100 million × (3/12) = $1,850,000. Assume 90-day LIBOR is now 6.2%.

June, pay the interest of 7.7% × $100 million × (3/12) = $1,925,000. Assume 90-day LIBOR is now 6.5%.

September, pay interest of 8% × $ 100 million × (3/12) = 2,000,000.

Total interest actually paid = $7,400,000.

Total interest that would have been paid if 90-day LIBOR did not change, on average (6.5% + 7% +7.3% +7.6%)/4 = 7.1%, $7,100,000.

So the loss due to increase in LIBOR is $400,000.</td><td>Short 100 DEC Eurodollar futures contracts at discount yield 7%, MAR 100 Eurodollars futures contracts at 7.3% discount yield, and JUN 100 Eurodollars futures at 7.6% discount yield.

Offset the DEC 100 Eurodollars futures contract at 7.40(1.5% + 5.9%) discount yield. This generates a profit of: 40 basis points × 100 × $25 tick size = $100,000.

Offset the MAR 100 Eurodollars futures contract at 7.70 (1.5% + 5.9%) discount yield. This generates a profit of: 40 basis points × 100 × $25 tick size = $100,000.

Offset the JUN 100 Eurodollars futures contract at 8.0 (1.5% + 5.9%) discount yield. This generates a profit of: 40 basis points × 100 × $25 tick size = $100,000.

Total profits produced from the hedge = $300,000.</td></tr>
<tr><td colspan="2">So, the company reduced the cost of increasing LIBOR by a gain produced from the hedge. Net interest expenses: 400,000 - 300,000 = $100,000.</td></tr>
</table>

LOS. Compare and contrast forward and futures contracts

Feature	**Forward contracts**	**Futures contracts**
Tradability	Over the counter contract (OTC). Traded outside an exchange market.	Traded only in the exchange market.
Contract terms	Non-standardized contracts. Can be on theoretically any asset and in any amount with any maturity agreed upon between the seller and the buyer.	Standardized contracts in terms of money size, maturities and settlements.
Marking to market	There is no marking to market. No initial or maintenance margin has to be maintained.	Positions are marked to market on a daily basis and both parties need to maintain a margin account with the clearing house.
Settlement	Delivery of cash settlement occurs mostly on expiry day.	Positions are mostly offset prior to expiration by taking the opposite position as in the contract (i.e. the long goes short and short goes long to exit the position).
Credit and counterparty risk	There is credit and counterparty risk because there is no intermediary between to guarantee the performance of the parties involved.	Theoretically no credit or counterparty risk because each position is ultimately held with the clearing house.
Pricing	Priced using cost-carry principle.	Priced using cost-carry principle.
Inception date	No money is paid for either party.	Initial margin account is opened.

Chapter 8. Swaps Market And Contracts

On completion of this chapter you will have learnt:

1. Swaps basics: definitions and terminology.
2. Types of swap contracts.
3. Risks and uses of swaps.
4. Swaptions.

8.1 Swaps Basics: Definitions and Terminology

LOS. Define a swap

A swap contract is a derivative contract in which one party agrees to exchange with another party a series of cash flows on future dates with no cash changing hands at the inception of the contract. These cash flows can be linked to equity, the movement of interest rates, index, or commodities. Typically, a swap contract involves one party paying a fixed stream of cash flows in exchange for floating ones.

LOS. List the key components of a swap agreement

Swap contracts include:

- The fixed rate that determines the size of fixed cash inflow (outflow).
- Periodicity of the payments.

- Notional amount (particularly in the case of an interest rate swap).
- Tenor of the swap contract (maturity).
- Currency of both legs of the contract.

LOS. Define swap rate and swap spread

- **Swap rate**: the rate that determines the fixed future payments in the swap contract. The swap rate should create fixed payments, the present value of which should be equivalent to the present values produced by the floating rate in the other leg of the swap contract.
- **Swap spread**: the difference between the swap rate and the interest rate on government securities with the same maturities.

LOS. Define the payer and receiver in swaps
LOS. Define the buyer of interest rate swaps

The **payer** is referred to as long, or the **buyer** of the swap contract; he is the counterparty in the swap contract which pays the fixed interest rate or payments. The **receiver**, on the other hand, is referred to as short, or the seller of the swap contract; he receives the fixed rate or payments in the swap contract.

8.2 Types of Swap Contracts

LOS. Discuss interest rate swap

Example 8.1: Interest rate swap cash flows

Assume you have the following information about an interest rate swap. Calculate the period cash flows for each leg of the contract.

Notional principle	200,000,000
Currency	USD
Tenor	4 years
Start date	10-Jun
Day count	Actual/365
Payment dates	1 June, 1 December
Reference rate	6-month LIBOR
Fixed payer	Party A
Fixed receiver	Party B
Fixed rate	4.61%

Solution

The transaction structure can be depicted as follows:

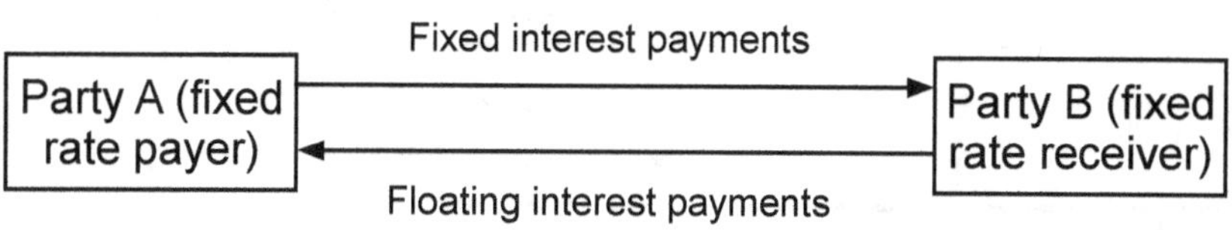

Net cash inflow (outflow) for Party A

Period	Date	Actual interest days	6-month LIBOR	Party A pays	Party A receives	Net payment
0.50	1-Dec	183	4.60%	4,622,630	4,612,603	(10,027)
1.00	1-Jun	182	4.50%	4,597,370	4,487,671	(109,699)
1.50	1-Dec	183	3.70%	4,622,630	3,710,137	(912,493)
2.00	1-Jun	182	5.50%	4,597,370	5,484,932	887,562
2.50	1-Dec	183	4%	4,622,630	4,010,959	(611,671)
3.00	1-Jun	182	4.60%	4,597,370	4,587,397	(9,973)
3.50	1-Dec	183	4.70%	4,622,630	4,712,877	90,247
4.00	1-Jun	182	5%	4,597,370	4,986,301	388,932

Net cash inflow (outflow) for Party B

Period	Date	Actual interest days	6-month LIBOR	Party B pays	Party B receives	Net payment
0.50	1-Dec	183	4.60%	4,612,603	4,622,630	10,027
1.00	1-Jun	182	4.50%	4,487,671	4,597,370	109,699
1.50	1-Dec	183	3.70%	3,710,137	4,622,630	912,493
2.00	1-Jun	182	5.50%	5,484,932	4,597,370	(887,562)
2.50	1-Dec	183	4%	4,010,959	4,622,630	611,671
3.00	1-Jun	182	4.60%	4,587,397	4,597,370	9,973
3.50	1-Dec	183	4.70%	4,712,877	4,622,630	(90,247)
4.00	1-Jun	182	5%	4,986,301	4,597,370	(388,932)

LOS. Discuss equity swaps

Equity swaps are an agreement in which two counterparties exchange cash flows based on an underlying asset of a stock portfolio or index. One counterparty will pay floating and receive fixed cash flows, while the other counterparty will pay fixed and receive floating cash flows. The fixed and floating cash flows are determined based on a notional principal representing the value of the stock portfolio or index.

For example, assume that you are a manager of a stock portfolio and you anticipate that the value of the stock portfolio will go down in the near future. You have several options to hedge your portfolio against this drop in value. You could buy put options on the portfolio, enter the futures markets or simply sell the stock portfolio now. But before taking any of these measures, you should answer the simple question that if your anticipation is correct and the stock value decreases, what effect will it have on your cash flows?

The effect would be that you would receive a reduced amount of cash flows. A swap contract can help you receive fixed cash from another investor in exchange for you paying them whatever you receive from this stock portfolio. This is called an equity swap. You swap what you receive from your current equity investment in exchange for getting a fixed amount. The following diagram depicts this idea.

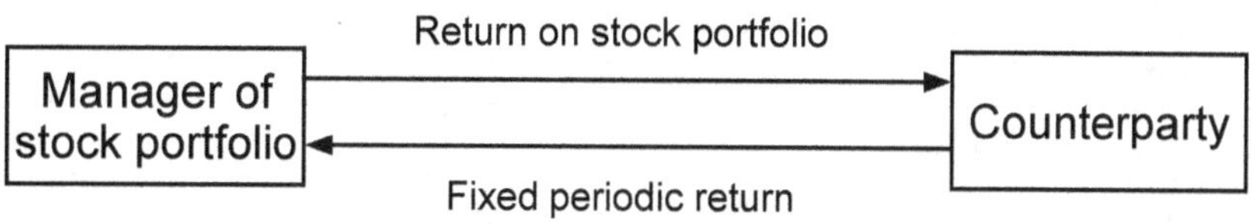

The following example illustrates how to calculate the cash flows in equity swaps.

Example 8.2: How to calculate cash flows in equity swaps

Assume a manager of a stock portfolio of $200 million is concerned about a decrease in the prices of the stocks in the portfolio. He is considering a one-year equity swap contract to mitigate this risk. He would pay the return on the portfolio on a quarterly basis in exchange for receiving fixed returns from the counterparty. The fixed rate is 6% and the returns on the portfolio by the end of each quarter are as follows (please note that these would not be known before the quarter-end). The day-convention of the equity swaps contract is actual/365:

- Return on 1 Jan 2011 = 1.5%.
- Return on 31 Mar 2011 = 1.7%.
- Return on 30 Jun 2011 = 1.6%.
- Return on 30 Sep 2011 = 1.9%.
- Return on 31 Dec 2011 = 1.4%.

Cash flow for portfolio manager

	Receive	Pay	Net	Net/Portfolio
March	2,958,904	(400,000)	2,558,904	1%
June	2,991,781	200,000	3,191,781	2%
Sep	3,024,658	(600,000)	2,424,658	1%
Dec	3,024,658	1,000,000	4,024,658	2%
Total	12,000,000	200,000	11,800,000	6%

The table below illustrates how the above cash flows were calculated:

	Receive	Pay
March	$200,000,000*6%*(90/365)	= -200,000,000(1.7%-1.5%)
June	$200,000,000*6%*(91/365)	= -200,000,000(1.6%-1.7%)
Sep	$200,000,000*6%*(92/365)	= -200,000,000(1.9%-1.6%)
Dec	$200,000,000*6%*(92/365)	= -200,000,000(1.4%-1.9%)

The tables indicate that at the year end, despite the changes in the return of the stock portfolio, it still enjoys an undisturbed 6% return. Also note that the portfolio manager pays only if the portfolio enjoys a positive return. In the case of negative returns, the counterparty pays the portfolio manager.

It is worth mentioning that the portfolio manager does not have to keep the stocks to enter into the equity swap. He can sell the stocks for cash and enter into the above contract. This is done by portfolio managers who need to liquidate the position for cash but still want an economic exposure to the stocks they sold. So, holding the assets is not necessary in this contract. Taking a short position in an equity swap contract is easier than taking a short position in an options contract because a short position in an options contract has to be covered with the underlying assets.

LOS. Discuss commodity swaps

In a **commodity swap**, the swap contract counterparties exchange net cash flows based on the price of a certain commodity. The commodity is not exchanged on the settlement dates, only the net cash flows. For instance, in a received-fixed pay-floating commodity swap contract, the received-fix party receives a fixed price during the life of the contract and pays the market price (hence floating).

So commodity swaps are structurally similar to interest rate swaps, with the difference being the commodity as a base or reference asset for determining the amount of cash flows, while it is a notional dollar amount in an interest rate swap.

LOS. Discuss currency swaps

A **currency swap** is a contract according to which one party makes a periodic payment in currency A in exchange for a periodic payment in currency B from another counterparty of the swap contract, for a certain tenor and according to a pre-agreed timetable.

Contrary to an interest rate swap, in a currency swap a notional amount is exchanged between the counterparties at the inception of the contract. It is exchanged again at the expiry date. In between, payments are exchanged based on the fixed and floating interest rates on these two currencies. So, a currency swap is an interest rate swap but with different currencies and an exchange of a notional amount at the inception.

LOS. Discuss basis swaps

Basis stems from basis risk: the risk that one side of a transaction is benchmarked against an interest rate (prime rate) while the other side is benchmarked against a different interest rate (such as LIBOR). For example, if an investor borrows at the floating LIBOR interest rate but lends at the prime rate he is exposed to basis risk.

So a **basis swap** is an interest rate or currency swap in which one of the counterparties of the swap would have to make a floating stream of cash flow payments based on different interest rates.

LOS. Discuss volatility swaps

A **volatility swap** is like an interest rate swap except that in this swap what is being exchanged is not an amount of a different currency or interest rate, but a measure of volatility multiplied by a notional amount. An example of volatility is the variance of the S&P 500 index return for the period of the swap contract.

LOS. Define par swap, accrual swap, commodity-linked interest rate swap, crack spread swap, overnight index swap, power LIBOR swap and extendible swap

- **Par swap** is an interest rate swap in which the initial and final payment is applied to a notional principle of 100.
- **Accrual swap** is a plain vanilla interest rate swap in which counterparties exchange floating LIBOR-based payments with only one difference from the plain vanilla swap. In an accrual swap contract the interest accrued to the floating-rate receiver will accrue only if LIBOR remains within a set range agreed at the time of initiating the contract.
- **Commodity-linked interest rate swap** is an interest rate swap in which one party pays a floating interest rate, say LIBOR, while the other pays

a fixed rate that depends on the movements of a commodity such as oil, gas, etc.

- **Crack spread swap** is a contract in which one party pays the floating price of a refined product while the other party pays the price of a crude product plus a fixed margin. This type of contract is typically used by companies in the oil and gas field.
- **A power LIBOR swap** is a contract that pays LIBOR squared or cubed or quadrupled, etc., less a fixed amount/rate, while the other counterparty pays a floating rate.
- **Extendible swap** is a contract in which one counterparty has the right to extend a swap contract's life beyond its original maturity.
- **Overnight index swap** is a swap contract that has a fixed and floating leg. The floating leg is indexed to an overnight floating interest rate such as the Federal Reserve Fund rate or any other overnight interest rate. The fixed leg is a fixed rate agreed upon at the inception of the contract.

8.3 Risks and Uses of Swaps

LOS. Discuss the risk of swaps

- **Credit risk/counterparty risk**: Parties in swap contracts do not exchange money at the inception of the contract. Hence, at the contract maturity neither of the two parties has to honor obligations to pay back any owed money. So typically in a swap contract there is no credit risk. There is, however, counterparty risk, which means if one of the two counterparties fails to pay at the time of the periodic cash flows being due as per the contract. This is of course due to the fact that swaps are traded in the OTC market.
- **Market risk**: Swap contracts have either two floating legs, two fixed legs, or one floating and one fixed leg in a contract. At each reset date, the value of the security would be equal to its par value, as we discussed in Chapter 5 under the FRN section. So, the floating leg of the contract is not exposed to market risk on these dates. The fixed leg of the contract, however, is exposed to the market risk as the value of the instrument would be valued according to the fixed rate in relation to the altered market rate.

LOS. Discuss the main uses of swaps

- **Balance sheet management**: A swaps contract helps firms balance out the negative impact of assets and liabilities by taking counter-positions that address the requirements of the assets or liabilities.
- **Hedging**: Swaps are used to hedge risks of interest rate, equity (fund and assets management), FX (typically in trade-finance currency exposures), commodity (such as oil and airline companies), and financial institutions (assets and liability management). Since they are OTC, swaps are not a costly tool as they do not require margin accounts with a clearing house or payments at the inception of the contract.

8.4 Swaptions

LOS. Discuss the pricing of swaptions

Swaptions are contracts that give a counterparty an option to enter into a swap contract according to a predefined notional principal or underlying asset, swap price and tenor. There are two types of swaps:

- **Receiver swaptions**: gives the holder the right to get into a swap contract to receive the fixed rate and pay the floating rate.
- **Payer swaptions**: gives the holder the right to get into a swap contract to pay the fixed rate and receive the floating rate.

Since it is a combination of two instruments – an option and a swap – a swaption has a unique quote to reflect this fact. The quote '2 into 6' for a swaption, for instance, means an option contract for two months to get into a six-month swap contract.

Identical to options contracts, pricing swaptions means finding the premium that must be paid at the inception of the swaption by the swaption buyer to the swaption seller. Swaptions are priced by a modified Black-Scholes model, binomial model or by Monte-Carlo simulation.

Also, the price of a swaption is affected by the same factors as the price of an options, such as:

- Interest rate volatility.
- Level of interest rate in the market (i.e. the shape of the yield curve).
- Expiry date of the option and the swap contracts of the swaption contract.
- Strike rate of the swap contract of the swaption contract.

Practitioners use the following formula to determine the swaption price:

$$\text{swaption price} = m^{-1}\left[BF\Phi(d) - BK\Phi(s - (nh)^{1/2}v)\right]$$

$$d = \frac{\log(F/K) + (nh)v^2/2}{(nh)^{1/2}v}$$

Where:

F = forward-starting swap rate

K = strike rate

m = number of payments per year

h = times between payments per year

n = maturity of swaption in length

nh = maturity of swaption in years

B = intrinsic values of the options

v = annualized volatility

Φ = cumulative normal distribution function

Chapter 9. Credit Derivatives

Upon completion of this chapter you will have learnt:

1. Basics of credit derivatives: definitions and objectives.
2. Types of credit derivatives.
3. Credit enhancement.

9.1 Basics of credit derivatives: definitions and objectives

LOS. Discuss the applications of credit derivatives

Credit derivatives are used by two types of market players: credit derivatives buyers and sellers. Credit derivatives buyers, such as commercial banks, have credit risk exposures arising from loans on their books. To reduce this credit risk, a credit derivative instrument is bought to transfer this credit risk from its books.

On the other hand, the protection seller uses credit derivatives to assume credit risk from the buyer for a fee. So, the seller uses them to enhance income.

LOS. Define reference entity, reference asset, credit event, settlement mechanism and deliverable obligation

Let us use an example of car insurance. A car accident is the event that triggers your use of your car insurance. The car is the subject of insurance, i.e. it is the object on which you bought the insurance. When an accident happens, you have a claim on the insurance company; the insurance company either gives you cash to repair it yourself or pays for its repair indirectly.

The accident is called an **event,** the car is the **reference asset** or **entity,** repairing the car directly or indirectly is called the **settlement mechanism.**

By the same token, a bank buys credit derivatives as an insurance against a loan. If the borrower fails to pay back the outstanding amount of the loan, then this is the **credit event** that triggers a claim on the protection seller. The loan is the **reference asset** on which the credit derivative is bought. In the **physical settlement mechanism,** the buyer would have to deliver to the seller the reference asset in exchange for the settlement/compensation. This is called a **deliverable obligation.**

LOS. Contrast technical default and actual default

When a borrower delays or fails to pay an installment on a loan or part of it when it falls due, however small the period of this delay, the loan is said to be in **technical default.** In technical default loans, the borrower does not intend not to make any payment and neither does he declare that he is in default and would not be able to pay the dues. But when the borrower announces that he is in default and also declares that he is not able to honor the obligations, then the loan is said to be in **actual default.**

LOS. Define and discuss funded and unfunded instruments

A **funded instrument** is when upfront payment is made by the protection seller (the investor) to a protection buyer (the issuer of the instrument). The instrument has a maturity date and redemption value. If a credit event does not take place, the redemption or maturity value of the instrument would be paid to the protection seller. On the other hand, if a credit event takes place, the redemption value adjusted for the recovered amount of the reference asset is paid to the investor.

In the case of an **unfunded instrument,** the protection seller does not make any upfront payment to the protection buyer. If a credit event does occur the protection seller would make a payment equal to the notional amount of the contract adjusted for the recovered amount of the reference asset.

LOS. List the types of credit events contained in a standard ISDA credit derivatives document

An International Swaps and Derivatives Association (ISDA) credit derivative document lists the following as credit events (but excludes a ratings downgrade from a ratings agency):

- Bankruptcy.
- Failure to pay.
- Obligation default.
- Debt moratorium or repudiation.
- Restructuring.

9.2 Types of Credit Derivatives

This section covers the LOSs related to the following types of credit derivatives:

1. Credit default swap (CDS).
2. Credit linked note (CLN).
3. Collateralized debt obligations (CDOs).
4. Collateralized loan obligations (CLOs).
5. Collateralized bond obligations (CBOs).
6. Synthetic CDOs.

LOS. Define and discuss credit default swaps (CDS) and their prospective cash flows

A **credit default swap (CDS)** is a contract between a protection buyer and protection seller. According to the contract, the protection buyer makes a periodic payment to the seller. If a credit event takes place on a reference asset, the seller would make a contingent payment to the buyer. The periodic fees are typically as a percentage (or basis points) on an agreed upon notional amount/principal.

Similar to options contracts, the maximum risk with the protection buyer in a CDS is the periodic fees (i.e. premium) when the credit event does not happen and no protection is needed. To the seller the maximum risk is the notional amount in the contract. The following diagram is a depiction of the CDS structure.

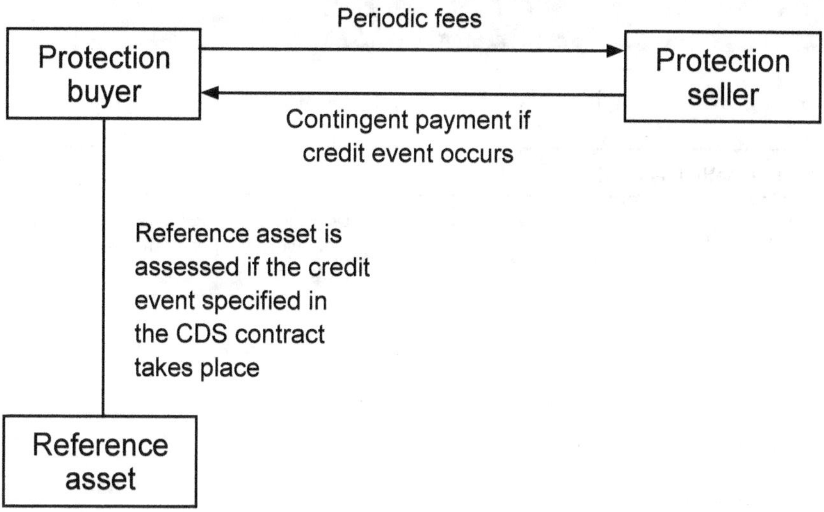

If a credit event takes place, the protection seller would compensate the buyer through either:

Cash settlement: In cash settlement, the seller would pay to the buyer an amount indicated in the CDS contract at the inception date. Such contracts are also called a *digital credit derivative*. Another mechanism of cash settlement is to pay to the buyer the reference asset's nominal value, less a recoverable amount. Recoverable amount is defined as the market value of the reference asset after the credit event according to the following equation:

payment from seller to the buyer of CDS after credit event = notional amount × [MAX(100-price after default (%)),0]

Physical settlement: In physical settlement the buyer, after the credit event, delivers the reference asset to the seller in exchange for its face value. The CDS may specify the reference asset or an alternative asset(s) to be delivered by the buyer. This is what I defined earlier in the chapter as *deliverable obligations*. For instance, in a CDS contract on bonds, the contract may specify physical delivery of Bond A, Bond B, etc.

LOS. Discuss some advantages of physical settlement vs. cash settlement in credit default swaps

The following table indicates the advantages of both mechanisms:

Physical settlement	Cash settlement
Requires administration and legal work to specify the deliverable obligations.	Does not require administration and legal work to specify the deliverable obligations.
If the buyer does not have the deliverable obligations at the settlement date, he would have to go the market to get them or accept a reduction in the settlement amount.	The buyer does not have to deliver any asset.
If the reference asset is delivered to the seller, and if the credit event is associated with restructuring or financial difficulties, the seller could increase its benefits (i.e. cost of compensation) if the issuer of the reference's financial situation improved.	Since there is no asset delivered, the seller cannot recover any amount from the asset.
Seller benefits from the recovery amount.	Seller does not have access to the recovery amount. It is enjoyed, if at all, by the buyer.
No need to estimate the size of the amount to be given by the seller to the buyer at settlement amount, as it would be the notional amount.	There is a need to estimate the amount to be given in cash to the buyer after the credit event.

LOS. Define and discuss loan-only credit default swaps (LCDS)

A **loan-only credit default swap (LCDS)** is a tradable contract in which the reference asset is a syndicated secured loan.

A syndicated secured loan means a loan under a syndicated loan agreement that has a designated priority stance in terms of liquidation. Since the reference asset is secured, the recoverable amount is typically assumed to be higher compared to an ordinary CDS. Due to this fact, an LCDS is traded with a higher spread than a CDS.

LOS. Define and discuss credit-linked notes (CLN) and their prospective cash flows

A **credit-linked note (CLN)** is a bond structure (maturity, present value, redemption value and maturity date) but the performance of this structure is linked to a performance of specified reference asset(s). A CLN is issued by a protection buyer and the investors buying the CLN are protection sellers.

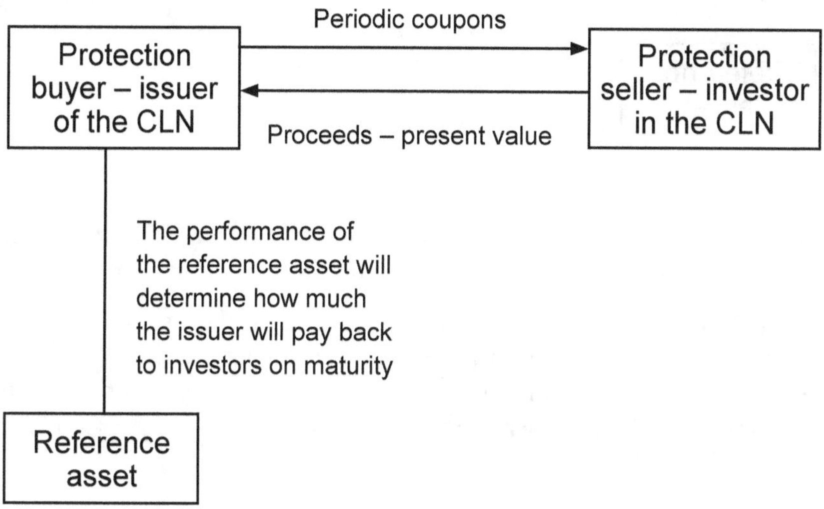

The above diagram depicts the definition of a CLN. The protection buyer has credit exposure to a reference asset. To hedge this risk, it issues a plain vanilla bond but the performance of the bond (size of future coupon payments and the amount paid back to the bond investor on maturity) depends on whether a credit event occurs or not. At inception, the investors pay the proceeds (typically CLN issued at par) to the protection buyer. Hence, a CLN is referred to as a *funded credit derivative*. During the life of the CLN the issuer pays periodic payments to the investors, as is the case in any plain vanilla bond structure.

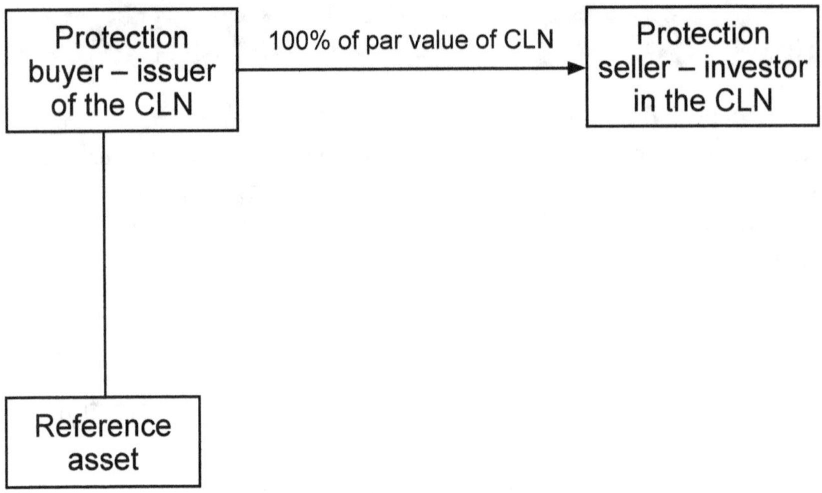

If no credit event takes place the issuer pays the investor 100% of the CLN face value, as depicted in the above diagram.

If a credit event does occur on the reference asset, the issuer will pay the investor the face value less the recoverable amount from the reference asset. Thus, as a protection seller the investor absorbs the credit risk in the reference asset. This is shown in the diagram below.

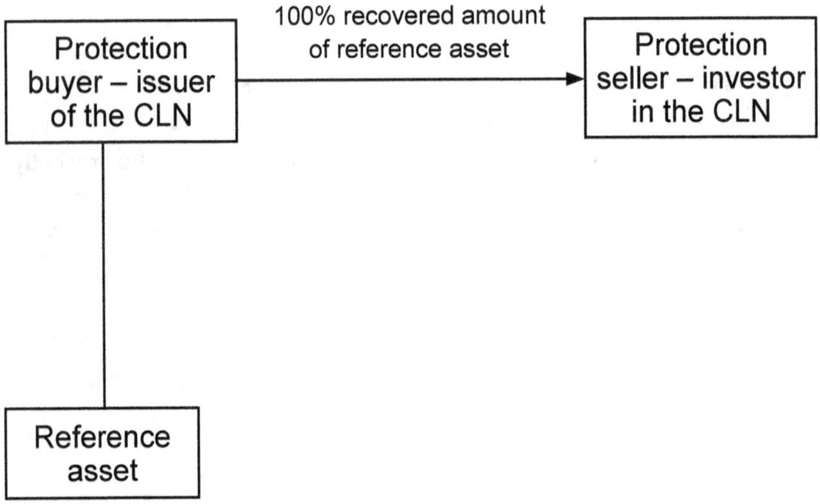

LOS. Define and discuss total return swaps (TRS) and their prospective cash flows
LOS. Discuss the risks of total return swaps

A **total return swap (TRS)** is a credit derivative contract in which protection buyers (owners of a reference asset) swap the returns and any appreciation in the value of the reference asset (e.g. capital gain) to the protection seller (total return receiver). In return, the total return receiver would make periodic floating payments (LIBOR-based) plus any depreciation in the value of the reference asset to the total return payer (protection buyer). The following diagram is a depiction of this structure.

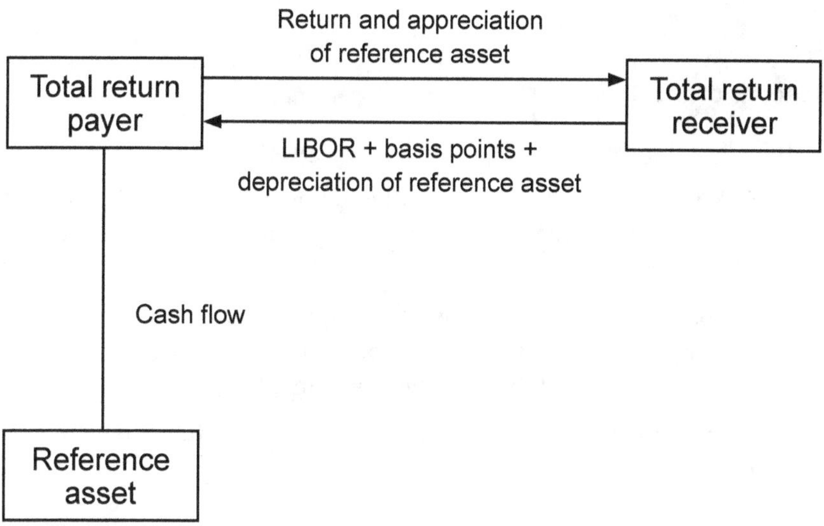

A TRS is typically structured with equity (or equity indexes) and bonds as reference assets. If the reference asset is equities, the TR payer will retain the voting rights.

Note the structure that parties – the TR receiver and payer – make payments for reduction and appreciation, respectively, of the reference asset. This means that the TRS not only caters for credit risk but also protects the total return payer from market risk.

Also note that this structure is not without risks. The TR payer is exposed to the risk of default of the total return receiver. This means he is still exposed to the reference asset and the loss of the periodic returns extended to the receiver. Another risk is that both the reference asset and TR receiver default in the same period.

If the TRS contract includes specification of any credit event, and a credit event takes place prior to the maturity of the TRS contract, the TRS typically terminates. If it terminates, the TR payer (protection buyer):

1. Receives payment from the TR receiver (protection seller); the amount will equal the notional amount of the reference asset minus the recoverable amount, or
2. Delivers the reference asset to the protection seller in exchange for the notional amount.

Choosing either one of the above mechanisms depends on the agreement in the TRS contract.

Benefits of the TRS

1. It hedges the credit risk exposure in the protection buyer's books.
2. It gives the protection seller a synthetic position in the reference asset in which he enjoys the cash flows and appreciation of its value without legally owning it.
3. It can be used as an alternative to a repurchase agreement with one difference in that the total receiver does not have to the buy the security back, as is the case in the repurchase agreement.
4. It helps financial institutions take some assets off their balance sheet, particularly those with a high funding cost.

LOS. Discuss the potential balance-sheet implications of different total return swap structures
LOS. Discuss the use of total return swaps as a funding vehicle

A TRS is used to help financial institutions get some assets off their balance sheet if these assets are funded at a high cost. A financial institution might have the intention of keeping certain assets on its balance sheet to enjoy the economic benefits from it. Due to the high cost of funding these assets and with the help of TRS, this financial institution could sell the assets to another institution (an investor) and enter into a TRS according to which the return on this asset is exchanged for periodic floating payments.

LOS. Define a credit option call and put

Similar to the concept of options discussed in Chapter 6, a **credit option** is a contract in which the underlying asset is the credit risk that is to be transferred from the option buyer to the option seller.

So, a credit put option grants the buyer the right to sell the *reference asset* to the seller at the strike price. A credit call option gives the buyer of the option the right to buy the reference asset from the seller at the strike price.

LOS. Define and discuss collateralized debt obligation (CDO), collateralized bond obligation (CBO) and collateralized loan obligation (CLO) and their prospective cash flows
LOS. Define senior note, subordinated note, mezzanine note and equity note, and how cash flows to each

A **collateralized debt obligation (CDO)** is an investment vehicle where the performance depends on the cash flows from debt securities. A CDO comes in two types:

1. Collateralized bond obligation (CBO).
2. Collateralized loan obligation (CLO).

A CLO is an investment vehicle in which the cash flows paid to investors flow from investment-grade loans. A CBO, on the other hand, is an investment vehicle in which the cash flows to investors flow from non-investment grade bond issues.

The steps for structuring CDOs are as follows:

1. Sponsoring firm appoints collateral manager.
2. Special purpose vehicle (SPV) is established.
3. SPV buys the collateral (commercial loans or bonds issues). The collateral is bought from proceeds collected from investors. Investors are classified into the following tranches, which are called *cash flow waterfalls*:
    - **Senior tranche investors**: Invest in senior notes, which are an investment-grade rated instrument. These investors get paid first in case there is a shortfall in the performance of the collateral. If there is a residual left after these investors have been paid, it is passed to the subordinated note investors tranche.

- **Subordinated note**: Investors in subordinated notes rank after the senior note in case of cash flows from the underlying asset and at times of liquidation. In terms of risk, subordinated notes are riskier than the senior notes because they are paid after the senior notes investors. The rating of the subordinated notes varies based on the level of collateralization.
- **Mezzanine investors**: As the name indicates, mezzanine is in between debt and equity. So, a mezzanine note is a hybrid instrument which has features of debt and equity. A mezzanine note is a subordinated note to other notes in senior tranches of the CDO structure. This entails getting paid after these senior tranches and in times of liquidity they also have lower priority to the underlying assets. Due to this risk, mezzanine investors require a higher rate of return than the senior tranche investors.
- **Equity investors**: Invest in equity notes, which is typically a not-rated tranche. Investors in this tranche get paid last. Due to this comparatively higher risk, investors in this tranche are compensated with a higher yield.

LOS. Discuss synthetic CDOs and their prospective cash flows
LOS. Define reference portfolio
LOS. Describe unfunded, partially funded, fully funded and fully unfunded synthetic CDOs
LOS. Define first-loss piece

In the cash CDO structure, the obligations are backed by real assets such as loans or bonds. The loans or bonds underlying the CDO are taken off the originator's balance sheet to a special purpose entity because the economic benefits from them as assets do not belong to the originator. A **synthetic CDO is not backed by real assets but by cash flows from a credit derivative instrument issued on them, such as a credit default swap.** In the synthetic CDO, the originator does not remove the assets from the balance sheet; this structure is designed to exploit a profit opportunity from interest differentials between the loans and bonds underlying the structure and the issued notes. Cash flow under the balance sheet CDO refers to the ability of the high-quality collateral in the structure to produce cash flows in excess of the principals and interest channeled to the investors in various tranches as well as covering all the administration and service expenses.

The diagram below shows the structure of a CDO.

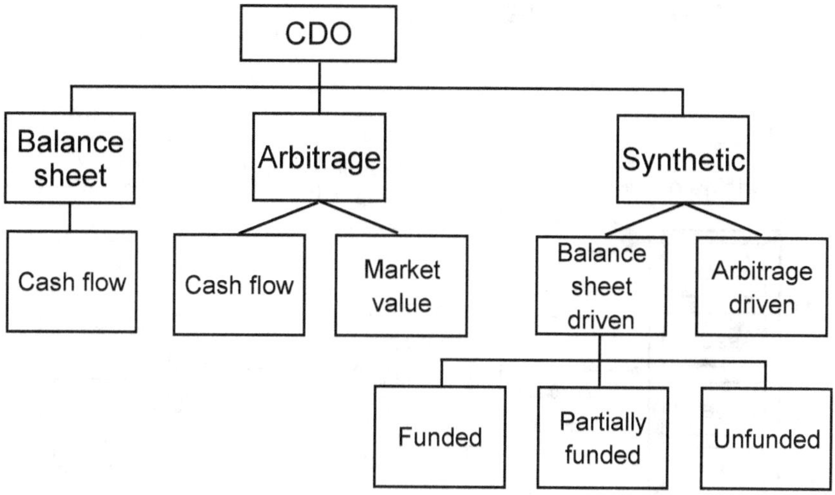

- **Funded synthetic CDO**: In this structure the investors pay upfront the proceeds of the notes issued for them to the SPV. The SPV channels these proceeds to invest them in high quality assets. Notes issued in this structure cover **all** the credit risk in the reference portfolio, i.e. a funded synthetic CDO transfers all the credit risk in the reference portfolio to investors.
- **Unfunded synthetic CDO**: As the name implies, unfunded means the investors do not make upfront payments of the proceeds, but receive periodic payments in exchange for payments if the reference portfolio allocated to their tranches defaults.
- **Partially funded synthetic CDO**: Similar to the funded synthetic CDO in which there is upfront payments from the investors, but these would cover only the highest credit risk in the reference portfolio and the originator would bear the rest of the **uncovered** credit risk.
- **Fully unfunded synthetic CDO**: A structure that has only a credit derivative contract, typically it is a credit default swap. Investors do not make upfront payments and there is no asset-backed part in the structure.

The following diagram illustrates the cash flows in the synthetic CDO. In this structure the asset packages comprising loans or bonds are the **reference portfolio** used in the CDS contract. These are the assets upon which the criteria of loss events are assessed to trigger payments from the SPV to the originator in case of default.

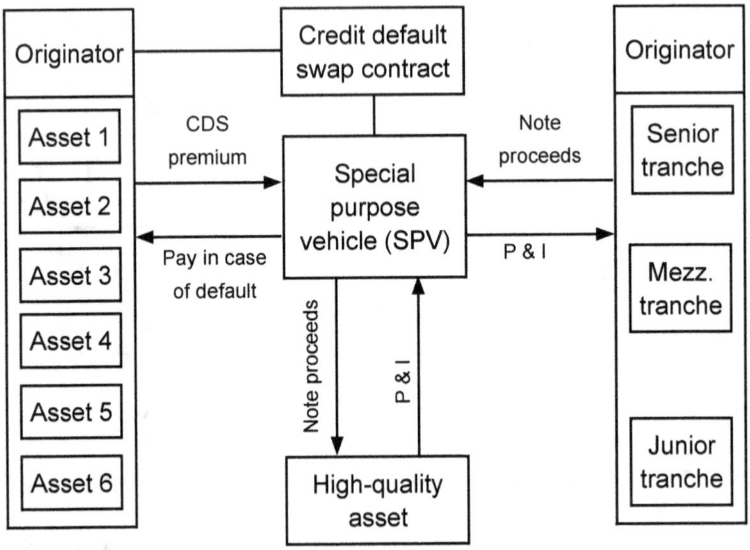

A junior tranche in the synthetic CDO structure is referred to as the junior or **first-loss piece** because it is the last tranche that gets paid from the cash flows generated from the collateral assets after the senior and mezzanine tranches have been paid. The first-loss piece is called this because it is typically retained by the originator and the originator will pay the value of this note plus/minus the residual of the cash flows produced by the collateral.

LOS. Discuss some general applications of credit derivatives
LOS. Discuss some uses, advantages and limitations of synthetic CDOs

Uses and applications of credit derivatives are categorized into two types:

1. Uses and applications for the protection buyer:
   - Managing credit risk without jeopardizing the relationship with the client. Through credit derivatives, the protection buyer, if a bank for instance, can hedge the credit risk that might seem imminent without indirectly informing the client that the loan would be sold due to high risk; bank clients consider the sale of a loan before it is actually in default as a signal of no trust.
   - Reduction of capital requirement: Under Basel 2 and 3,[5] non-rated corporations attract a 100% risk weight and unrated banks attract a 50% risk weight. If corporate loans are sold to a bank, the capital charge will be reduced from 8% to 1.6%.
2. Uses and applications for the protection seller:
   - Access to different markets: As discussed earlier, a TRS involves receiving returns on a reference asset. In some circumstances, institutional investors might face difficulties in accessing investments in some markets or countries. TRS allows this access by investing in a structure that uses foreign investments as a reference asset in the TRS deal.
   - Leverage and measures to improve profitability: TRS allows investors to benefit from the returns on the reference assets without actually holding this investment on balance sheet (credit derivatives are off-balance sheet). This improves the profitability measures and reduces the capital requirements, cost of capital and leverage of the position.

Synthetic CDOs are used to relieve the sponsor from regulatory capital requirements because reference assets in the structure attract a low risk-weight. The sponsor can achieve that while keeping the assets on its balance sheet. They are used by firms which are more cautious about transferring the credit risk than funding the assets. By not removing the assets from

---

5 Basel 2 and 3 are recommendations issued by the Basel Committee of Banking Supervision (BCBS) at the Bank of International Settlement (BIS) in Basel, Switzerland. These recommendations are collectively called Basel accords. They are designed as international standards for bank capital regulation and supervision.

the balance sheet, a synthetic CDO is an effective insturement of hedging credit risk while maintaining the relationship between the sponsor and its clients, particularly if the sponsor is a bank. Sponsors are attracted to synthetic CDOs because of ease of adminstration, issuance and lower legal costs compared to cash CDOs.

Besides their useful applications, synthetic CDOs do suffer from some limitations. Synthetic CDOs are intricate structures issued by complex financial institutions. Investors might not be fully congnizant of all the underlying risks and concepts in this structure so they rely heavily on the rating agencies in this respect. The crisis that began in 2007 revealed that even rating agencies face difficulties in sufficiently understanding the intricacies of these instruments and assessing their risks. So, investors are exposed to a risk of information asymmetry. Due to their intricacies and specific tailoring to the investor and sponsor, synthetic CDOs are not liquid instruments that can be foreclosed easily in the market.

LOS. Discuss some possible unintended risks of credit derivatives

The most important risk of credit derivatives is the dispute on the definition of credit events and the realization of the factors that constitute an event that triggers payments from the protection seller and buyer.

Another risk is counterparty risk: a protection buyer might be exposed to counterparty risk with an aggressive protection seller. In times of crisis or market slowdown, the excessive or frequent occurrence of loss events might jeopardize the protection seller's ability to honor the payments needed during the event.

LOS. Define tranche, tranching and credit enhancement
LOS. List various credit enhancements

Tranche is a French word which means slice. In the credit derivatives context, **tranching** means issuing securities with different tranches. Each tranche represents a financial instrument with its own risk profile and return structure, but with the same issuer and within the same issue. A financial instrument is structured into tranches to customize the risk and reward of the issue to various investors.

Investors in structured securities, such as a CDO, are exposed to the credit of the issuer. **Credit enhancement** is a method issuers of financial instruments or structured securities, such as CDOs, apply to enhance the credit risk of the issue. The following are examples of these methods:

1. **Overcollateralization**: Issuing of securities with a nominal value that is considerably lower than the nominal values of the bonds or loans used as collateral for the structure.
2. **Cash reserve**: Part of the proceeds collected from the investors in various tranches are maintained with a dedicated reserve account which contains high-quality financial securities.
3. **Excess spread**: If the cash inflows collected from the collaterals of the CDOs exceed the cash outflows that have to be paid to the investors in the tranches, this excess is kept by the SPV to cater for any future cash flow shortages.
4. **Insurance wraps**: Cash flows to the CDO investors are guaranteed by an insurance company. This protects these investors from a lack of performance that could result from non-payment from the collaterals of the CDO structure. Only investors in the senior tranche enjoy such a guarantee.

Chapter 10. Stock Market

Upon completion of this chapter you will have learnt:

1. The fundamentals of financial markets.
2. Types of stocks.
3. Terminology and mechanics of trading stocks.
4. Stock valuation.

10.1 Fundamentals of financial markets

> **LOS.** Compare and contrast financial exchanges and OTC markets
> **LOS.** Describe the role of exchanges
> **LOS.** Describe the role of the OTC market

An **over the counter (OTC)** market is an unorganized market in which the buyer and seller deal with each other directly, without intermediaries such as banks, dealers or brokers. The buyer and the seller bear the credit risk for each other. Since it is merely a direct dealing between the seller and the buyer and there is no standardized type of contract, product or characteristics of the contracts between the buyer and the seller, there is typically and theoretically no limit on the types of contracts or the underlying assets of these contracts in the OTC. That is to say, the buyer and seller can have a financial contract on any asset for any size of transaction, any volume, any amount and for any maturity.

The equity **exchange and OTC markets** perform the following main functions:

1. **Benchmarking of economic performance**: The index movements reflect the trust, liquidity and credit appetite of the market players in the economy.
2. **Raising capital**: The exchange is a platform through which companies can raise new capital or trade shares already issued.
3. **Matching orders**: The exchange matches the orders to buy and sell from buyer and sellers.
4. **Price discovery**: The exchange gives all market participants a chance to quote their bid/ask prices as best fits their profile.

LOS. Define inter-dealer market and inter-dealer broker

1. **Inter-dealer market**: The OTC market is only accessible for financial institutions. Interactions take place not in a physical location, but through systems or platforms.
2. **Inter-dealer broker**: In the OTC market there are no clearing houses or exchange houses monitoring and regulating the financial transactions. There is, however, a facilitator that facilitates transactions amongst the dealers and brokers, which are themselves financial institutions (brokerage houses, banks, etc.). An inter-dealer broker is only allowed to facilitate transactions amongst financial institutions, not with individual investors.

LOS. Discuss the importance of market liquidity

Liquidity is defined as the market participants' ability to trade in volume and search for the prices of a particular security with ease. The larger the orders in the trading book on the exchange (buy or sell), the higher the security's liquidity, and vice versa.

Liquidity of a security in the market place is impacted by the following drivers:

1. **Funding**: Players typically prefer to place transactions that do not require initial margin or upfront payment (funding). The higher the funding, the more market players shift their liquidity toward transactions that do not

require funding, such as interest rate swaps and other OTC derivative contracts.

2. **Credit risk:** The higher the credit risk market players associate with the issuers of a security, the less liquid is this security. An indicator of the players' assessment of this risk is the size of the spread required on top of the risk-free rate in order to invest in the security.

LOS. Describe a repo and a reverse repo and their roles as sources of liquidity

A **repo** is a short-term contract in which one counterparty sells an asset and buys it later on at a higher price. A **reverse repo**, on the other hand, is taking the opposite position to the repo contract: buying the asset and selling later at a higher price.

The purpose of the repo or reverse repo as defined here is as a source of financing for the parties involved. A party might not be able to seek financing through bank loans, for instance, so he can pledge an asset with a seller and receive the amount required so that afterwards he repurchases again at a higher price. It is repurchased at higher price because this extra amount is the profit enjoyed by the seller. A repo, and a reverse repo, is considered a source of liquidity in the marketplace because:

1. It is a tool through which the central bank implements the lender of last resort operations.
2. It facilitates short selling, with lower costs.
3. It is a viable source of funding other than traditional credit facilities from banks, such as loans.

LOS. Describe an electronic communication network (ECN)

An **electronic communication network (ECN)** is a trading platform somewhere between a formal exchange market and an OTC market (i.e. it is not a formal exchange, nor an OTC). In this platform, brokerage houses connect to match and cross their orders without the need to go through intermediaries such as the exchange. Examples of ECNs are *Island* and *Archipelago*.

10.2 Types of stocks

LOS. Compare and contrast ordinary and preference shares

There are two different types of shares: ordinary shares and preferred shares. The terms ordinary shares and common shares are used interchangeably. **Ordinary shares** represent ownership in a firm with a voting right and claim on the profit in the form of dividends. Ordinary shareholders are entitled to dividends only in an accounting year in which the firm distributes dividends. Dividend distribution is a decision made by the board of directors, which represents the shareholders, and is based on the percentage of shares owned.

Preference or **preferred shares** are ordinary shares with some additional characteristics:

1. **Seniority**: Preferred shares are senior to ordinary shares in times of dividends and liquidation, but they come after debtholders. Superiority in dividends comes into play with cumulative or non-cumulative dividends. In the case of cumulative dividends, in the years an organization pays dividends it would pay to the preferred shareholders all the dividends that were not paid in the past years, if there were any dividends not paid already for any reasons. For this reason, preferred stocks are treated in the financial analysis as debt-like instruments, because they create a financial burden on the organization.
2. **Voting rights**: Preferred shareholders do not have the right to vote in the general assembly meetings.
3. **Duration**: While the life of the ordinary shares are for the life of the firm, if the ordinary shareholder decides to keep the share and not to trade on it, the life of the preferred shares depends on the firm's policy. A firm issuing preferred shares might have a limited life for the preferred share before it is redeemed at a pre-agreed price.

LOS. Describe the common characteristics of a stock

A stock:

1. Represents ownership in the issuing organization.
2. Represents claims of the holder on the issuing company's earnings and assets.

3. Represents, in the balance sheet, the capital paid to run the organization.
4. Gives its holder the right to vote for the board of directors, the organization's policies and management issues, where applicable.
5. Can be traded and its ownership transferred to any other buyer.
6. Gives its holder annual income from the positive earnings of the issuing company in the form of dividends.
7. Does not expire – if held by the owner it stays valid as long as the organization is in business.

LOS. Discuss shareholder rights

There are two main rights discussed in the PRMIA outline, as follows:

1. **Voting rights**: Shareholders have the right to vote for a nominated board of directors in the annual general meeting (aka general assembly meeting). The board of directors would then nominate the executive management to run the organization. The voting right is proportionate to the number of shares (i.e. percentage of ownership of the total shares issued by the organization).
2. **Dividends**: As holders of claims on the organization's earnings and assets, shareholders have a right to receive periodic portions of the earnings, proportionate to their respective ownership.

10.3 Terminology and Mechanics of Trading Stocks

LOS. Define market capitalization

The **market capitalization** of a company whose shares are listed on the exchange market is the amount equal to a multiplication of the total number of shares issued by the market share price.

$$\text{market capitalization} = \text{number of issued shares} \times \text{market share price}$$

LOS. Discuss stock indices

A **stock index** is a composite of the values of all companies listed on the index. It is created and used as a benchmark for specific and overall market performance. The composite is typically price-weighted or market capitalization-weighted.

In a price-weighted index, the value of the index is calculated as a simple average of the prices of the listed companies. Dow Jones and Nikkei 225 are examples of this index. A major disadvantage of this index is that since it is only based on price of the shares, it can easily be manipulated by traders in order to benefit from fluctuations in the index value. For example, by using derivative instruments that have an index as an underlying asset.

A market capitalization index, on the other hand, is created as an average of the market capitalizations of each listed company. This makes the index difficult to manipulate because the traders would have to buy many shares of a specific company in order to alter the value of the whole index in their favor. NASDAQ and FTSE 100 are example of market-cap indices.

LOS. Discuss the types of stock market participants

Participants in the stock markets are: issuers, investors and intermediaries.

1. **Issuers** are companies which wish to offer their shares to the public through a process called an initial public offering (IPO). The initial offering of the shares takes place in a primary market (a market in which securities are offered for the first time). Subsequently, the company's

shares get listed on the exchange after satisfying all the regulatory requirements. Issues of stocks are then bought by investors.

2. **Investors** are those individuals or institutions which buy the issued stocks in the primary market and/or trade on these stocks in the secondary market (a market in which securities are traded after their initial offering).
3. **Intermediaries** help the issuers get the stocks offered to the investors. Intermediaries are typically investment banks, dealers or brokerage houses, which operate either on their own behalf (proprietary trading), for their clients (wealth management), or as an intermediary underwriter for the stocks offered by companies.

LOS. Define listing and float

Listing and **floating** both refer to the issuance of a company's shares to the public for the first time as new capital. This process requires a lot of legal and compliance work as an issuing company would need to adhere to the listing requirements of the stock exchange as well as the regulatory bodies supervising the exchange. Issuing companies typically hire an investment bank to help them in the float process.

LOS. Compare and contrast matched market and market maker

A **market maker** is a market participant that holds financial instruments in inventory (virtually) and is able to quote the buy and/or sell prices of the instruments. He/she benefits from the spread between the buy and sell price. By having instruments in inventory, the market maker creates liquidity in the market and facilitates buy and sell orders.

The **matched market**, on the other hand, is the process of quoting either a buy or sell price into the trading system that will systemically be matched with a sell or buy order from another participant to execute the deal.

LOS. Define T+1 and T+3 settlement

There is a lapse of time between the trading day (the day the orders to buy or sell are crossed and matched between the buyers and sellers) and settlement day (the day of finalizing the administration and financial procedures to transfer the ownership of the traded instrument).

T = trade day. **T+1** denotes one day's delay between the trading day and settlement day and **T+3** means three days' delay between the trade and settlement day.

LOS. Define private placement and seasoned new issue
LOS. Describe the process of a private placement

Private placement is the issuing of shares of a company to selected investors, but not to the public. Private placement, since dealing with a limited number of investors, does not require the same level of legal and administration work as is the case with an IPO. So, from the issuer's perspective, private placement is cheaper than an IPO. The issuer might face difficulties placing a large issue to a small number of select investors due to their risk profile and appetite. From the investors' perspective, they might deem private placement to be riskier than an IPO because of liquidity risk. In the private placement an investor would face difficulty, due to a limited number of holders, in finding a buyer for his holdings. Advantages of private placement are that it has a lower cost than an IPO and the issuing company does not have to make extensive disclosure about the company, so there are less complex legal procedures compared to an IPO. A **seasoned new issue** is a listed company issuing more of its shares to the public.

The private placement offering process has the following steps:

1. The issuer should determine if the offering will be made directly to the investors or through a specialized firm such as a registered broker or dealer.
2. A due diligence study is made. Investors in the private placement need to see the minute detail of the company, its history, current performance and forecast results, as well as its governance structure, sources of funds, market share, etc.
3. The issuer should select the desired types of investors to be sought for the placement. Criteria of selection depends on the size of the investors, industry orientation and the stage on the industry life cycle.
4. The offering document is assembled. This document is also called the private placement memorandum. It encompasses the executive summary of the offer and due diligence.

5. Investment solicitation: at this stage the issuers approach the targeted investors in an individualized process to solicit their investment into the offer.
6. The legal administration matters are finalized with the interested investors.

LOS. Define the bid-offer spread

Bid is the price quoted among market participants to buy an asset; ask is the price quoted by market participants to sell an asset. The difference between the bid and ask is the **bid-offer spread.**

LOS. Discuss margin trading

Some investors trade using borrowed money, either due to a lack of sufficient funds or for arbitrage. When an investor takes a loan from his dealer/broker to buy a certain instrument, he is **margin trading**. Interest and a fee would be paid to the dealer/broker for the borrowed amount and the instrument would remain the custody of the dealer/broker as collateral.

Once the loan is agreed, the investor has to deposit an amount as a percentage of the position with the dealer/broker, called initial margin. As the position value changes every trading day, the margin amount will change. If the margin amount decreases below a certain level – the *maintenance margin* – the investor would be required to top up his account with the dealer/broker.

Example 10.1: Margin trading

Assume an investor wishes to buy what is equal to $20,000 in stocks with borrowed money from his broker. The broker states that 50% as initial margin must be deposited by the investor in the account with the broker.

initial margin = 50% × $20,000 = $10,000

So the investor pays $10,000 of his own money into the investment and the broker lends him the remaining $10,000.

After striking the agreement, the value of the position will fluctuate; if it decreases the investor would suffer a drop in his own equity account as the position is marked to market on a daily basis. Assume the next day the equity position has dropped in value to $16,000. In this case the value of the investor's equity is only $6,000 and the size of the percentage is:

$$\frac{\text{investor equity}}{\text{value of the position}} = \frac{6{,}000}{160{,}000} = 37.5\%$$

The more the equity position drops, the more the margin percentage will drop until it reaches a level at which the broker will ask the investor to pay extra money in addition to that which he initially added to the account (i.e. $10,000). Say, for instance, the broker requires that an investor injects money into his account if the margin reaches 10%. The 10% is called the maintenance margin.

LOS. Discuss short-selling and borrowing stocks

If the investor observes that a financial instrument is relatively highly priced and he expects the price to drop in the future, this is considered an opportunity to benefit from selling this instrument now at a higher price and buying it later on when the price has fallen.

If he does not already own the instrument now he can still benefit from this through a short sale. **Short selling** is an act of selling an asset that one does not own, by borrowing it, at a higher price and buying it back later at a lower price, returning the borrowed asset to the broker/dealer and pocketing the difference after paying the interest and administration expenses of the transaction.

The process of short selling does not, however, always go as smoothly as in this simplified example. The expectation of a decrease in prices might not be accurate, and in this situation the investor would have to go to the market to buy the borrowed instrument at a higher price to pay it back to the investor and thus would incur a loss.

Due to its riskiness, some countries put restrictions on short selling. For instance, in the US there is a rule of uptick, which means that short selling is only allowed on instruments whose price has shown positive movement in the last trading day.

Market participants borrow and lend stocks to each other at an interest rate. They lend and borrow stocks in numbers, not values. Similar to cash loans, interest rates, administration and arrangement fees apply and these are handled by the broker/dealer.

LOS. Define dividend and ex-dividend trading

Dividends are a share of earnings generated during the accounting year and distributed to shareholders by a resolution of the organization's board of directors. Dividends are distributed if the organization has generated a positive income. The size and frequency of dividends varies amongst firms. Some have a fixed dividends policy, while for some it varies based on annual earnings. For some firms, such as financial institutions, dividend distribution is subject to regulatory approval or notification.

The procedures for dividend payments are as follows:

1. **Declaration date**: The date the board of directors approves and announces the dividend distribution.
2. **Ex-dividend date**: Once the dividends are announced, a record of the shareholders entitled to receive the dividends payments is prepared. The date on which this record is prepared is called the holder-of-record date. The record does not, by practice, include all shareholders who bought the shares within two business days prior to holder-of-record date. Thus, there is a cut-off date for investors to be entitled to receive the dividends payments. This cut-off date is called the ex-dividend date. Buying and selling of the company shares on the ex-dividend date is called ex-dividend trading.
3. **Payment date**: Cash disbursement is made to the eligible shareholders on this date.

10.4 Stock Valuation

LOS. Define the dividend discount and Gordon growth model of stock valuation

A basic idea in finance is that one way to find the value of any asset is to find the present values of all the cash flows that are generated from this asset. By this basic idea we value a share as the present value of the cash flows that are expected to be generated from it, namely dividends and its estimated sale price (*Pn*). This method of calculating the value of the share is called the **dividend discount model (DDM).**

$$\text{share present value} = \frac{D1}{(1+i)} + \frac{D2}{(1+i)^2} + \frac{D3}{(1+i)^3} + \cdots \frac{Dn+Pn}{(1+i)}$$

If the dividends are assumed to be constant or to grow at a constant rate, we can find the price of the share using the **Gordon growth model (GGM)** as follows:

$$\text{share present value} = \frac{D}{r-g}$$

Where:

r = required rate of return

D = expected dividends to be paid in the next period

g = growth rate of the dividends

Chapter 11. Money Markets

Upon completion of this chapter you will have learnt about:

1. Definitions and terminology of money markets.
2. Types of deposits.
3. Money market instruments.

11.1 Definitions and Terminology of Money Markets

LOS. Define add-on interest

Add-on interest is the interest banks pay on Eurocurrency deposits. The interest is not paid periodically but added to the deposits once – at maturity. Hence the name.

LOS. Define LIBOR

LIBOR is an acronym of London Interbank Offered Rate. On a daily basis, the British Bankers' Association (BBA) gathers interest rates quoted by banks among themselves for accepting deposits or giving loans to each other in dollars and then create an average called LIBOR. The BBA solicits the quotes from about eight to ten banks who are active in the Eurocurrency market.

LOS. Define term, principal, interest rate, secured and unsecured

1. **Term**: Life of the contract between the borrower and the lender until the borrower returns the whole principal amount borrowed. Put differently, it is the number of months/years until the borrower pays all its debt to the lender. This is also known as the *maturity*.
2. **Principal**: The amount of money borrowed from the lender by the borrower. This is also known as *face value*, *future value*, *par value* or *redemption value*.
3. **Interest rate**: The price that the borrower needs to pay to the lender for providing the loan and waiting to get it back during the term. It is typically quoted as an annual percentage applied to the principal amount of the loan. Interest payments could be paid monthly (in the case of consumer or mortgage loans), quarterly (e.g. FRAs) or semi-annually (e.g. bonds).
4. **Secured loans/debt**: A debt or loan is secured if it is collateralized by an asset or guaranteed by an entity. In the case of the borrower's default, the lender has a claim on the collateral, either to liquidate it to receive his money back or claim ownership on it. A loan that is collateralized or guaranteed is said to be secured (e.g. it gives security to the lender that the loan amount is not lost).
5. **Unsecured loans/debt**: A debt or loan that is not secured by collateral or guarantee.

LOS. Define a reference rate

A **reference rate** is a benchmark against which the minimum or maximum level of a floating rate on a financial instrument is set. Famous reference rates are the prime rate, LIBOR and the US 90-day Treasury bill rate. Interest based on a floating rate loan can be quoted as: LIBOR + 50bps, or Prime Rate + 1%, etc.

LOS. Describe a credit facility

Borrowing from banks, in terms of size, frequency and types of products, differs amongst borrowers. An individual borrower will not need a credit line like a corporation and does not need a size of loan as big as a corporation may need.

Corporations need to borrow funds in different forms, for example as a line of credit (LC), letter of guarantee (LG), overdraft, or plain vanilla loan, etc. These forms of borrowing are called **credit facilities** and are offered to corporates by the bank. Banks design these credit facilities for their clients based on the history of the relationship, credit worthiness, the client's line of business, the collateral structure provided by the client, etc. In this customized design, and in light of the above factors, the bank determines the size of its commission, fees and interest rate on these credit facilities.

LOS. Define basis point

A **basis point** is a unit of change used in the financial markets to denote a change in interest rate, currencies and equity indexes. It is 1/100th of 1%.

11.2 Types of Deposits

LOS. Describe the types of deposits (demand, notice and fixed-term)

1. **Notice deposits:** A savings account in which the depositor can only withdraw his/her deposits after giving prior notice, hence the name. Interest paid on these deposits is very low.
2. **Demand deposits:** An account in which the bank does not pay interest and the depositors do not have to give any prior notice to the bank before withdrawing, i.e. deposits can be withdrawn at any time.
3. **Fixed-term deposit:** Also known as *term deposits* or *time deposits*. In this account, deposits are kept with the bank for a fixed, predetermined contractual period. Interest is paid on these deposits as fixed or floating.

LOS. Describe the Eurocurrency market, particularly the Eurodollar market

Banks accept deposits or extend credit facilities to customers in currencies other than the bank's local functional currency. These types of transactions are called the *Eurocurrency market*. For example, an American bank can give a loan in Mexican pesos to a client in the US. The Eurodollar is a market in which the loans and deposits are made and accepted in dollars by banks operating outside the US. Eurodollar is considered the dominant type of Eurocurrency market for loans and deposits. Deposits in this market are typically term or time deposits.

LOS. Describe the characteristics of fixed-income instruments

In the financial market and in terms of funding, there are two types of market players: those who have a shortage of funds (borrowers) and those who have a surplus of funds (lenders).

Lenders provide funds to borrowers for a certain period of time, called maturity. In return, the borrower pays back the borrowed funds plus interest. This interest is considered the price of the lender's money. Lenders and borrowers could be banks (through loans), corporations, governments and individual investors (through investing in a bond issue, for instance). The interest on the borrowed funds is either paid periodically through the life of the contract, paid in full on maturity, or paid at the inception date.

This interest is also called income. This is typified in bond markets or contracts. Income/interest comes either in the form of fixed payments (this is why bonds are also called **fixed-income**) throughout the life of the contract or floating payments. A bond with floating coupon payments is called a floating rate note (FRN). An FRN is also part of the fixed-income market because typically an FRN includes a fixed margin on top of floating index rate, such as in the following form: 20bp + LIBOR. It is possible to have fixed-income instruments with neither fixed nor floating period coupon payments, as in the case of zero-coupon bonds.

Prices of fixed-income instruments move conversely with the market interest rate, i.e. the price increases as the interest rate decreases. In regard to maturity of these instruments, there are three categories:

1. Short-term fixed-income instruments with maturity of less than five years.
2. Medium-term notes with maturity between five and ten years.
3. Long-term bonds with more than ten years to maturity.

Bond contracts might be embedded with options or be option-free (also called a plain vanilla bond contract). Options in the bond market give bondholders the right, for instance, to put (sell) the bond, call (buy) the bond, or convert the bond to common shares. In terms of risk to the holders of fixed-income instruments, they are ahead of shareholders in times of liquidation.

11.3 Money Market Instruments

In this section I will discuss the following instruments:

1. Commercial paper.
2. Promissory notes.
3. Banker's acceptance.
4. Certificates of deposit.
5. Repurchase agreement.

LOS. Describe different types of money market securities
LOS. Define commercial paper and promissory notes

Money market securities are traded with a maturity of one year or less. We can classify money market securities based on the types of interest rate paid on them (discount or coupon type), or whether they are negotiated between the lender and borrower.

There are two categories of money market securities in terms of types of interest rate: interest-bearing securities, and securities issued at discount. Examples of interest-bearing securities are reps and certificates of deposit. Examples of discounted securities are commercial paper, Treasury bills and banker's acceptance.

If big corporations need funds, one alternative is to borrow from a bank or banks. Another alternative is to issue **commercial paper (CP)** and collect proceeds from investors. The maturity of the CP is typically not more than 270 days. It is issued at discount (no periodic interest or coupon will be paid by the corporations to the investors). Investors in the CP are not given any collateral or guarantee for their investment, i.e. they are exposed to credit risk, even if CP is normally issued by big-name corporations. Due to the credit risk, which is higher than for other money market instruments, CP is traded at a higher spread than T-bills.

There are four types of commercial paper: drafts, checks, certificates of deposit and promissory notes. All of these types are issued without financial backing of the issuer.

Banker's acceptance (BA) is a short-term debt instrument transacted for commercial purposes (import and export). It is issued by a company advised by another company and its performance is guaranteed by a commercial bank. Similar to Treasury bills and Eurodollars, BA is quoted and traded at a discount.

LOS. Calculate the bond-equivalent yield of a T-bill

Investors typically compare securities in order to determine the best viable alternatives in light of constraints, time horizon and investment objectives. When securities have different structures it is difficult to compare between them. For example, it is difficult to compare interest-bearing securities with zero-interest (discounted) securities.

If we want to compare T-bills with any interest-bearing securities, we use the bond-equivalent yield, calculated as follows:

$$\text{bond equivalent yield} = \frac{FV - P}{P} \times \frac{365}{N}$$

Where:

FV = redemption value

P = price of Treasury bills

N = number of days to maturity

Chapter 12. Foreign Exchange (FX) Market

Upon completion of this chapter you will have learnt:

1. Definitions and terminology of the foreign exchange market.
2. Theories of foreign exchange rate determination.
3. Exchange rate calculation.

12.1. Definitions and Terminology of the Foreign Exchange Market

LOS. Define an exchange rate

An **exchange rate** is the price in one currency paid to get the other currency. For example, an exchange rate of USD/EUR 1.5 is the price to be paid in USD (1.5) to get one unit of EUR.

LOS. Describe the interbank market
LOS. Define decentralized, continuous, open bid and double-auction

As the name suggests, the interbank FX market is the buying and selling of currencies in large volume amongst financial institutions. It is a virtual over-the-counter market in which the counterparties transact by telephone and through banking systems. Thus, it is a 24-hour market. The FX interbank market has no clearing house or regulator. Controls and governance on this market take place, however, based on guidance and the minimum requirements of the financial institutions through central banks or prudential authorities. This is why the FX interbank market is called a **decentralized** and **continuous** market. The FX market is self-regulated as there is no regulator between the seller and the buyer.

- **Open bid**: A counterparty in the FX market which quotes the bid/ask spread on request. It does not need to specify the amount that is desired to be exchanged for another currency.
- **Double auction**: A counterparty in the FX market which offers the bid/ask quote (in this case being the market maker) also calls another counterparty to receive a bid/ask quote on the same currency (in this case being a market taker). The position of being both market maker and taker is called *double auction*.

LOS. Define direct and indirect quotations

A **direct quote** of an exchange rate is the number of your local currency that you need to pay for one unit of a foreign currency. If you are an American investor who would like to buy British pounds, USD/GBP 1.5 is called a direct quote for you as you have to pay 1.5 of your currency to get 1 unit (1 GBP) of foreign currency.

To the UK counterparty, this exact quote is an **indirect quote** as it indicates the amount of foreign currency that he would get for each unit of his domestic currency. To make the quote direct for the UK counterparty we would need to reciprocate the quote to be GBP/USD 0.667. To change from direct to indirect, or vice versa, we use the following equation:

$$\text{foreign} / \text{domestic} = \frac{1}{\frac{\text{domestic}}{\text{foreign}}}$$

Practitioners also use the terms **American quote** and **European quote**. An American quote is the price of a foreign currency in terms of dollars. For example, GBP/USD 1.5 is an American quote, which means you have to pay USD 1.5 to get GBP 1. A European quote is a reciprocal of the American quote, so USD/GBP 0.667.

So far we have been talking about one-way quotes, i.e. the price of one currency in relation to another. GBP/USD 1.5, for instance, is a one-way quote. Practitioners also use two-way quotes, which are quotes that include how much a dealer is willing to sell a currency for (the ask price), and the price she is willing to buy the currency for (the bid price).

So, a two-way quote is termed as follows: GBP/USD 1.5430-1.5435. In this quote, GBP is called the base currency. A dealer buys the base currency at the price written on the left (1.5430) and sells the base currency at the price on the right of the quote (1.5435). In summary the dealer is saying: I buy the GBP by paying 1.5430 but I sell it by receiving 1.5435. The 0.0005 (1.5435-1.5430) is my spread, or my profit.

LOS. Compare and contrast direct dealing, foreign exchange brokers and electronic systems

As in any financial transaction, a deal can either be through direct contact between the buyer and the seller (i.e. **direct dealing**) or through a broker. Dealing through a broker takes place via an electronic brokerage system. As we defined the FX interbank market as being virtual and decentralized, an FX deal can be transacted through **electronic systems** as well. Dealing through a **foreign exchange broker**/dealer involves payment of commissions as a percentage of the amount involved in the FX deal. Direct dealing is the most usual way of dealing by banks. Each bank sets limits of FX positions with the other banks in order to curb excessive exposure to market risk. Direct dealing might be preferred to broker dealing because it helps create open lines of business (i.e. easy access to borrow or lend, credit line, etc.) with banks.

LOS. Define the trading terms 'mine' and 'yours'

At the trading desk of a financial institution where there are dealers/brokers quoting the best bid/ask offer for one or multiple currencies, they would communicate amongst themselves using shortcut terms. When one broker shouts to another **mine**, he is informing the other broker that "I want to buy the currency," but if he shouted **yours** he is saying "I want to sell the currency to you."

LOS. Define the trading term big figure

The bid/ask is typically quoted as a four-digit decimal, such as 1.1234 - 1.1246. Brokers communicate among themselves by quoting the last two digits only of the bid/ask quote (34-46, in this example). In the documentation of the transactions the quote would be indicated as a four-digit decimal, which is called the **big figure** by practitioners.

12.2 Theories of Exchange Rate Determination

LOS. Define covered-interest arbitrage/interest rate parity

If an interest rate in country A is lower than the interest rate in country B, this would be reflected in the exchange rate between the two countries. The currency in country A would be weaker than the currency of country B. This is because the country with the high interest rate would attract more foreign investments that seek to enjoy this high level of interest rate than the country with the lower interest rate.

So, the country with lower interest rate would trade at a forward premium in relation to the country with the higher interest rate. This is called **interest rate parity**. If interest rate parity does not hold, an arbitrage opportunity occurs.

Example 12.1: Interest parity arbitrage

Assume the MXN/USD spot price is 0.0766. The interest rate in the US is 5% while the interest rate in Mexico is 4%. Also, assume that the 30-day forward rate for MXN/USD is 0.0763. Examine if covered interest parity holds and, if not, examine how can interest parity arbitrage be exploited.

Solution

The interest rate in Mexico is lower than that in the US. So, Mexican pesos *should trade at forward premium* in relation to the USD. Let us see if MXN is, according to the given information, trading at a premium in relation to the USD:

$$\frac{0.0763 - 0.0766}{0.0766} \times \frac{360}{30} = -4.6\%$$

So, MXN is trading at forward discount.

An arbitrage opportunity is possible by taking the following steps (assume using $1,000,000 as a notional amount for the arbitrage transaction):

a. Borrow MXN 1,000,000 at 4%.

b. Exchange the MXN 1,000,000 to USD = MXN 1,000,000 × 0.0766 = USD 76,600

c. Invest the USD 76,600 at 5% in the US for 30 days: 76,600(1+4%)1/12 = USD 76,850.77

d. After the 30 days, exchange the USD 76,850.77 to MXN: USD 76,850.77/0.0763 = MXN 1,007,218.

e. Pay the MXN 1,000,000 borrowed plus the interest: MXN 1,000,000 (1.04)1/12 = MXN 1,004,074.

f. Arbitrage profit = MXN 1,007,218 - MXN 1,004,074 = MXN 3,144.336

From Example 12.1 we then need to know how we can determine the forward exchange rate, according to covered interest parity, that eliminates the arbitrage opportunity. The following formula determines the zero-arbitrage forward exchange rate:

$$F_{x/y} = S_{x/y} \times \frac{1 + r_x \times \frac{n}{360}}{1 + r_y \times \frac{n}{360}}$$

$$F_{x/y} = 0.0766 \times \frac{1 + 4\% \times \frac{30}{360}}{1 + 5\% \times \frac{30}{360}}$$

Where:

$F_{x/y}$ = Forward currency exchange rate between country x and y

$S_{x/y}$ = spot currency exchange rate between country x and y

r_x= interest rate in country x

r_y = interest rate in country y

Thus, the forward exchange rate that produces zero-arbitrage in MXN/USD is 0.076536.

LOS. Describe some economic factors that might affect exchange rates

The value of a country's currency, i.e. its foreign exchange rate in relation to other currencies, depends on many factors. Market players assess these factors in historical and future terms. For instance, gross domestic product (GDP) is a crucial factor in determining the strength of an economy and subsequently the strength of the currency. Market players assess the GDP of past quarters as well as looking at the forecast future figures to assess growth and stability. I discuss below some of the economic factors that affect exchange rates.

1. **Gross domestic product (GDP)**: GDP measures the value of the goods and services produced by economic agents within a country. The impact of GDP on the foreign exchange price should be analyzed in a comparative sense, i.e. the performance of country A as measured by its GDP in relation to the GDP of country B. If the GDP of country A is higher than the GDP of country B that would make the currency of country A stronger than the currency of country B, holding other factors constant.
2. **Inflation rate**: Inflation decreases the purchasing power of a currency. So, if the inflation in country A is higher than the inflation in country (B), the currency of country A would be weaker because it takes a high amount of units of country A currency to get a unit of country B currency.
3. **Productivity**: Similar to the conclusion derived about the impact of GDP on the strength of a currency, increases in a country's productivity, supported by innovation, a skillful labor force and technology, contribute to a stable price level and increased demand on this country's goods and services. That would eventually make the currency of this country stronger in relation to other currencies.
4. **Employment**: A high level of employment leads to a high level of production, a high level of GDP and eventually a stronger currency in relation to other currencies.
5. **Balance of payments (BoP)**: The balance of payments is comprised of two accounts: the currency account and capital account. These two accounts include the transactions between the residents of the country

and the rest of the world. The higher the exports (sales from residents to the world) compared to the imports (purchases by residents from elsewhere in the world), the higher the balance of payments. The higher the balance of payments, the higher the demand on the country's currency in the international market and the stronger the currency and exchange rate.

6. **Political risk**: Political instability in a country erodes the possibility of foreign investment flowing into the country as political uprising almost always negatively impacts production, employment, inflation, etc. International market participants would reduce their demand on the currency of this country – in turn increasing its supply – which would eventually lead to a weaker currency. (And that would exacerbate the economic difficulties of the country.)

12.3 Exchange Rate Calculations

LOS. Define a cross rate and a cross trade
LOS. Calculate a cross rate given two exchange rates

One does not find a quote for every single currency against every other currency in the FX market. For example, you might not find a quote for Indian rupees against the Algerian dinar, i.e. you will not see a quote like this: DZD/INR.

So, if you are an Algerian merchant who wishes to buy DZD and get INR you need a third currency to complete the deal. For instance, you might buy USD and sell DZD, then you convert the USD into INR. This deal is called a **cross trade**. So, the cross trade is the use of a third currency to complete a deal between two other currencies. The foreign exchange rate used in this cross trade is called the **cross rate.**

Before we look at the example below, it is very important to note that for the purpose of the exam you need to know that the exchange rate given between two currencies is as follows: price currency/base currency. So, for instance, BHD/USD 0.377 means that each 1 USD (base currency) is worth 0.377 BHD (price currency).

When given a bid-ask quote, remember to follow these two rules:

- Buy the base currency at the ask price and sell the base currency at the bid price.
- Buy the price currency at the bid price and sell the price currency at the ask price.

For example, the quote BHD/USD 0.375-0.377 means the following:

- If you have 100 USD and want to convert to BHD, you would multiply 100 by 0.375 and receive BHD 37.5.
- If you have BHD 100 and want to convert to USD, you would divide 100 by 0.377 and get USD 265.350.

An easier way to remember this while in exam is:

- If you are moving from the base to price, use the bid and multiply.
- If you are moving from the price to base, use the ask and divide.

Example 12.2: Cross rate

Assume you have the following quotes: MXN/USD 13.32 and USD/BHD 2.67. Calculate BHD/MXN.

Solution

$$\frac{MXN}{USD} \times \frac{USD}{BHD} = \frac{MXN}{BHD}$$
$$13.32 \times 2.67 = 35.56$$

But since the required rate is BHD/MXN, we take the inverse of MXN/BHD as follows:

1/(MXN/BHD) = 1/35.56 = 0.0281 = BHD/MXN

LOS. Discuss central bank intervention

A central bank may intervene in the foreign exchange market if it notices that its currency is traded in the international market in a way that will erode its strength or current maintained level. It is not typical that central banks intervene directly; rather, central banks, including industrialized countries, intervene indirectly through adjustments in the economic factors that affect the exchange rate, such as the interest rate, inflation rate, short-term liquidity in the market, etc.

LOS. Discuss spot and forward markets
LOS. Define currency swap rate, forward premium and forward discount
LOS. Calculate the forward premium or discount

There are two types of contracts in the FX market: spot and forward/future.

1. A **spot** FX transaction is a deal involving an exchange of two currencies with the settlement between the buyer and seller of these currencies taking place within two business days.
2. In the **forward** FX market, two counterparties agree to exchange two currencies at a foreign exchange rate agreed on today but for a future delivery on an agreed-upon date.

The characteristics we mentioned in section 12.1 relating to the FX market (e.g. continuous, decentralized) apply to both the spot and the forward FX market.

The *absolute* difference between the spot and forward exchange rate is called the **currency swap rate.** The relative difference between the spot and forward rate is called the **forward premium and discount.**

swap currency rate = Fn - S

annualized forward premium and discount =

$$\frac{F_n - S}{S} \times \frac{360}{n}$$

Where:

n = maturity of the contract

F_n = forward premium

s = spot price

Example 12.3: Spot and forward exchange

Assume the USD/MXN spot price is 13.050 and the 30-day forward price is 13.100. The 30-day swap currency rate between USD and

MXN is 13.100 - 13.050 = 0.050. Traders call this a swap rate of 500 points.

$$\text{annualized forward premium} = \frac{13.100 - 13.050}{13.050} \times \frac{360}{30} = 4.6\%$$

So, USD is trading at a premium of 4.6% on the Mexican peso. Inversely, MXN is trading at a discount of 4.6% to the USD.

Chapter 13. Commodity Market

Upon completion of this chapter you will have learnt:

1. Definitions and terminology of the commodity market.
2. Types of commodities.
3. Issues of pricing commodities.

13.1 Definitions and Terminology of the Commodity Market

LOS. Define on the spot and settlement of difference

Commodities are traded in two distinct markets:

- **Spot OTC market**: This is an OTC market in which a buyer and seller of the commodity transact directly without an intermediary. In this market, terms of the contract are implemented in the spot even if the cash settlement of the difference takes place within 45 days.
- **Organized exchange**: Buyers and sellers in this market transact according to a set of standardized terms and legal contracts with the presence of a clearing house in the middle between the buyer and seller.

An **on the spot** cash transaction means an exchange of a commodity for cash in the spot market, i.e. instantly. The difference between the forward or future price and the actual cash price at maturity for a commodity is called the **settlement of difference**.

LOS. Define in store, ex store, free on board (FOB), free alongside ship (FAS), cost insurance & freight (CIF) and exchange for physicals (EFP)

1. **In store:** The seller of the commodity delivers the commodities to a mutually agreed warehouse. After delivering to the warehouse, a warrant document is produced as a legal claim to the commodities in the warehouse. At the settlement date of the contract, the seller hands the warrant to the buyer and finalizes the transaction. Warrants are tradable to other parties.
2. **Ex store:** The same as the in store arrangement, plus the seller pre-pays the warehouse keeper for loading the commodities on to the buyer's transportation. Obviously an ex store arrangement is more expensive than in store.
3. **Free on board (FOB):** The seller is responsible for delivering the commodities over the ship rail but is not obliged to pay for the insurance during the shipment or claims on any damages to the commodities during the shipment.
4. **Free alongside ship (FAS):** Similar to FOB except for one difference. In FAS, the seller is not responsible for loading the shipment on board the ship, but just for keeping it alongside the ship. So, the seller in FAS does not pay for insurance, damages, VAT or loading on to the ship.
5. **Cost insurance & freight (CIF):** This mechanism of delivery involves FOB, paying the insurance on the shipped goods and the transportation to the warehouse.
6. **Exchange for physicals (EFP):** Sellers and buyers have the option to exchange a future position for a physical delivery, i.e. instead of delivering a load of wheat physically, this is exchanged for a futures contract on wheat.

13.2 Types of Commodities

LOS. List four general types of commodities
LOS. Contrast base, strategic, minor and precious metals
LOS. Contrast grains, oilseeds and fibers

Commodities in the financial markets are bifurcated into the following categories:

1. **Metals:**

There are four types of metals: base, minor, strategic and precious metals. Base metals include: zinc, aluminum, copper, and lead. Minor metals include cobalt and chromium. Practitioners distinguish between base and minor metals by the size of production and form of extraction. Minor metals are categorized as such because they are produced in lower quantity than the base metals and they are extracted as by-product from base metals.

Strategic metals include bismuth and vanadium, while precious metals include silver, gold and palladium. Strategic metals are *strategic* because they are mined for daily manufacturing needs, i.e. they are the basis for modern industry. They are traded, as physical products, in large quantities and they are the underlying asset of different types of financial contracts, such as futures. Precious metals, on the other hand, are not mined for daily manufacturing and industrial needs. Even though silver and gold can potentially be used in industrial projects they are regarded as stores of value so they are not mined and used for manufacturing.

2. **Softs**: Coffee, sugar, cacao, tea, rubber, pepper, etc.
3. **Livestock**: Live animals and meat products.
4. **Grains and oilseed**: Grains includes barely, wheat, oats, rice, while oilseeds includes soybeans. Seeds are planted in order to grow a fruit while grains are harvested to produce food. Soybeans are either used directly as meals or crushed to produce consumable products for humans and animals.

LOS. Discuss the uniqueness of the gold market and the lease rate

Gold is used as a store of value and as a reserve at central banks. It is used as such because it does not erode or corrode and the quantity available of it in the market is much more than the demand. For this very reason, it was used as the underlying asset of exchange rate determination until 1971.

Gold was used as an international standard system for currencies, i.e. money was totally backed by gold from the year 1870 until World War I. In that era, investors, borrowers and lenders were protected from the impact of inflation. People could exchange their money for ounces of gold at any time. This system was suspended in 1933 because of growing concern of the availability of enough gold to back the amount of money circulating in the financial system. Mismatch between the money in circulation and the gold resulted in problems of unemployment and recession.

In 1944 the Bretton Woods System was created and a monetary fixed exchange rate was introduced. According to this system, all countries (except the US, since it was the major architect of the system and the only country surviving World War II with huge gold reserves) would peg their currencies to the USD. The USD was in turn pegged to gold, at $35 for an ounce of gold.

Also, central banks in these countries were to observe the market for their local currency. If the currency deviated from the level it was pegged to, the central bank would intervene to either buy or sell its currency in relation to the USD. This system was suspended in 1971 and since then the USD has been a floating currency.

Although the gold standard is no longer in place to determine the value of currencies, it is still significantly used by central banks as a reserve for the same reason indicated above, as a store of value. Gold kept in the reserve is loaned to earn a return. The lease rate is the interest charged by central banks to lend out their gold.

LOS. Define contango, backwardation, carrying cost (cost of carry)

Naturally, the future/forward price of any goods in the future is expected to be higher than its spot price for various economic reasons. Commodities are exceptions to this rule. Typically, commodities trade for a future/forward price lower than the spot price. In a commodity forward/future contract in which the forward/future price is lower than the spot price, the contract is said to be in **backwardation**. If the spot price is lower than the forward/future price, the contract is said to be in **contango**. Gold has almost always been in contango, except in some rare occasions.

- Backwardation: future or forward < spot
- Contango: future or forward > spot

The **carrying cost** model implies that a commodity is bought in the spot market, stored and then delivered in the future. Storing the commodity entails a lot of costs, depending on the type of commodity and maturity of the contract. The storage cost is called the carrying cost or cost of carry. These costs should be factored into the determination of the future price. So:

future or forward price = commodity spot price + cost of carry

Cost of carry or storage costs include: interest cost, warehouse cost, storage and transactions.

13.3 Issues of Pricing Commodities

LOS. Discuss the impact of shortages on commodity prices and the history of short squeezes
LOS. Define short squeeze and demand for immediacy
LOS. Discuss the convenience yield theory

Shortages in the commodity markets mean the size of supply of the commodity is lower than the size of demand for the commodity. This shortage will push the price of the commodity up considerably. As a result of that, the short party in a futures or forward contract might be in a position in which he does not have the commodity and cannot acquire it from the market in order to deliver it to the long position. This situation is called a **short squeeze**.

Users of commodities, such as farmers or producers, cannot afford to stay without a certain level of commodity inventory. This leads them to pay a higher price now to attain and maintain the level of inventory than they would pay if they waited to buy it in the future. This demand is called **demand for immediacy**, i.e. demand to have immediate access to the commodity now. It is due to this particular reason that *backwardation* occurs. Users of a commodity would like to enjoy the convenience of having the commodity with them now, even if that means paying the currently higher price, rather than wait for the commodity to be delivered in the future. This convenience is called **convenience yield**.

LOS. State the no-arbitrage equation for commodity pricing
LOS. Discuss the decomposition of risk factors in commodities

Arbitrage is a chance to make a risk-free return with zero cost of investment. Arbitrage takes place in a non-efficient market. The typical type of arbitrage is cross-market arbitrage in which the arbitrageur buys a product from a market and spontaneously sells in another market. Pricing of financial and physical assets should be determined at a level, and in light of all the relevant factors, that minimizes arbitrage opportunities. The no-arbitrage equation for commodity price is equal to:

$$\frac{\text{future price} - \text{spot price}}{\text{spot price}} = \text{RF} + \text{C} - \text{q}$$

Where:

Q = convenience yield

C = storage cost

RF = risk-free rate

The right-hand side of the equation is the carrying cost while the left-hand side is the expected capital gain. If we decompose the above equation and analyze the relationship between the factors on each side of the equation we can make the following observations:

1. If the expected capital gain from an asset is higher than the inventory cost of carrying it, an investor would rather store the asset.
2. If the convenience yield is higher than the storage cost and risk-free rate, the future price would tend to be lower than the spot price because consumers and investors put more value in current possession of an asset. If this happens the market of this asset will be in backwardation.
3. If convenience yield increases, capital gain tends to decrease as a result of a decrease in future price in relation to the spot price.
4. In practice, convenience yield is more volatile than the storage costs or risk-free rate. Therefore, convenience yield plays the greater role in determining the value of the basis (the difference between the future and spot) and the overall cost of carry.

LOS. Discuss the importance of non-normality in commodity price distributions

The normal distribution is inconsistent to the reality of factors affecting the price movements of commodities. Commodity prices are exposed to the short squeeze, justified by the convenience yield, harvest failures, etc.

Chapter 14. Energy Market

LOS. Describe various options on energy

Consumption of crude oil and petroleum products approaches 90 million barrels a day. The value of this consumption is about $1 trillion. The value of the consumption and the volume of production motivate both the buyer and the seller of these products to hedge their exposures to the price risk. Futures contracts, options and swaps are viable hedging tools for all concerned parties.

The active physical and financial markets of energy products invite investors and speculators to participate in the markets without being directly involved with the physical assets. This means, for instance, an investor takes a position in futures contracts of the underlying asset – crude oil or natural gas – without being either a supplier or consumer of these products, but to profit from fluctuation in prices.

Futures, options and swaps on energy products might hedge the price risk but they expose the long and the short positions to counterparty risk, liquidity risk, legal risk, operational risk, market risk and regulatory risk. At the beginning of the 1990s, the energy markets expanded to include futures contracts on electricity.

In addition to the traditional options (American or European call and put options), there are various other options contracts traded on energy, as follows:

1. **Asian options**: The strike price of the contract is not settled against the prevailing market price as in American or European options, but it is settled against the average prices of the underlying energy commodity asset for a certain period in the contract. This contract, by taking the average of the underlying asset's price, reduces the option risk of volatility.

2. **Calendar spread option**: This option contract involves buying a call and put option on the same underlying asset at the same strike price, but with different expiry dates. *Long calendar spread* means, for instance, buying an option on oil with a six-month expiry date and selling another option with a nearer expiry.
3. **Crack spread option**: Crack spread means the difference between crude oil and its refined products. An option on crack spread involves taking simultaneous positions in derivatives contracts for the underlying assets of crude oil and refined products from crude oil.

LOS. Discuss using futures markets to hedge energy risk
LOS. Construct an energy hedge using futures contracts

Example 14.1: Hedging using futures energy contracts

In December 2013 XYZ Electricity Company anticipates that it will have excess production and storage by the beginning of year 2014. To hedge against a drop in the spot markets in the future, the chief risk officer (CRO) at the company considers selling futures contracts. So he decides to buy futures contracts for the excess in storage in the upcoming three months: January, February and March. The prices for the three contracts are:

- January: $29 per megawatt-hour (MWh).
- February: $30.
- March: $31.

Calculate the benefits of the futures contracts sold when:

The January spot price per MWh is $27

Spot market: 10 × 736 × 27 = -$198,720

Payoff from futures contracts = 10 × 736 × 29 = +$213,440

So the CRO saved $213,440 - $198,720 = $14,720 by selling futures contracts.

The January spot price per MWh is $33

Spot market: 10 × 736 × 33 = -$242,880

Payoff from futures contracts = 10 × 736 × 29 = +$213,440

So the CRO would lose +$213,440 - $242,880 = -$29,440 by selling futures contracts with unmet expectations.

It is very important to notice the - and + signs in the above calculations. Why did we consider the spot market cash outflow (i.e. the negative sign) if XYZ is in short futures contracts?

The answer is that the energy futures contracts are rarely physically delivered; they are offset and cash settled. Offsetting means if XYZ is short electricity futures contracts for the January contract, before the last of the month of January it would have to go to the market and take a long position in the contract to offset its position and avoid the physical delivery. So, if the prevailing price is $33, it would have to go long on futures contracts at $33 to offset the futures contract it sold before at $29 ($4 loss).

Note: 736 is a fixed number applied by the exchange to calculate the pay off of such contracts. 10 is the multiplication by the number of contracts assumed.

LOS. Discuss physical delivery in energy markets

About 2% of the underlying commodities in the futures markets get delivered physically. This percentage is because 98% of the market participants trade in futures contracts not to guarantee supply of materials but to hedge/arbitrage and speculate on energy product prices.

LOS. Discuss the role that Platts plays in the energy market

Platts is a platform that provides assessment of the prices of energy-related products. These assessments provide a benchmark for prices of such products. Assessments are undertaken by collecting various information and news, as well as disclosed financial results. Platts was founded by Warren C. Platts in 1909.

LOS. Define heating degree day (HDD) and cooling degree day (CDD)

- **Heating degree day (HDD)**: As the name indicates, HDD refers to the day in which the average temperature requires buildings to be heated (i.e. people need to use heaters inside buildings). In the weather derivatives markets, an average temperature below 18 Celsius (65 Fahrenheit) is the HDD.
- **Cooling degree day (CDD)**: CDD refers to the day in which the average temperature requires buildings to be cooled (i.e. people need to use cooling air conditioning inside buildings). In the weather derivatives markets, an average temperature above 18 Celsius (65 Fahrenheit) is the CDD.

About the author

Jaffar Mohammed Ahmed is a professional trainer, lecturer and consultant. Jaffar is the General Manager at JMA Business Consulting & Financial Learning.

Jaffar's consulting services focus on instilling international best practices in risk management, Basel Accords implementation, compliance and corporate governance in financial institutions all over the Middle East. Jaffar also coaches staff of banks to equip and prepare them to handle their responsibilities efficiently. In particular, Jaffar works with his clients in the design and implementation of their enterprise risk management framework and the integration between risk management, internal control, internal audit and strategy.

Some of the in-house and public training courses that Jaffar offers to various financial institutions and learning centers are:

- PRM Preparatory Program
- Assets & Liability management
- Operational Risk Management
- Corporate Valuation
- Basel 3
- Developing Effective ICAAP
- Auditing ICAAP
- Strategic Planning and Enterprise Value
- Accounting and Finance to Non-Finance Managers.
- Executive Course to Board of Directors: Enterprise Risk Management
- CFA Level I Preparatory course
- PRM Preparatory Course
- Basel 2
- Corporate valuation
- VaR and Risk Management
- Introduction to Foreign Exchange
- Corporate Governance
- Audit of Central Banks Corporate Governance.

Jaffar pursued his doctorate study in Economics at Newcastle University in the UK, earned a Master of Science in Finance from DePaul University in the US, a Baccalaureate in Accounting from the University of Bahrain and he is holder of the designation Financial Risk Manager (FRM). He can be reached on: jaffar@jma-consulting.org.

www.ingramcontent.com/pod-product-compliance
Lightning Source LLC
LaVergne TN
LVHW022156200926
848481LV00006B/1764